THE BUSINESS GUIDE
TO
JAPAN

THE BUSINESS GUIDE TO
JAPAN

Edited by
Gerald Paul McAlinn

The Business guide to Japan

Asia, an imprint of
Reed Academic Publishing Asia,
a division of Reed Elsevier (Singapore) Pte. Ltd.
1 Temasek Avenue
#17-01 Millenia Tower
Singapore 039192

ISBN 981 00 7077 2

Cover design by Heymans Tho, Sellagraphic
Typeset by Linographic Services Pte Ltd.
Printed in Singapore by KHL Printing Co Pte Ltd

ABOUT THE GENERAL EDITOR

Gerald Paul McAlinn is a professor of law on the Faculty of Law of Aoyama Gakuin University. He is Chairman of the Legal Services Committee of the American Chamber of Commerce in Japan. He was formerly Senior International Counsel and Director of the Law Department of Nippon Motorola Ltd. and a Visiting Professor at the Faculty of Law of Tokyo University. He is a graduate of the University of Pennsylvania Law School, has an LL M degree from Trinity College, Cambridge University and has studied at Keio University.

ABOUT THE CONTRIBUTORS

Jeffrey P. Clemente is a foreign law consultant at the Tozai Sogo Law Office. He is a graduate of the Seton Hall University Law School and has an MBA degree from Cornell University.

Glen S. Fukushima is a Vice President of the American Chamber of Commerce in Japan and Vice President, AT&T Japan Ltd. He was formerly Director of Japanese Affairs and Deputy Assistant US Trade Representative for Japan and China at the Office of the US Trade Representative. He has been a visiting professor at Sophia University. He is a graduate of Stanford, Harvard and Harvard Law School, and has studied at Keio University and as a Fulbright Fellow at the Faculty of Law of Tokyo University.

Robert F. Grondine is a Vice President of the American Chamber of Commerce in Japan, and Executive Partner in the Tokyo office of White & Case. He is a graduate of Boston University Law School.

W. Temple Jorden is an associate in the Tokyo office of White & Case. He was a Fulbright Research Fellow at the Faculty of Law of Tokyo University. He is a graduate of Cornell Law School and has an LL M degree from the University of Washington School of Law.

Noboru Kashiwagi is a professor of law on the Faculty of Law of Tokyo University. He was formerly Deputy General Manager of Mitsubishi Corporation. He is a graduate of the Faculty of Law of Tokyo University.

Robert McIlroy is a professor of international politics in the School of International Politics, Economics and Business of Aoyama Gakuin University. He is a graduate of the Harvard Law School.

George L. Miller is Managing Director and Regional Counsel in the

Tokyo regional headquarters of Federal Express Corporation. He is a graduate of the Georgetown University Law Center and has a MIM degree from the American School of International Management.

Masashige Ohba is a senior partner in the law firm of Yuasa and Hara. He is a graduate of the Faculty of Law of Chuo University, and of the Legal Training and Research Institute of the Supreme Court of Japan.

John P. Stern is President of Japan Market Engineering. He is the first foreign member of the more than 15 policy and standard committees run by the Ministry of International Trade and Industry and the Ministry of Posts and Telecommunications. He was formerly President, Asian Operations, American Electronics Association. He is a graduate of the Harvard Law School.

Charles R. Stevens is a partner in the Tokyo office of Freshfields. He is a member of the Advisory Council, Department of East Asian Studies, Princeton University, and has taught at Harvard and Columbia Law Schools. He is a member of the Executive Committee, Asia-Pacific Council, London Court of International Arbitration, and an Arbitrator, Japan Commercial Arbitration Association. He is a graduate of the Harvard Law School.

Yoshikazu Takaishi is the founding partner of the Takaishi Law Office. He was formerly General Counsel and Managing Director of Law, Intellectual Property and Security of IBM Japan. He is a graduate of the Faculty of Law of Nihon University, and of the Legal Training and Research Institute of the Supreme Court of Japan. He has an LL M degree from New York University School of Law and an MCL degree from Columbia University School of Law.

Norifumi Tateishi is the founding partner of the Tozai Sogo Law Office. He is a graduate of the Faculty of Law of Tokyo University, and of the Legal Training and Research Institute of the Supreme Court of Japan. He has an LL M degree from Harvard Law School.

Christopher P. Wells is the Administrative Partner in the Tokyo office of White & Case. He is the Vice Chairman of the Financial Services Committee of the American Chamber of Commerce in Japan. He is a graduate of the University of California at Los Angeles School of Law and has an MBA degree from UCLA.

E. Anthony Zaloom is a partner in the Tokyo and Beijing offices of Skadden Arps Meagher & Flom. He is a graduate of the Harvard Law School.

CONTENTS

INTRODUCTION

by Gerald Paul McAlinn

This book is not a "how to" guide, nor is it a scholarly tome. The reader will not find within its pages a complete explanation of the many details of the law necessary to successfully complete a specific business project. For that it is still necessary to consult and rely on the many lawyers, accountants and other professional advisers available in Japan to assist foreign businesses. The book will, however, be of material assistance to the reader in identifying the right questions to be asked and in avoiding some of the more common pitfalls of doing business in Japan.

What this book seeks to do is to guide the reader on an entertaining and enlightening journey across the sometimes rugged terrain of Japanese business law and practice. Our mission in preparing this book was to provide the reader with the basic parameters of the law along with the practical insights which give the law meaning. Each of the contributors was asked to convey the information and advice a real client would need in order to appreciate the legal and practical issues likely to be encountered "in the trenches" of business in Japan.

The contributors are all leading experts on their topics (and could do an equally creditable job on any of the other chapters as well). The insights and information they have generously shared in these pages reflect their substantial expertise and experience. Each chapter is packed with the kind of information and advice usually available only to elite clients with large budgets for outside consultants.

Japan is a constitutional democracy with a modern civil law system. In addition to the Constitution, five other major laws make up the core of the civil law system. These laws are the Civil Code, the Commercial Code, the Code of Civil Procedure, the Penal Code and the Code of Criminal Procedure. Together they comprise what is called the *Roppo* (literally, six laws). Purchasing an English Language translation of the *Roppo* is a worthwhile investment for anyone doing business in Japan.

While Japan has had other constitutions, the present Constitution is relatively new having been prepared in English by the Occupation Forces, translated into Japanese and then adopted as the supreme law of the land in 1946. The other five basic laws of the *Roppo* date back to the Meiji Era (1867–1912). All share in common the fact that their basic structure and contents have been imported into Japan. In this sense, the fundamental statutory law of Japan cannot be said to have sprung directly from the history, traditions and culture of the Japanese. Rather, the law was "borrowed" from abroad in response to the real or perceived need to modernise the country. It was then subjected to a prolonged and on-going process of adaptation and interpretation. It is in this process of "Japanisation" that a true understanding of the dynamics of Japanese law is to be found.

A similar history pertains with respect to the other major laws likely to be encountered by foreigners doing business in Japan. These laws are the Foreign Exchange Law, the Antimonopoly Law, the Securities Law and the various laws concerning taxation, intellectual property rights and labour.

Before concluding this introduction, a few general words about the role of law in Japanese society are in order to assist the reader in understanding the backdrop for much of what follows in this book. Law in Japan (and in much of Asia) is not the vibrant social force that it is in the West. The Japanese simply do not look to law as a primary tool for ordering their relations, whether in business or otherwise. Far more important are the social conventions, customs, norms and beliefs on which Japanese society is constructed. Japan can be a permissive society so long as these mores are understood and respected.

Professor John Haley has brilliantly and thoroughly explored this fertile topic in his book, *Authority Without Power, Law and the Japanese Paradox*. He demonstrates throughout his book the lack of effective legal sanction in formal Japanese law. He explains the role of law in Japan as follows:

> "[Law in Japan] serves as a means for legitimising norms while it remains relatively ineffective as an instrument of coercive control. Substantive legal norms thus operate as principles — *tatemae* — that both shape and reflect consensus. As *tatemae* legal norms may not command obedience, but they do demand respect and induce some level of outward conformity."

Tatemae (literally, the exterior facade) and its flip-side concept of *honne* (literally, the real sound, but meaning one's true feelings, beliefs or intentions) are central to preserving the harmony so deeply cherished by Japanese society. In short, *tatemae* is the visible or outward appearance, whereas *honne* represents the underlying and more determinative reality of the situation. In the business context, being able to distinguish between *tatemae* and *honne* is critical for understanding the true outcome of meetings and the decision making process of the Japanese.

Japanese society must rely on a variety of extralegal methods for compelling appropriate behaviour from its participants since it lacks effective legal sanction. Principal among these are the strong and deeply internalised desire on the part of Japanese to avoid confrontation (arguably the *sine qua non* of Western law), the ultimate threat of being made an outcast in a very close, highly group oriented society, and the concept of duty. It can safely be said as to the latter that Japan is a duty-, as opposed to a rights-, based society.

These principles apply with equal force in the business environment. Contracts, for example, are performed faithfully less out of a fear of being sued for breach, than from a realisation that a failure to do so will result in irreparable harm to one's name and reputation. At the same time, a party to a contract is not expected or permitted to abuse its right (a principle embodied in Article 1 of the Civil Code) by enforcing the terms and conditions of the contract without regard to the actual circumstances. Both parties to a contract have a duty (more social than legal) to make the arrangements work smoothly to their mutual benefit even if this means altering previously negotiated provisions to meet changing circumstances.

To be sure a large body of positive law exists in Japan and it would be wrong to suggest that it can be ignored with impunity. At the same time, a person new to Japan would profit from focussing his or her attention at least initially on the customs and culture of Japan as they exist at large in society and in particular in the business environment. This effort will pay handsome dividends and go a long way towards increasing understanding of situations where Japanese law is relevant. In this respect, it is the hope of the authors that this book will live up to its title and serve the reader as a meaningful and highly useful *Business Guide to Japan.*

PART I
THE SETTING

CHAPTER 1

ECONOMIC TRENDS, INTERNATIONALISATION AND DEREGULATION

by Glen S. Fukushima

INTRODUCTION

This chapter provides a general overview of the economic, business, and political environment surrounding foreign companies that wish to do business in Japan. It does so by discussing

(a) the postwar economic "miracle" that catapulted Japan from a defeated and prostrated nation in 1945 to the status of a world-class economic competitor by the 1970s;

(b) the "bubble economy" of the late 1980s and its aftermath;

(c) the current business and political climate for foreign companies;

(d) the often-discussed but usually misunderstood notion of "deregulation" in Japan; and

(e) future prospects for foreign companies in Japan.

Because other chapters in this book discuss in considerable detail specific aspects of Japanese business and law, this chapter seeks to provide the general context in which business is conducted in Japan. This context is especially important for non-Japanese, in particular Westerners, to understand, since Japan is unique. This is intended to be a value-free statement of fact: Japan is the only non-Western country that has attained the status of an advanced industrialised nation. As such, it combines the rational, efficient, scientific, goal-directed approach to material production characteristic of the United States and Western Europe on the one hand with the personal, relationship-focused modes of business behaviour often found in Asia, Latin America, the Middle East, and other non-Western regions on the other.

Indeed, some observers have gone so far as to argue that Japan has adopted Western-style organisations and institutions but has used them to invent a form of capitalism quite unlike that found in the United States or even Western Europe. Some take this argument even further to say that this Japanese form of capitalism is more applicable than is the American form to the countries of Asia, Eastern Europe and Russia.

What are the elements of this Japanese form of capitalism? Space limitations do not permit a full discussion here, but the essential elements of the Japanese model involve a different notion of "the market" than that usually ascribed to Western economic theory. That is, the product markets, labour markets and capital markets function differently from those in the United States, and the role of the government is seen in a more favourable light. In fact, the government is expected to take a more activist approach to the economy because the "invisible hand" of the free market cannot be trusted to produce the most constructive — as opposed to "efficient" — outcome. In the Japanese model, competition must be "tamed" and "guided" to create outcomes that are societally desired (e.g., preserving employment) even if economic efficiency is sacrificed in the process. One Japanese scholar has even termed this the "1940 System" to indicate the central role of government in the economy, a holdover from the system that came to maturation in 1940 to wage the Second World War.

Although international and domestic changes over the past 50 years have brought about certain modifications to this basic model, most Japanese are persuaded that it has served their country well in promoting the remarkable economic growth that has attracted the world's admiration. What follows is a brief survey of economic developments over the 50 years since the end of the Second World War and the economic, business and political environment facing foreign firms in Japan today.

THE POSTWAR ECONOMIC MIRACLE

Japan's postwar economy has been characterised by remarkably rapid growth. Between 1950 and 1973, the economy grew at an average rate of 10% per year, doubling in size every seven years. Or, seen in another way, Japan's per capita GNP grew from $276 in 1950 to $23,463 in 1989, making it among the richest of the G-7 countries. This is perhaps the highest sustained rate of increase ever seen of a major world economy. [see chart on page 10]

The sources of this increase are generally considered to be the following:

(1) The private sector generated high and rising savings to feed the strong investment demand.

(2) Japan has been politically stable since the war, with a popularly supported, non-coercive government that, until 1993, was

essentially one party, the Liberal Democratic Party.

(3) The Japanese government provided supportive economic policies, both macro and micro.

(4) Japan faced a favourable world environment including a free-market liberal trade regime based on the General Agreement on Tariffs and Trade (GATT).

(5) The Japanese have long valued education, hard work, resourcefulness, and loyalty — all of which were channelled to increasing productivity in the workplace.

(6) Labour-management relations evolved in a relatively non-confrontational way, minimising strikes and maximising the identity of interests between workers, managers and companies.

(7) The postwar occupation by the United States brought a number of political and economic reforms that may have been very important to economic growth.

RECONSTRUCTION (1945–1952)

The Second World War destroyed a fourth of Japan's national wealth and assets, a fourth of its structures, and 82% of its ships. When the U.S. occupation forces arrived in Japan in August 1945, inflation, unemployment, and shortages of energy and food were serious concerns.

Among the "democratisation" and "demilitarisation" measures carried out by the U.S. occupiers, three stand out as key foundations of Japan's postwar economic growth:

(1) zaibatsu dissolution,

(2) land reform, and

(3) labour reform.

The prewar *zaibatsu* were groups of large companies across different industries controlled by family-owned holding companies. At the end of the war, major *zaibatsu* groups held about 40% of equity, or paid-in capital. The occupation forces required the auctioning off of the shares owned by their holding companies, thus technically dissolving the groups in 1946 and 1947. In addition, in April 1947 the Antimonopoly Law was passed, and in December 1947 the Elimination of Excessive Concentration of Economic Power Law was passed. These anti-concentration measures are credited with making many markets in Japan more competitive, prompting investment demand, and enhancing consumer welfare.

Chart 1 Annual GNP Growth Rate (%), 1950–1973

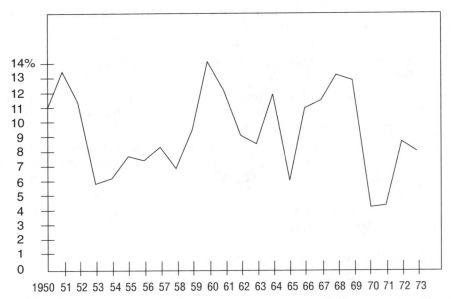

Land reform began in 1946 and 1947 with the confiscation of land from absentee landlords with little compensation, and reselling the land to tenant farmers at bargain prices. This drastic redistribution of wealth contributed to a considerable convergence in the standard of living. The percentage of farmland cultivated by tenant farmers declined from 46% in November 1946 to 10% in August 1950. Land reform helped to create a middle class, thus contributing to income equity and political stability in the agricultural sector. It also led to a rapid increase in agricultural production, so that Japan's food supply was stable a few years after land reform was instituted.

The Labour Union Law of 1946 granted workers the right to organise in unions and to engage in collective bargaining. The percentage of unionised workers rose from 3.2% in 1945 to 41.5% in 1946 and 53.0% in 1948. This unionisation led to an improvement in working conditions and real wages. From a macroeconomic perspective, the improved working conditions and higher wages achieved by the labour unions expanded domestic consumption markets and, in combination with increased farm incomes, made significant contributions to the development of the economy.

Another important policy measure during the Occupation was the

Dodge Plan, named after the Detroit banker Joseph Dodge, who was assigned to work in Japan in 1948 to combat inflation. Put into effect in 1949, the Plan was to stop inflation by tightening the fiscal budget so that the government would not need to print money in order to finance its spending. The exchange rate of $1 to ¥360 was set, and steps were taken to encourage exports.

RECOVERY (1952–1964)

Japan's sovereignty was restored on April 28, 1952, when the San Francisco Peace Treaty, signed the previous year, became effective. A severe recession looming in 1949-50 was reversed mainly by export demand created by the outbreak of the Korean War in 1950. This surge in orders for Japanese goods continued until 1952.

The period from 1952 to 1964 was characterised by full recovery from the wartime years. From around 1954 there was significant increase in large-scale capital investment, and the "Jinmu boom" of 1956 led the Japanese government's White Paper on the Economy for Fiscal 1956 to declare confidently that "the postwar era is over."

The rapid economic growth in the 1960s was at the heart of the postwar Japanese economic "miracle." When Hayato Ikeda became the prime minister in July 1960, he declared the goal of "income doubling in 10 years." Although many skeptics doubted that this could be achieved, in fact the doubling of national income, measured by real GNP, was accomplished in seven years.

In 1964 Japan signed Article 8 of the International Monetary Fund (IMF) and joined the Organisation for Economic Development (OECD), symbolising the country's joining the ranks of the industrialised nations. In October of the same year, Japan hosted the Olympic Games amid much fanfare and national pride. Just 20 short years after the end of World War II, Japan had made a gigantic leap to the forefront of economic development.

CONSOLIDATION AND EXPANSION (1964–1973)

The period between 1965 and 1970 saw economic growth of 10% per year sustained. Trade surpluses also became the norm during this period. And consolidation reversed some of the Occupation period measures in industry: in the wake of the merger of three companies to reconstruct Mitsubishi Heavy Industry Co. in 1964, a wave of big mergers took place — Nissan and Prince in 1966, Yawata Steel and Fuji Steel in 1970, and the Daiichi Bank and Nihon Kangyo Bank in 1971.

By the early 1970s, the Bretton Woods fixed exchange rate regime came to an end, to be replaced by a system of floating exchange rates. On August 15, 1971, President Nixon suspended the gold convertibility of the dollar. After an adjustment period from December 1971 (when the yen was pegged at 308 per $1) to February 1973, the major currencies began to float in the spring of 1973.

INTERNATIONALISATION (1973–1988)

In October 1973, the fourth Middle East War erupted, leading to the oil embargo by the OPEC countries. Goods in Japan became in short supply, and prices of many products skyrocketed. Drastic measures to restrict credit slowed down inflation, which had reached 30% in 1974. Wages increased by more than 20% in that year, since prices were also rising, but in turn the increase in wages fuelled inflation, resulting in a classic example of a price-wage spiral.

Japan suffered its worst postwar recession during this period. Mining and manufacturing production dropped 18% between the end of 1973 and the start of 1975. In early 1977 the yen strengthened sharply owing to a huge trade surplus, reaching 170 per $1 by October 1978, and export industries entered a temporary slump period.

The era of high growth had come to an end through a combination of oil crises (in 1973–74 and 1979–80), a decrease in investment, and a slowdown in technological progress. Yet the average growth rate only dropped from about 10% to about 5%. And by 1981, exports were surging and imports stagnating, leading to persistent trade friction with trading partners not only in North America but in Europe and Asia as well. [see chart on page 14] The Plaza Accord of September 1985 led to the yen reaching a level of 150 per $1 by December 1986, but trade surpluses continued to mount. The strong yen also led to massive investments abroad, creating yet another source of friction with trading partners that faced barriers in their attempts to invest in Japan.

THE "BUBBLE ECONOMY" AND AFTERMATH

The "bubble" started to form in 1985 and had burst by 1990. The high yen that resulted from the Plaza Accord led to what was termed a "high-yen slump." The Japanese government reacted with a series of cuts in the official discount rate beginning in 1986, bringing it down to a postwar low of 2.5% by February 1987. Related to this policy, there are at least four causes which explain the formation of the "bubble."

First, the easy-money policies adopted to combat the high-yen slump were kept in place for well over two years. When prices remained stable despite the low interest rates, investors grew overly optimistic about the economy. Low interest rates meant that both interest costs and risk premiums were lower, so share prices rose. By December 1989, the Nikkei stock index hit its historical high of ¥39,000.

Second, corporations and financial institutions also started to invest more aggressively based on optimism about the future. For industries this meant higher capital investment, and for institutional investors and financial institutions it meant further loans and equity shares. Larger companies began to raise funds directly from the capital markets, which forced banks to turn to non-bank lenders, who dealt mostly with smaller businesses and real estate ventures as the principal borrowers of their funds.

Third, experts in securities houses and other seasoned investors began to engage in short-term trading, which sent prices soaring far beyond what the fundamentals justified.

Fourth, Japanese financial institutions — used to fixed fees and government protection — became lax in their screening and examination of lending and underwriting proposals. They became overly aggressive in their efforts to place loans and cavalier in their underwriting. A vicious circle ensued: easy lending caused the prices of land and shares to rise, which increased their collateral value, which convinced institutions to loan even more money against the "new" collateral.

It was only after the "bubble" reached its maximum expansion that the Bank of Japan stepped in with tighter credit. It took until 1990 for stock prices to begin to fall, and real estate prices continued their upward spiral until 1991.

The current recession is seen as Japan's longest recession in the postwar period. Yet exports are strong, and Japan's huge trade surpluses in part led to a strengthening of the yen to the level of ¥79.75 per $1 on April 19, 1995. Since that time, however, intervention in the currency markets by the G-7 countries has brought the yen to a level of ¥107 per $1 as of early 1996.

CURRENT BUSINESS CLIMATE

"OPENNESS" OF THE JAPANESE MARKET

"Is the Japanese market 'open' or 'closed'?" Perhaps the most accurate, though cliched, answer is, "More open than many foreigners think but

Chart 2

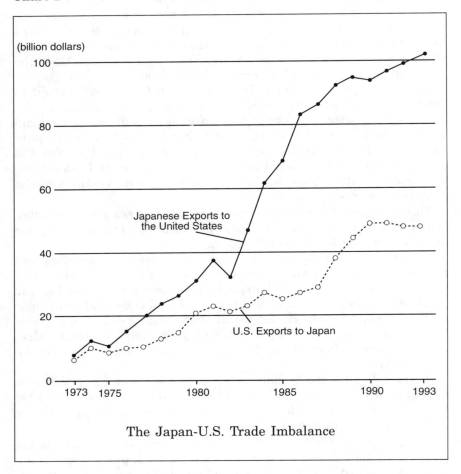

The Japan-U.S. Trade Imbalance

more closed than most Japanese believe." There are, in fact, at least six economic asymmetries that lie at the root of Japan's relationships with its trading partners:

(1) global current account surplus,

(2) bilateral imbalances,

(3) low level of manufactured imports,

(4) sectoral barriers,

(5) company-specific barriers, and

Chart 3

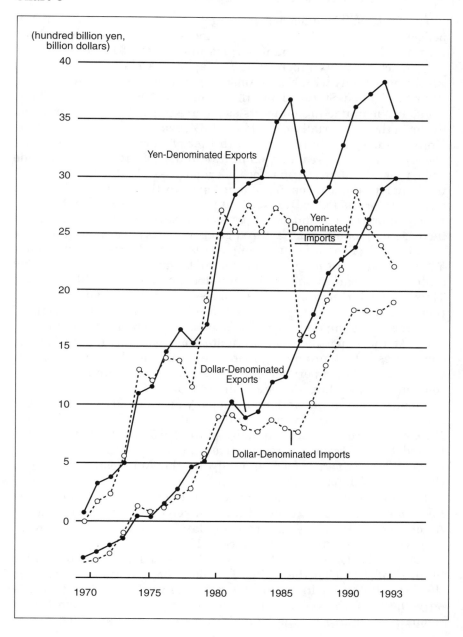

(hundred billion yen, billion dollars)

Yen-Denominated Exports

Yen-Denominated Imports

Dollar-Denominated Exports

Dollar-Denominated Imports

(6) low level of foreign direct investment.

The first two asymmetries are largely a product of macroeconomic policies in Japan and its trading partners. The past few years have seen a global current account surplus in excess of $100 billion every year, reaching $130 billion in 1994. Japan has maintained bilateral surpluses not only with North America but also with Europe and Asia. With the United States alone, the surplus in 1994 was $66 billion.

Japan's manufactured imports as a percentage of GDP is the lowest by far in the industrialised world — at 3%, roughly one-half that of the United States, one-third to one-fifth that of European countries, and one-sixth that of Korea. And empirical studies of intra-industry trade show that — unlike, for instance, Germany — what Japan exports it tends not to import, leaving Japan open to the accusation by such commentators as Peter Drucker that it practices "adversarial trade."

Yen appreciation and other pressures have resulted in a recent increase in Japan's manufactured goods imports. Before long, Japan's overall level of manufactured imports is likely to rise substantially. Yet, this will result largely from exports to Japan by Japanese-capital affiliated companies that have invested abroad, especially in Asia. Thus although macroeconomists will see the aggregate data and claim that Japan is "converging" with the other advanced industrialised countries in its import behaviour, microeconomists are likely to point out that the imports do not originate from foreign capital-affiliated companies, thus providing evidence that the Japanese market continues to be impervious to industrial goods manufactured by companies under foreign ownership and control.

Japan's sectoral barriers and company-specific barriers have been discussed at length in such publications as the *National Trade Estimates Report*, issued annually since 1985 by the Office of the United States Trade Representative, and the *United States-Japan Trade White Paper*, issued annually by the American Chamber of Commerce in Japan (ACCJ).

The imbalance between inward and outward foreign direct investment is even starker than between imports and exports. According to Japanese government data, Japan's outward/inward foreign direct investment imbalance in 1993 was 17 : 1. This compares to 1.4 to 1 for Germany, 1.3 to 1 for France, 1.1 to 1 for the United States, and 1 to 1 for the United Kingdom. According to U.S. data, in the early 1990s Japan occupied 16% of the world's GDP but took in only 0.8% of the world's foreign direct investment, while the comparable figures for the United States were 26% and 29%.

THREE LEVELS OF BARRIERS

How do these macroeconomic data manifest themselves in concrete day-to-day business transactions in the Japanese market? Here we see a disjunction between foreigners, many of whom would claim that the Japanese market is "closed" — or at least not as open as that of other industrialised nations — and Japanese, most of whom argue that their market is "completely open." Foreigners and Japanese who debate this issue often talk past each other, since they are prone to use different definitions of the same word, "open."

To most Japanese, their market is "open" if the Japanese government has not imposed laws, rules or regulations specifically to discriminate against foreign firms, products or services. To many foreigners, on the other hand, well-established Japanese companies are inordinately favoured in the Japanese market through three sets of barriers: (1) governmental; (2) structural, organisational and institutional; and (3) attitudinal and psychological.

(1) Governmental barriers — including tariffs, quotas, standards, import procedures, certifications, etc. — have been reduced or eliminated over the past three decades through bilateral and multilateral trade negotiations. Some, however — such as administrative guidance and the lax enforcement of antitrust laws — still persist, often to the detriment of foreign firms.

(2) Structural, organisational and institutional barriers include long-term supplier-user ties, banking ties, distribution channels, corporate cross-shareholding, *keiretsu* ties, *amakudari* ("descent from heaven" by senior government bureaucrats to Japanese firms after retirement) and other structural features of the Japanese economy that make it difficult for newcomers, especially foreign newcomers, to penetrate the market. Japanese counter that these features were not established for the purpose of excluding foreigners. This may be true, but the results have been exclusionary. (Interestingly, Japanese analysts have pointed out that in the 1960s and 1970s the Japanese government actively encouraged corporate cross-shareholding as a defense against possible foreign acquisition attempts.)

(3) Attitudinal and psychological barriers — manifested in a "buy Japan" mentality — comprise several aspects. One is the notion that Japan, being a small island nation devoid of natural resources, must import vast quantities of raw materials, add value in Japan, and export equally vast quantities of manufactured products in order to survive. This sense of vulnerability

contributes to the Japanese obsession with self-sufficiency, of wanting to make everything itself and not be dependent on foreign suppliers. There is even a Japanese word to denote this premium on self-sufficiency: *jimaeshugi*.

A second aspect of this attitudinal barrier is the myth that Japanese products are superior to foreign products across the board. Although certainly not as strongly held now as during the "bubble" period of the late 1980s, there is still a sense in Japan that foreign workers are incompetent, foreign firms uncompetitive, and foreign products unreliable. Where it is widely conceded that foreign products *are* competitive — as in telecommunications — the Japanese response is to circle the wagons, create a siege mentality, retrench, and undertake cooperative efforts among domestic industry, government and academia to "catch up with and overtake" the pioneers — in this case, the United States.

A third aspect is the conceit that Japan is "unique": Japanese intestines are longer than Western intestines, so Japanese are unable to consume imported beef; Japanese snow is different from foreign snow, so Japanese ski standards must be changed, to the detriment of foreign ski manufacturers; and Japanese soil is different from foreign soil, so foreign construction companies are unfit to work on Japanese public works projects. Some Japanese actually believe these statements, whereas others merely use them as arguments to justify their protectionist policies, practices and preconceptions.

DIFFERING DEFINITIONS OF "COMPETITIVENESS"

Another difficulty faced by foreign companies selling industrial products or services to organisations (companies or government agencies) is that the term "competitiveness" carries a definition different in Japan than that found in most other countries. The Japanese definition has three components: (1) product factors, (2) support factors, and (3) relationship factors.

(1) Product factors comprise the core of what most people around the world mean when they say that a product or service is "competitive":
    (a) Quality (including technology); and
    (b) Price

(2) Support factors comprise the following:
    (a) Before the sale, the vendor offers to the potential customer ample advice, consultation, explanations, persuasion, wining

and dining, favours, and efforts to develop a close business relationship;

(b) When the transaction is agreed to, the vendor commits himself to the delivery time and conditions, and installation conditions requested by the customer; and

(c) After the product is delivered and installed, the vendor provides to the customer dedicated service, repair, maintenance, etc.

(3) Relationship factors include:

(a) Reputation of the vendor in Japan;

(b) Track record of the vendor in Japan;

(c) Perceived reliability and responsiveness of the vendor;

(d) Past transactions and relationships between the vendor and the customer;

(e) Potential future transactions and relationships between the vendor and the customer;

(f) Investment and cross-shareholding ties between the vendor and the customer;

(g) Third-party relationships that might be affected by the transaction;

(h) Banking ties;

(i) School ties;

(j) Marriage or other relative ties;

(k) Whether the customer feels indebted to the vendor;

(l) Whether buying or not buying from a particular vendor would pose risks to the customer;

(m) Whether there is a sense of trust (*anshinkan*) felt by the customer toward the vendor; and

(n) General sense of comfort, ease, and familiarity felt by the customer toward the vendor.

These and other "noneconomic" factors play an important, and at times decisive, role in the purchasing decisions by Japanese organisations. Thus newcomers — especially foreign newcomers — are often faced with huge disadvantages unless their products or services are so outstanding and unique (and there are no significant domestic competitors) that they penetrate the market through their sheer competitive advantage in product terms.

ACCJ TRADE AND INVESTMENT FORUM OF JULY 1993

Some of the above points were illustrated when U.S. President Bill Clinton and his economic advisers attended the Tokyo Summit in July

1993. On the morning of July 9, the ACCJ hosted a "Trade and Investment Forum" in a Tokyo hotel in which nine American country representatives described their company's experiences in Japan. Of the nine, three (representing Warner-Lambert, Pitman-Moore, and Domino's Pizza) expressed satisfaction with their business in Japan. The other six (representing Intel, DEC, Apple Computers, Teradyne, Chemical Bank and White & Case) all expressed varying degrees of dissatisfaction with formal or informal barriers in Japan. They urged the President to conclude results-oriented agreements with Japan and to monitor them closely to ensure compliance and results.

Interestingly enough, the factors that distinguished the three satisfied companies from the six dissatisfied companies were at least three:

(1) the first three deal with consumer products or services while the latter six deal with industrial or institutional products or services;

(2) the first three deal with products or services not considered "strategic" in Japan while the latter six deal with products and services that are widely considered strategic and thus important for Japan's future to develop an independent Japanese capability without having to rely on foreign suppliers;

(3) the first three sell to Japanese consumers while the latter six sell to institutions and organisations.

Many of the foreign companies touted as "success stories" in Japan can be categorized as having the three attributes discussed above; that is, they deal with: (1) consumer products that are (2) not strategic, sold to (3) individual consumers, not organizations or institutions.

WASHINGTON, D.C. "DOORKNOCK"

The annual ACCJ "Doorknock" visit to Washington, D.C. took place in 1995 from March 6 though 10. Six ACCJ leaders — including the President, Vice President, and Executive Director — spent four days meeting with officials in the Administration and members of Congress and their staff to discuss issues of concern to the American business community in Japan.

This visit was timed to coincide with the release on March 2 of the *ACCJ United States-Japan Trade White Paper 1995*, which catalogues market barriers in 35 sectors, ranging from consumer products such as cosmetics to industrial components such as semiconductors to services such as insurance. A press conference held in Tokyo on

March 2 resulted in several newspaper articles carrying such headlines as the following: "Access Still Key Hurdle for U.S. Firms: ACCJ" (*Japan Times*, March 3) and "Uphold Pacts, U.S. Firms in Japan Urge" (*International Herald Tribune*, March 3).

This year's Doorknock focused on four broad themes:

(1) the continuing importance of the Japanese market;

(2) the need to implement existing U.S.-Japan trade agreements;

(3) the benefits of accelerating deregulation of the Japanese economy; and

(4) the desirability of promoting foreign direct investment in Japan.

Why did the ACCJ leadership choose to focus on these themes? Because they are important subjects, they are not fully appreciated in Washington, and they strike a responsive chord in some of the ongoing debates in Washington about U.S. domestic policy.

Importance of the Japanese market. To those of us who live and work in Japan, it is self-evident that the Japanese economy dominates East Asia. With a GNP of over \$5 trillion, Japan constitutes more than 70% the total GNP of East Asia and over eight times the GNP of China. As the world's second largest economy, Japan currently stands at about 80% the GNP of the U.S. Per capita income is roughly 36% higher than that of the U.S. Thus, to divert resources away from Japan to other Asian markets — i.e., "bypassing Japan," as some American corporations appear to be doing — is silly at best and suicidal at worst. It is, as one prominent industrial strategist recently put it, as if a Japanese company interested in the Americas decided to "bypass" the U.S. and focussed resources on the rest of the region because there the competition was less intense and the growth prospects appeared more attractive. All of this, coupled with the "Japan fatigue" in Washington one hears about so often, led the ACCJ delegation to dwell on the importance of the Japanese market during our Doorknock.

Implementing Trade Agreements. During the past three years, 20 trade agreements have been signed between the U.S. and Japan. Four of these, including the rice agreement, are multilateral, reached as part of the GATT Uruguay Round negotiations. The others are based on bilateral negotiations, including construction, apples, cellular telephones, NTT procurement, government procurement of telecommunications equipment, government procurement of medical equipment, intellectual property rights, financial services, insurance, flat glass, and auto and auto parts.

Americans tend to put most of their efforts into negotiating the agreements and, once reached, assume that they are self-executing. Japanese, on the other, tend to view the agreements as merely one phase in a prolonged negotiation. Thus many Americans do not realise the resources required to monitor and implement trade agreements in order to produce concrete results. The ACCJ, mindful of this, urged our Washington, D.C. colleagues to devote the necessary resources to ensure that the agreements yield tangible results.

Accelerating Deregulation. Although as discussed below deregulation by itself is unlikely to cure the major economic asymmetries between Japan and its trading partners, there are some sectors where the existence of government regulations has seriously impaired the ability of foreign companies to penetrate the market or to expand their business in Japan. In addition to the potential benefits to foreign companies, the fact that deregulation can benefit Japanese consumers and Japanese producers means that it is considered to be a "win/win" proposition that is plus-sum rather than zero-sum. Another source of its appeal at this particular time is the Republican Congress, which generally views the reduction of government involvement in the economy as a desirable trend, whether in the United States or abroad.

Promoting Foreign Direct Investment. As discussed earlier, even more than in trade, U.S.-Japan asymmetries in foreign direct investment are extraordinary. Japan's investment in the United States has been roughly 16 times U.S. investment in Japan in recent years. At one point during the "bubble" economy of the late 1980s, this imbalance reached 25 times. Recent studies have indicated that Japan's low investment intake contributes to Japan's low level of manufactured imports, since investment often stimulates trade. Thus increasing foreign direct investment is seen as one way to boost Japan's imports of manufactured products.

DEREGULATION

"Deregulation" is often mistranslated into Japanese as *kisei kanwa*. Whereas the English term, according to *Webster's New Collegiate Dictionary*, denotes "the act or process of removing restrictions and regulations," the Japanese term, according to *Kenkyusha's New Japanese-English Dictionary*, denotes merely an easing or relaxation of regulations. Thus perhaps a more accurate translation of deregulation would be *kisei teppai* or *kisei haishi* — abolishing or removing regulations.

This difference illustrates the profound gap that separates people in the West and Japanese in their vision of what constitutes the ideal relationship between government and business. To put it simply, in Western systems, people tend to assume that everything is permitted unless explicitly proscribed, whereas in the Japanese system, people tend to assume that everything is proscribed unless explicitly permitted. Ever since the "Action Program" announced by the government of Prime Minister Yasuhiro Nakasone in July 1985, Japanese officials have proclaimed that in economic activity, Japan will adopt the philosophy of "Freedom in principle, restrictions only as exception." Unfortunately, the past 10 years have shown that the predominant mode of thought and behaviour among Japanese government bureaucrats is still "Restrictions in principle, freedom only as exception."

Yet, it cannot be denied that some small steps toward easing — if not removing — regulations have taken place in Japan in recent years and that some in the Japanese business community, political world, mass media and public favour further relaxation. Why is this so? Because *kisei kanwa* is seen by Japanese to benefit Japan. These benefits are primarily seen as threefold.

The first benefit is producer-centered: the need to stimulate the economy, develop new areas of business, and overcome the current recession. It is widely perceived in Japan that the existence of regulations can impede the ability of businesses to form new companies and enter new ventures. Some Japanese fear that their country may fall behind its trading partners in economic vitality and innovativeness as a result of onerous regulations. In this sense, a significant number of Japanese who advocate deregulation do so because they believe it will enhance Japan's international competitiveness.

The second benefit is consumer-centered: the desirability of lowering prices and raising the standard of living of the average Japanese. Some believe that easing regulations will help close the gap between the national wealth of Japan on the one hand (as demonstrated by Japan having the world's highest per capita GNP) and the comparatively low standard of living, especially in housing, of many Japanese on the other.

The third benefit is international: the hope that easing regulations will serve to diffuse trade and investment friction with Japan's trading partners. But this benefit is usually seen to be merely a byproduct of actions that should be taken to benefit Japanese producers and consumers. In this sense, the international benefits are peripheral rather than at the core of the current Japanese interest in *kisei kanwa*, much more so than at the time of the Maekawa Commission Report issued in April 1986. Indeed, the formal name of this Commission was "The Advisory Group on Economic Structural Adjustment for International Harmony."

Despite these three benefits, *kisei kanwa* (let alone true deregulation) faces opposition from four sources in Japan. The first is producers who fear that relaxing regulations will destroy industries and jobs. In the distribution sector, for instance, it is often claimed that a rationalisation of the system would produce thousands of unemployed workers.

The second opposition force is the government bureaucracy, which wants to maintain its jurisdiction and regulatory control as a means to retain power and to ensure jobs in the private sector for retiring bureaucrats, known as *amakudari*, or "descent from heaven." In this regard, the political leadership's recent failed attempt to consolidate major public corporations demonstrated just how difficult it is to bring about drastic change in the face of entrenched bureaucratic opposition.

The third opposition force is consumer groups, who resist easing regulations often based on health and safety considerations. It was widely reported, for instance, that in the Murayama Cabinet's committee to recommend specific proposals for *kisei kanwa*, the most vocal opponents of regulations came not from the producers or government bureaucrats but from those purporting to represent consumer organisations.

The fourth opposition force is the general dependence by the Japanese public on the government — to provide jobs, protect and promote industry, determine and maintain health and safety standards, set the general future direction of the Japanese economy, etc. The public's expectations of the government are high, feeding the tendency of the government bureaucrats to think and act toward the public in a patronising mode. As long as this heavy dependence on the government continues, it will be difficult in Japan to realise the philosophy of "freedom in principle, restrictions only as exception."

Given the priority order of the three benefits and the four sources of opposition to *kisei kanwa* discussed above, it is unlikely that major changes will be undertaken in the regulatory area in Japan that will truly benefit a large number of foreign firms. Rather, to the extent that the relaxation of regulations takes place at all, these changes will primarily benefit domestic interests, whether they be producers or consumers.

This is because *kisei kanwa* is, for many Japanese, fundamentally a question of how to modify existing regulations to increase the international competitiveness of Japanese industry. Thus, without denying the overall long-term benefits to the Japanese economy of *kisei kanwa*, it behooves foreign firms to analyse concretely and empirically the extent to which specific regulatory changes can concretely improve their ability to expand their presence in this market.

Otherwise, we can easily end up in the situation so often repeated in the past: the U.S. government asks the Japanese government to undertake certain regulatory changes, Japan resists but in the end grudgingly accepts in the form of a negotiated agreement, both sides declare victory, and a year later the U.S. industry is once again asking the Administration to do something to rectify the continued asymmetries. Clearly, it is often not government regulations per se but rather the practices and attitudes of the private sector and public sector that impede foreign access to this large and potentially lucrative market.

PROSPECTS

The late Edwin O. Reischauer, former Harvard professor and U.S. Ambassador to Japan, wrote on the last page of *Japan: Past and Present*, published in 1946: "No one can yet tell what the new age in Japan will mean in the long run — democracy or authoritarianism; liberalism, fascism, or communism; international cooperation or blind nationalism. The outcome is of concern to the whole world, for the success or failure of the attempt to create a peaceful and democratic Japan inevitably will influence the cause of peace and democracy in other parts of the world."

When measured against this standard, Japan's course in the postwar period has been a resounding success — so much so that by the late 1980s, Chalmers Johnson, another authority on Japan, could write, "The Cold War is over, and Japan won." Creating a "peaceful" and "democratic" Japan — the two greatest concerns of 50 years ago — has been realised. Furthermore, the United States made significant contributions to realising this favourable outcome. How is it that two countries so different in history, culture and psychology have managed to work so well together over the past 50 years?

First was the will, determination and effort of the Japanese people never to repeat the tragedy of the wartime experience and to regain rapidly Japan's place in the world politically and economically.

Second was the magnanimity of the U.S. in providing Japan assistance to recover — including food, raw materials, education, technology, and a huge export market. By providing for Japan's military security, the U.S. allowed Japan to focus almost single-mindedly on economic recovery and development.

Third was the Cold War, which increased Japan's dependence on the U.S. for military and economic security. The Cold War also enhanced Japan's importance in the minds of Americans as a reliable ally in the common struggle against Communism. The Cold War provided the context for the "Grand Bargain" that was struck between the two countries: in return for Japan's cooperation politically and militarily to "contain" Communism, the U.S. offered to Japan economic resources — including a huge market for Japanese exports.

Now, 50 years after the end of the Second World War, the relationship is undergoing a fundamental transformation.

First, the relative power of the two countries has seen tremendous change. Whereas in 1955 the size of Japan's GNP was merely 6% that of the U.S., by 1996 it was 80%.

Second, this growth in Japan's economic power has led the U.S. to treat Japan as an equal partner rather than as a vanquished nation. This means the U.S. expects Japan to shoulder more responsibilities as the world's second largest economy, including opening its markets to manufactured products and to foreign direct investment.

Third, this growth in economic power has led to an increased sense of confidence by Japan to pursue its own course in the world, sometimes independent of what the U.S. says or does.

Fourth, the end of the Cold War has strengthened this sense of Japanese autonomy from the U.S. and, coupled with the passage of time from the Second World War, an increased interest in "returning to Asia."

Fifth, the end of the Cold War has caused the U.S. to focus more of its attention and resources to domestic issues. The U.S. can no longer afford to be the world's policeman and now expects allies, including Japan, to share more of the political and military burden for maintaining world order, stability and peace.

As we approach the 21st century, the U.S. and Japan both need to create a future vision for the relationship. This includes planning for the next five, 10, 20 and 50 years: What kind of relationship do we expect and desire? How can this be promoted? What concrete measures should be taken to realise this?

The desirability of such a vision was evident even in the 1980s, when I worked for five years (1985-90) at the Office of the U.S. Trade

Representative in the Executive Office of the President, deeply engaged in U.S.-Japan trade negotiations. The need for a vision is even greater now that the end of the Cold War has caused both Japanese and Americans to reassess the bilateral relationship and to question whether the erstwhile bilateral division of labour makes sense in the post-Cold War world.

Given the complexity of the relationship, we are likely simultaneously to see the three "C's" of cooperation, competition and conflict. Political and economic leaders in the two countries should find ways to promote cooperation, channel competition to mutual benefit and, when possible, act to prevent or reduce conflict. A "methodology of cooperation" should be established in order to maximise the potential for mutual benefit from cooperative endeavours.

It should not be taken for granted that the U.S. and Japan will naturally be able to sustain in the future the close and cooperative relationship they have enjoyed over the past 50 years. The vast domestic changes in the two countries, coupled with the transformation of the international environment surrounding them, require that the U.S. and Japan consciously formulate a future vision that will help guide them into the 21st century. As Proverbs 29:18 reminds us, "Where there is no vision, the people perish."

REFERENCES

American Chamber of Commerce in Japan, *United States-Japan Trade White Paper, 1995*

Anchordoguy, Marie, *Computers Inc.: Japan's Challenge to IBM*, Cambridge: Harvard University Press, 1989.

Aoki, Masahiko & Ronald Dore, *The Japanese Firm: Sources of Competitive Strength*, Oxford: Oxford University Press, 1994

Fallows, James, *Looking at the Sun: The Rise of the New East Asian Economic and Political System*, New York: Pantheon, 1994.

Fingleton, Eamonn, *Blindside: Why Japan Is Still on Track to Overtake the U.S. by the Year 2000*, Boston: Houghton Mifflin, 1995.

Fruin, W. Mark, *The Japanese Enterprise System*, Oxford University Press, 1992.

Fukushima, Glen S., *Nichi-Bei Keizai Masatsu no Seijigaku* [The Politics of U.S.-Japan Economic Friction], Tokyo: Asahi Shimbunsha, 1992 (in Japanese).

Imai, Kenichi & Ryutaro Komiya, ed., *Business Enterprise in Japan: Views of Leading Japanese Economists*, Cambridge: MIT Press, 1994.

Johnson, Chalmers, *MITI and the Japanese Miracle*, Stanford: Stanford University Press, 1982.

Johnson, Chalmers, *Japan: Who Governs? The Rise of the Developmental State*, New York: W.W. Norton, 1995.

Lincoln, Edward J., *Japan: Facing Economic Maturity*, Washington, D.C.: Brookings Institution, 1988

MITI, *Trade White Paper, 1995*

Murphy, R. Taggart, *The Weight of the Yen*, New York: W.W. Norton, 1996.

Noguchi, Yukio, *1940 Nen Taisei* [The 1940 System], Tokyo: Toyo Keizai Shimposha, 1995. *(in Japanese)*

Office of the United States Trade Representative, *National Trade Estimates Report, 1995.*

Prestowitz, Clyde V., *Trading Places*, New York: Basic Books, 1988.

van Wolferen, Karl, *The Enigma of Japanese Power*, New York: Knopf, 1989.

Yanagida, Yukio, et. al, *Law and Investment in Japan: Cases and Materials*, Cambridge: Harvard University Press, 1994.

CHAPTER 2

TRADE
by Robert McIlroy

STATISTICAL OVERVIEW [1]

1980 was, if one may believe the Ministry of International Trade and Industry's (MITI) statistics, the last year that Japan suffered a trade deficit. According to MITI, in 1980 Japan had $129.8 billion of exports and $140.5 billion of imports, for a trade deficit of $10.7 billion. On the other hand, according to the Ministry of Finance's (MOF) statistics, reproduced in the table on page 30 in 1980 Japan enjoyed a trade surplus of $2.1 billion. What could account for such a major difference in the statistics compiled by these two ministries? Both ministries compile their statistics from customs clearance data, which show exports generally at their invoice price (which would include the value of usance) adjusted to f.o.b. at the point of export, and imports generally at their invoice price (which would include the value of usance) adjusted to c.i.f. to the point of import. MITI reports these data without further adjustment. The MOF, on the other hand, following IMF guidelines on the subject[2], adjusts both exports and imports to their value f.o.b. at the customs frontier of the exporting country and then discounts such value to remove the value of usance. In 1980, the net result of such adjustments (the reduction of export value to remove usance, and the reduction of import value to remove insurance, freight, and usance) was, evidently, $12.8 billion, changing a trade deficit of $10.7 billion into a trade surplus of $2.1 billion.

This does not necessarily mean that the MOF's statistics are better than MITI's. For making comparisons with the statistics of other countries, the MOF's statistics may be more convenient[3], whereas for the analysis of exports or imports country-by-country, commodity-by-commodity, or month-by-month it may be more convenient to use MITI's statistics. But the more important point is that trade statistics, whether MITI's or the MOF's, are rough and sloppy things. Because they are based on customs clearance data, they capture only a part of the exports and imports arising from international direct marketing, and they capture hardly any of the exports and imports arising from the carrying home by travellers of goods purchased abroad. These are major omissions. (As further evidence of the roughness and sloppiness of balance of payments statistics, look at the size of entries in the Errors & Omissions column below.)

C.Y.	Average Exchange Rate	Trade Balance	Invisible Trade and Unrequited Transfers	Current Balance	Capital Movements	Errors & Omissions	Overall Balance	Net External Assets at Year End	Trade Balance as Percent of GDP
	¥/$	$bn	$bn	$bn	$bn	$bn	$bn	$bn	
1980	226.74	+2.1	-12.8	-10.7	+5.5	-3.2	-8.4	+11.5	+0.1%
1981	220.54	+20.0	-15.2	+4.8	-7.4	+0.5	-2.1	+10.9	+1.8%
1982	249.09	+18.1	-11.2	+6.9	-16.6	+4.7	-5.0	+24.7	+1.7%
1983	237.51	+31.5	-10.7	+20.8	-17.7	+2.1	+5.2	+37.3	+2.7%
1984	237.52	+44.3	-9.3	+35.0	-53.9	+3.7	-15.2	+74.3	+3.5%
1985	238.54	+56.0	-6.8	+49.2	-65.5	+4.0	-12.3	+129.8	+4.1%
1986	168.52	+92.8	-7.0	+85.8	-133.0	+2.4	-44.8	+180.4	+4.6%
1987	144.64	+96.4	-9.4	+87.0	-112.7	-3.8	-29.5	+240.7	+4.0%
1988	128.15	+95.0	-15.4	+79.6	-111.4	+2.8	-29.0	+291.7	+3.3%
1989	137.96	+76.9	-19.7	+57.2	-68.4	-22.1	-33.3	+293.2	+2.7%
1990	144.79	+63.5	-27.7	+35.8	-22.1	-20.9	-7.2	+328.1	+2.2%
1991	134.71	+103.0	-30.1	+72.9	+11.3	-7.8	+76.4	+383.1	+3.1%
1992	126.65	+132.3	-14.7	+117.6	-35.5	-10.5	+71.6	+513.6	+3.6%
1993	111.20	+141.5	-10.1	+131.4	-92.8	-0.2	+38.4	+610.8	+3.4%
1994	102.18	+145.9	-16.8	+129.1	-90.9	-17.8	+20.4	+689.0	+3.2%

Exchange rates affect trade, a point nicely illustrated by these statistics. During the first half of the 1980s, unprecedentedly high real interest rates in the United States, in combination with other factors[4], caused the yen to remain weak against the dollar, and this in turn helped Japan's trade balance to grow from 0.1% to 4.1% of GDP. Then came the Plaza Accord of September 1985, at which the G5 finance ministers agreed on concerted market intervention to weaken the dollar. The ensuing rise of the yen against the dollar caused Japan's trade balance first to rise during 1986–1988[7] and then to fall during 1989–1990[8] (the J-curve effect, to be discussed further below).

The converse point, that trade affects exchange rates, is also illustrated by these statistics. Like any other price, the yen/dollar rate is ultimately a function of supply and demand. In the above statistics, the column that represents (albeit roughly and sloppily) "real" demand for yen is the Overall Balance column. Theoretically, as long as Japan keeps recycling its trade earnings into foreign investments (the Capital Movements column) and keeps the Overall Balance column small or negative, the yen can remain weak forever. But speculators, of course, are free to guess otherwise. They are free to guess that, before long, Japanese investors will (a) tire of recycling all of Japan's trade earnings into foreign investments, (b) start to repatriate the earnings on their accumulated foreign investments (the earnings generated by the Net External Assets column would be no small number, and it would show up as a positive input to the Invisible Trade column), (c) start to repatriate some of the investments themselves (this would show up as a positive input to the Capital Movements column), or (d) all of the above. In other words, they are free to speculate that "real" demand for yen will increase, before it actually does. This is exactly what happened in 1987–1988. In the Louvre Accord of February 1987, the G7 finance ministers announced that the yen had risen far enough and that they would attempt to stabilise the yen/dollar rate at its then level of 150–160. But this time, the speculators ignored the ministers and continued to buy yen, despite the fact that there was no "real" demand for it, and such speculative activity kept the yen above the ministers' target zone. (In 1991–1994, the speculators' guess was finally proven correct, as the Overall Balance moved firmly into the black, indicating an increase in "real" demand for yen. Whether the speculators who bought yen in 1987–1988 were still around to enjoy the fruits of their perspicacity is unknown.)

Despite the continuous strengthening of the yen from 1991 through 1994 (and, though not shown in the above statistics, through mid-1995), Japan's trade balance has continued to grow. At the time of the

Plaza Accord, the expectation on all sides was that (a) a stronger yen would make Japanese exports more expensive in dollar terms and therefore less competitive, leading to a fall in exports in volume terms and yen terms, and the percentage fall in volume terms would be greater than the percentage rise in dollar unit price, so that total exports in dollar terms would fall, and (b) a weaker dollar would make imports cheaper in yen terms and therefore more competitive, leading to a rise in imports in volume terms and dollar terms, and the percentage rise in volume terms would be greater than the percentage fall in yen unit price, so that total imports in yen terms would rise. In other words, it was expected that Japan's trade balance, whether measured in yen terms or in dollar terms, would fall by a large margin. It was also broadly understood that, because of market inertia, changes in export and import volumes would take some time to materialise and, in the interim, exports and imports would continue at the old volumes but at the new unit prices, causing a temporary surge in Japan's trade surplus. From the viewpoint of Japan's trading partners, their trade deficit with Japan would (temporarily, they hoped) head South before (permanently, they hoped) heading North, delineating a curve in the shape of a reclining J: thus the name "J-curve effect." From 1986 through 1990, Japan's trade behaved more or less in accordance with expectation, and, from the viewpoint of Japan's trading partners, their trade deficit with Japan delineated a curve in the shape of the first part of a reclining J, but, before getting very far along the long stem of the J, the curve broke and, since 1991, has headed the other direction: this might be called the "broken J-curve phenomenon." What caused it?

The obvious explanation is that, even at the 120–150 range, the yen was still undervalued against the dollar. According to this school of thought, even a doubling in the value of the yen from the 240s to the 120s was not enough to create the hoped-for changes in export and import behaviour: the fall in Japan's trade surplus in 1989–1990[8] resulted not from any J-curve effect but rather from the fact that Japan's economy was booming during those years whereas the economies of America and Europe were sluggish. This school of thought does not deny the logic of the J-curve effect but rather argues that further appreciation of the yen, say, to the 70–90 range, will be required to create it.

Another explanation is that Japan's trade surplus is structural, so that import and export volumes are not easily affected by changes in the terms of trade[5]. According to this school of thought, the commodities that Japan imports are mostly foodstuffs, fuels, raw materials, and semi-finished manufactured goods, and the domestic demand for all of these commodities is somewhat inelastic: in other words, even a large decrease in yen unit price produces only a small increase in import volume. Meanwhile, the commodities that Japan exports are mostly high-technology manufactured goods that are essential to the purchaser and whose production Japan has a virtual monopoly over[6], so that the overseas demand for such commodities is highly inelastic: even a large increase in dollar unit price produces little if any decrease in export volume.

This second explanation is supported by the evidence. According to MITI's statistics, since 1990 Japan's imports, though they have grown in volume and dollar terms, have steadily decreased in yen terms (evidence that domestic demand for import commodities is somewhat inelastic). Meanwhile, since 1990, Japan's exports have been about flat in volume and yen terms despite the strengthening of the yen (evidence that overseas demand for Japanese export commodities is highly inelastic). Furthermore, although consumer goods played a conspicuous role in the huge growth of Japan's exports during the first half of the 1980s, since the Plaza Accord the share of consumer goods in total exports has decreased and that of capital goods has increased, so that now Japan's exports consist of about 1/3 consumer goods and about 2/3 capital goods (demand for which is, putatively, relatively less elastic).

Before leaving the subject of statistics, one closing thought: global trade statistics (statistics for Japan's trade with all its trading partners) may be rough and sloppy things, but bilateral trade statistics (statistics for Japan's trade with a particular trading partner) are rough, sloppy, and dirty. If a Japanese trading company, rather than importing gold bullion directly from Country A, decides to import the bullion via Country B, should this count as a Country B export to Japan? If a Japanese financial institution purchases a new aircraft made in Country C and then leases the aircraft to an airline in Country D, should this count as a Country C export to Japan? If a Japanese manufacturer sets up an assembly shop in Country E and ships finished products, which by value are 90% made-in-Japan, from there to Country F, should this count as a Country E export to Country F? Such games as these cannot affect global trade statistics, but they can, and do, affect bilateral trade statistics, and, accordingly, one should not give the latter much credence.

PROMOTION, RESTRICTION, AND SUBSIDISATION OF EXPORTS

The promotion of Japanese exports, as a governmental activity, has pretty much ceased. The Japan External Trade Organisation (JETRO), which was established in 1951 to promote Japanese exports by gathering information about market opportunities overseas and communicating this information to businesses in Japan, shifted its emphasis 180° during the 1980s, and nowadays JETRO engages primarily in promoting Japanese imports by gathering information about market opportunities in Japan and communicating this information to businesses overseas. The promotion of Japanese exports continues, but it is now undertaken mostly by private-sector institutions, such as the Japan Automobile Manufacturers Association, the Japan Machinery Federation, etc.

The opposite concept, the restriction of Japanese exports, is so antithetical to traditional thinking as to have little support within the private sector, but in fact the Government of Japan has imposed restrictions on Japanese exports in two situations. The first situation relates to security: Japan prohibits the export of weapons as such, and Japan also participates in the various multilateral arrangements regarding the export of commodities and technologies that can be used in the development of weapons of mass destruction and missiles. The second situation relates to trade friction: when Japanese exports of a particular product to a particular foreign market have achieved such a high market share that there was deemed to be a danger of some sort of corrective action by the foreign government concerned, the Government of Japan has sometimes imposed voluntary export restraints. This latter kind of export restriction is, however, of historical interest only; under the Agreement on Safeguards (one of the multilateral trade agreements annexed to the Agreement Establishing the World Trade Organisation), such voluntary export restraints are generally required to be phased out within four years from January 1, 1995.

Subsidisation of Japanese exports by the Government of Japan takes two forms.

The first is the subsidisation that results from administering a value-added like VAT tax in the usual way, namely exempting exports from the application of VAT tax and, in addition, refunding the upstream VAT tax borne by exports. This form of export subsidisation is widespread in the world, largely because the GATT shields from retaliation a country that subsidises exports in this manner[7].

The second is the subsidisation that results from lax enforcement of transfer pricing rules, combined with the existence, throughout Asia, of tax havens, free trade zones, tax holiday schemes, and other tax-based incentives to promote inbound foreign direct investment and trade diversion. This form of export subsidisation is also widespread in the world, but is seldom remarked upon, and therefore a few pages will be devoted to it here.

So as not to injure anyone's feelings, let us invent the mythical country of Maha. It is a developing country, located somewhere in Southeast Asia with good access to shipping lanes. The regular income tax rate in Maha is 50%, but, so as to promote inbound foreign direct investment and trade diversion, Maha has enacted legislation providing that enterprises newly established by nonresidents shall pay tax not at the regular 50% tax rate but rather at a special preferential tax rate of 10%. Lest there be any doubt about the intention of the legislation, the Government of Maha has invited delegations of Japanese industrialists to Maha and has explained to them that, if, rather than shipping products directly from Japan to third countries, they establish subsidiaries in Maha, which assemble such products in Maha from components shipped in from Japan and then ship such products from Maha to the third countries, they will gain the benefit of Maha's special preferential tax rate of 10% on the income attributable to the assembly operations in Maha.

Note that the effective corporate income tax rate in Japan is approximately 55%. Therefore, the offer of a 10% preferential tax rate will succeed in gaining the attention of a Japanese industrialist. But there is something more important than the level of the preferential rate: it is the amount of income that can be sheltered at that preferential rate. Suppose that the product in question is produced in ten stages, each of which generates a cost of 80, and that the export price to the third country is 1000. If the Japanese industrialist keeps the first nine production stages in Japan and establishes a subsidiary in Maha to perform only the tenth stage, how much of the profit will be sheltered at Maha's preferential rate? According to common sense, since 1/10 of the total cost is attributable to the operation performed in Maha, 1/10 of the profit should be attributable to the operation performed in Maha. Since the total profit (export price to the third country minus total cost) is 200, the profit attributable to the operation performed in Maha should be $200 \times 1/10 = 20$, and the industrialist's tax saving (assuming that the profit is left in the Maha subsidiary and not dividended up to the parent corporation in Japan) should be $(55\% - 10\%) \times 20 = 9$. Is a tax saving of only 9 (less than 1% of the export price to the third country) going to be enough to persuade the Japanese industrialist to go to all the trouble of setting up a Maha subsidiary and channeling exports through it? Not likely.

But suppose that the parent corporation in Japan establishes 740 as the price at which it sells the semi-finished product to the subsidiary in Maha. If this transfer price is not challenged by Japan's

National Tax Administration (NTA), it will produce an allocation of 1/10 of the profit to the parent corporation in Japan (740 minus the cost of the operations performed in Japan equals 20, which is 1/10 of the total profit) and 9/10 of the profit to the subsidiary in Maha (export price to the third country minus 740 minus the cost of the operation performed in Maha equals 180, which is 9/10 of the total profit), and the industrialist's tax saving (assuming that the profit is left in the Maha subsidiary and not dividended up to the parent corporation in Japan) will become $(55\% - 10\%) \times 180 = 81$. Is a tax saving of more than 8% of the export price to the third country going to be enough to persuade the Japanese industrialist to go to the trouble of setting up a Maha subsidiary and channeling exports through it? Very likely yes.

As this hypothetical example illustrates, the attractiveness to Japanese corporations of the various schemes established by Japan's neighbouring countries for promoting inbound foreign direct investment and trade diversion hinges on the question of whether Japan's NTA is likely to challenge a transfer price between a Japanese parent and its subsidiary in one of these countries. There is no definitive answer to such a question, of course, but the following points are suggestive: (a) Japan never even had transfer pricing legislation until 1986, (b) based on the debate at the time and on actual practice by the NTA to date, it appears that Japan's transfer pricing legislation was adopted mainly so as to create a means whereby Japan could, when Japanese multinational enterprises were subjected to transfer pricing investigations by another developed country, retaliate by instituting transfer pricing investigations against that developed country's multinational enterprises in Japan[8], (c) the NTA is understaffed in general and has assigned only a handful of staff to transfer pricing matters, and (d) diplomatic considerations militate against Japan's taking a strong position vis-a-vis certain countries, especially those that have memories of Japanese military occupation. In fact, it seems that the likelihood of the NTA's challenging a transfer price between a Japanese parent and a subsidiary such as that described in the hypothetical example above is extremely small. And, if so, it follows that virtually all of the profits associated with exports to third countries that are channelled through such a subsidiary can gain the benefit of the preferential tax rate or other tax-based incentives applicable to the subsidiary.

The official position of the WTO is that such laxity in enforcement of transfer pricing rules is an export subsidy prohibited by Article XVI of the GATT. Specifically, in December 1981 the GATT Council stated its "understanding that ... Article XVI: 4 requires that arm's-length pricing be observed, i.e., prices for goods in transactions between exporting enterprises and foreign buyers under their or the same control should for tax purposes be the prices which would be charged between independent enterprises acting at arm's length."[9] The problem is that, although the GATT Council's understanding may be eminently correct as an abstract proposition, as a practical matter it seems impossible to enforce. If Japanese manufacturers channel their exports to Country X through assembly shops that they have set up in Maha, and manipulate their transfer prices between Japan and Maha so as to gain the benefit of Maha's 10% tax rate on virtually all of the profits associated with such exports, how is Country X going to complain? Country X has no means even of learning what the transfer price between Japan and Maha is, let alone of obtaining the data that would be required in order to ascertain whether it is an arm's-length price. There seems to be no effective way under the GATT to prevent export subsidisation by schemes such as this.

In fact, Japan takes such subsidisation of exports one step further, by allowing the Japanese parent, through the "tax sparing credit", to gain the benefit of a preferential tax rate applicable to its subsidiary even if the profit of the subsidiary is dividended up to the parent.

Tax sparing is a concept that may be unfamiliar to most readers, but, as the export subsidy effect is substantial, it is worth explaining.

In countries that, like Japan, use a residence-based system of corporate income taxation, the income attributable to the foreign branch of a domestic corporation will normally be subject to two corporate income taxes: first it will be subject to tax in the foreign country where the branch is located, and then it will be subject to domestic tax. To eliminate the tax increase arising from this double taxation, domestic law provides a foreign tax credit. For example, if the income attributable to the foreign branch is 100, the foreign tax rate is 50%, and the domestic tax rate is 55%, the foreign tax will be 50 ($=100 \times 50\%$), and the domestic tax will be 5, computed as follows:

Income	100
Tax rate	$\times.55$
Tax before foreign tax credit	55
Foreign tax credit	-50
Tax	5

Thus, the total tax borne by the 100 of income will be 55 ($=50$ of foreign tax $+5$ of domestic tax).

Suppose, now, that the foreign country, so as to promote inbound foreign direct investment and trade diversion, passes a law providing that enterprises owned by nonresidents shall pay tax not at the regular 50% tax rate but rather at a special preferential tax rate of 10%. If the income attributable to the foreign branch is still 100, the foreign tax will now be 10 (=100 × 10%), and the domestic tax will be 45, computed as follows:

Income	100
Tax rate	×.55
Tax before foreign tax credit	55
Foreign tax credit	−10
Tax	45

Thus, the total tax borne by the 100 of income will still be 55 (=10 of foreign tax +45 of domestic tax): through the normal working of the foreign tax credit mechanism, the reduction in foreign tax will have been completely offset by an increase in domestic tax. But if this is so, the incentive that the foreign country intended to provide to inbound foreign direct investment and trade diversion is vitiated. What is a developing country that wants to pursue this path to development supposed to do?

The tax sparing concept was invented in response to this question. Under tax sparing, a developed country agrees in its tax treaty with a developing country that, if the developing country, so as to promote inbound foreign direct investment and trade diversion, establishes a preferential tax rate for enterprises owned by nonresidents, the developed country shall allow its corporations to compute their foreign tax credit as if they had paid tax in the developing country at the old, non-preferential rate. Thus, if the income attributable to the foreign branch is still 100, the foreign tax will still be 10 (=100 × 10%), but the domestic tax will be back to 5, computed as follows:

Income		100
Tax rate		×.55
Tax before foreign tax credit		55
Foreign tax credit:		
Regular foreign tax credit (foreign tax actually paid)	10	
Tax sparing credit (foreign tax deemed to have been paid)	+40	− 50
Tax		5

The total tax borne by the 100 of income will now be 15 (=10 of foreign tax +5 of domestic tax): the benefit of the developing country's preferential tax rate will have been passed through to the taxpayer, presumably resulting in the intended incentive to foreign direct investment in and trade diversion via the developing country.

Tax sparing, from an economic point of view, is bad policy because it encourages multinational enterprises to allocate capital not based on gross ROI, as would be optimal for world economic welfare, but rather based on ROI net of local taxes. Primarily for this reason, tax sparing is not sanctioned by the OECD model tax treaty and has been steadfastly opposed by the United States. Nevertheless, all of the G7 countries except the United States have entered into numerous tax treaties providing for tax sparing.

Tax treaties providing for tax sparing are currently in effect between Japan and the following 15 countries: Bangladesh, Brazil, Bulgaria (tax sparing to be phased out after 2001), China, India, Indonesia, Korea, Malaysia (tax sparing to be phased out after 1996), Pakistan, the Philippines, Singapore (tax sparing to be phased out after 2000), Sri Lanka, Thailand, Turkey (tax sparing to be phased out after 2004), and Zambia. All of the treaties except those with India, Pakistan and the Philippines provide for both a direct tax sparing credit (for the foreign tax deemed to have been paid by a branch or withheld on dividends) and an indirect tax sparing credit (for the foreign tax deemed to have been paid by a subsidiary). The only statistics available for the usage of tax sparing credits by Japanese taxpayers are for corporations capitalised at ¥30 billion or more, and these statistics show that the total usage of tax sparing credits annually by such corporations has been in the ¥40–50 billion range in recent years[10].

To summarise the situation, a Japanese manufacturer of products for export has, as a practical matter, the option of shifting most of its export profits to an assembly shop that it sets up in a country that (a) is one of the 15 countries that Japan has a tax sparing treaty with and (b) has established a preferential tax rate for such assembly shops, and thereby of substantially reducing the effective tax on such profits, even if they are repatriated to Japan. The export subsidy effect is apparent, but, for the reason set forth in the text above, mounting a legal challenge to it would be difficult.

BARRIERS TO AND PROMOTION OF IMPORTS

In October 1985, right after the Plaza Accord, Prime Minister Nakasone appointed a group, led by Haruo Maekawa, a former governor of the Bank of Japan, to advise him on nothing less than "the way in which our country's economy should be structured, and its economic affairs should be conducted, in the future". The resulting Maekawa Report was issued in April 1986. It pointed out that, during the first half of the 1980s, Japan's current balance, as a percent of GNP, had grown to a level that was unprecedented in the world and that was so high as to have created a crisis in terms of the harmonious development of the world economy. It stated that the fundamental cause of this was the export-oriented structure of the Japanese economy, and it called for a national commitment "to reform the structure of the Japanese economy into a structure oriented toward international concert".

More specifically, the Maekawa Report called for domestic-demand-led (as opposed to export-led) economic growth, but at the same time it cautioned against deficit spending, implying that monetary policy (i.e., low interest rates) should be the main policy tool. The Report envisioned the Japanese people living in more spacious residences closer to their jobs, working fewer hours, saving less, and consuming more, and it proposed various policies to promote these objectives. Finally, the Report envisioned an "international division of labour", with restructured, information-intensive Japanese corporations providing technological leadership and investment capital to developing countries as well as a market for components and finished products made in such developing countries.

In the years that followed, the Japanese establishment accepted the parts of the Maekawa Report that it found palatable (the parts about monetary policy[11] and the "international division of labour") but totally rejected the parts that it did not (the parts about the Japanese people saving less[12] and consuming more)[13].

Today, ten years after it was presented to the world, the Maekawa Report is still frequently cited as the last word on the restructuring of the Japanese economy, but this writer would demur. The "international division of labour" envisioned in the Maekawa Report is based on the premise that access to the domestic Japanese market will continue to be controlled by the Japanese corporations at the top of the pyramid, and components and finished goods will be imported into Japan only if and when these corporations have made arrangements to produce them overseas. This seems to be a recipe for an even greater concentration of production in Japan of the kind of commodities described in the text above, overseas demand for which is highly inelastic. Such a restructuring of the Japanese economy, far from reducing Japan's current account surplus, will only make it more intractable. The prescription for restructuring set forth in the

Maekawa Report needs to be reformulated, and the new prescription should (a) recognise that the "international division of labour" is not an acceptable surrogate for true market opening and (b) state clearly something that the Maekawa Report studiously avoided stating, namely that Japan needs to increase its imports of manufactured goods from other developed countries.

But, even without a new report to tell it so, the Government of Japan is well aware that Japan's trading partners, both developed and developing, regard the Japanese market as far from open, especially to manufactured goods. Though Japan has raised the share of manufactured imports in total imports from about 20% in 1980 to about 50% today, in most of the other OECD countries the share is about 80%.

The most authoritative and up-to-date list of Japan's barriers to imports is found in National Trade Estimate Report on Foreign Trade Barriers, issued every year at the end of March by the United States Trade Representative.[14,15] The complaints are probably familiar to every reader: blatant protection of the agricultural sector, technical standards and procurement specifications designed to discriminate against non-Japanese products, and, most of all, cosy and opaque relationships that effectively exclude non-Japanese companies from a huge proportion of the business-to-business market. Too often, the official Japanese response to such complaints is that the complainant is misinformed or lazy, so let it be stated clearly here that this is rarely so. Virtually all the complaints are well founded, the complainants legitimately aggrieved.

Such systemic protectionism is like the Lernean hydra, and there is no Heracles to slay it, least of all the Government of Japan. Yet the Government has taken some significant steps to promote imports. This is not really contradictory. It is difficult for the Government to do battle with systemic protectionism because such protectionism is merely the outward aspect of the web of vested interests that holds Japan together and keeps its politicians in power. The promotion of imports, on the other hand — especially imports for the consumer market — can often be done in such a way as not to gore anyone's ox.

JETRO's transformation into an import-promoting agency was mentioned earlier. Specifically, JETRO maintains JETRO Centres in major cities in North America, Europe and Australia, where local business persons can receive information and expert counseling about market opportunities in Japan; maintains Business Support Centres in Tokyo and other major cities in Japan, where foreign business persons can receive free office space and support for import-related activities; maintains "antenna shops" in several Japanese cities for test-marketing imported consumer goods; organises import trade fairs throughout Japan; maintains a permanent exhibition of imported housing; and organises buying missions overseas for Japanese business persons and selling missions in Japan for foreign business persons.

The Manufactured Imports Promotion Organisation (MIPRO), which is, like JETRO, a MITI auxiliary, has a large exhibition hall in Tokyo where it hosts import trade fairs, usually in cooperation with the Tokyo embassies of the foreign governments concerned. MIPRO also maintains an information centre where Japanese consumers can receive counseling about opportunities and procedures for "personal importing" (ordering directly from overseas catalogs) and Japanese business persons can access JETRO's database for connections to business persons overseas that are interested in exporting to Japan.

Several agencies of the Government of Japan make financing available on preferential terms to enterprises in Japan that are engaged in import-related activities as well as to enterprises overseas that are engaged in exporting to Japan. Also, Foreign Access Zones have been or are in the process of being established adjacent to most of Japan's major harbours and airports (the prominent exceptions being Narita and Haneda Airports), and import-related facilities within such zones are eligible for accelerated depreciation in addition to the aforementioned preferential financing.

Finally, as a temporary tax measure, Japanese wholesalers, retailers, and manufacturers that increase (in yen terms) their imports of manufactured goods are eligible for deferrals of taxable income or for tax credits equal to certain percentages of the amount of such increase.

What more could Japan be doing to increase imports? In light of the Japanese establishment's total rejection of the Maekawa Report's vision of an epochal transformation of Japan from a nation of savers to a nation of consumers, there is no room for optimism that such a transformation will occur anytime soon. Thus, Japan will continue to have a huge current balance. But, huge though the current balance may be, it is small in comparison with the non-yen-denominated investment opportunities that are available to Japanese investors around the world. Thus, as long as there is reasonable diversification so as to prevent "over-presence" by Japanese investors in a particular market[16], the MOF can continue to pursue its policy of encouraging the recycling of Japan's trade earnings into non-yen-denominated investments overseas. Japan's net external assets can grow into the trillions of dollars, yet the yen's appreciation can be slowed down or even reversed.

If this seems unreal, ask yourself: if you were the world's biggest currency speculator, would you go head to head with the MOF? Even if you analysed the fundamentals and concluded that the yen was undervalued, would you take a speculative long position in yen, knowing that (a) the MOF could influence the Bank of Japan to keep real interest rates in yen far below the real interest rates available in other currencies and (b) the MOF could influence Japan's financial institutions — the world's largest — to make non-yen-denominated investments so as to create a negative "real" demand for yen indefinitely into the future?

So, what more could Japan be doing to increase imports? Here is a proposal: exempt imports from VAT. Although the GATT permits a country to collect VAT on imports[17], the GATT does not require a country to do so.[18] Japan's spokespersons often claim that the GATT ties Japan's hands, preventing it from acting aggressively to increase imports (this is the stock response to suggestions that Japan should establish numerical targets for imports), but this proposal is guaranteed 100% GATT-legal. Moreover, it is non-sector-specific and accords most-favoured-nation treatment to all, and it is the kind of fiscal policy that (as of this writing in the spring of 1996) Japan should be pursuing in any event.

PROSPECTS OF JAPAN'S JOINING A FREE TRADE AREA

The rules under which members of the WTO may establish limited-membership free-trade areas (FTAs) are set forth in Article XXIV of the GATT. Essentially, the proponents of an FTA are supposed to establish to the satisfaction of the WTO, in advance, that the net effect of the creation of the FTA will be to lower barriers and increase trade, including trade with non-members of the FTA. Unfortunately, compliance with the procedures of Article XXIV has been deficient. Members have failed to submit information about new FTAs in time to allow them to be analysed by working parties before their entry into effect, and members have refused to submit any information at all about the ongoing operation of existing FTAs.[19]

In such circumstances, it is understandable that countries that are not currently members of any FTA should be concerned about the danger of the existing FTAs developing into outsider-excluding trade blocs, and that such countries should conclude that their only defense against such a development is to join FTAs themselves. Thus, particularly since the creation of the FTA between the United States and Canada in 1989, there has been a boom in FTAs: from 1990 through the end of 1994, the GATT was notified of the creation of no less than 33 new FTAs or accessions to existing FTAs.

Japan, as the country that has reaped the greatest benefit from a generally free world trading system, and as a country that has generally placed trade ahead of all other strategic considerations, is not enthusiastic about FTAs. Japan much prefers the principle of most-favoured-nation treatment, adulterated only by preferences for developing countries. Nevertheless, it is conceivable that trade blocs elsewhere may develop to a point where Japan feels that it has no choice but to join an FTA. In such a case, the three possible configurations that are most often bruited are: (a) Japan plus China plus most of the rest of East Asia and Australasia, (b) Japan plus the United States, Canada, Mexico, etc., and (c) Japan plus China plus most of the rest of East Asia and Australasia plus the United States, Canada, Mexico, etc. Of these three, it should be obvious which Japan would prefer. The larger the grouping, the less the likelihood of substantial departures from the principle of most-favoured-nation treatment, and the greater the defense against departures from that principle by trade blocs elsewhere.

---

[1] Statistics is an area where inability to read the Japanese language is not a major handicap for the foreign observer of Japan, because most of the important statistics are published with captions in English as well as in Japanese. The *Trade White Paper* (通商白書 TSŪSHŌ HAKUSHO), edited by MITI and published in May every year, contains large pull-out spreadsheets showing Japan's exports and imports country-by-country and, within each country, commodity-by-commodity, for the preceding calendar year. For the same statistics on a more current basis, see *Japan Trade Monthly* (日本貿易月表 NIHON BŌEKI GEPPYŌ), published by Nihon Kanzei Kyōkai. *Balance of Payments Monthly* (國際收支統計月報 KOKUSAI SHŪSHI TŌKEI GEPPŌ), published by the Bank of Japan under the authority of the Ministry of Finance, supplements the export and import data with information about — n.b., beginning in January 1996, the taxonomy will change slightly — invisible trade (investment income, transportation, travel, and other services), grant aid and other unrequited transfer payments, direct investment and other long-term capital movements, and short-term capital movements.

[2] International Monetary Fund, *Balance of Payments Manual, 5th Edition* (Washington, 1993).

[3] Beginning in January 1996, the MOF will issue its balance of payments statistics in yen only, without translation into dollars, so that the degree of convenience will decrease.

[4] Other factors include the MOF's pressuring Japanese financial institutions to invest in dollar-denominated securities, the Bank of Japan's keeping yen interest rates low, and the United States' repeal (effective after July 18, 1984) of tax on US-source, portfolio-debt interest received by nonresident aliens and foreign corporations.

5   The "terms of trade" is defined as export unit value divided by import unit value.
6   For specific examples of such commodities, see Eamonn Fingleton, *Blindside: Why Japan Is Still on Track to Overtake the U.S. by the Year 2000* (London, 1995).
7   Article VI:4 of the GATT provides, "No product of the territory of any contracting party imported into the territory of any other contracting party shall be subject to anti-dumping or countervailing duty by reason of the exemption of such product from duties or taxes borne by the like product when destined for consumption in the country of origin or export, or by reason of the refund of such duties or taxes." See also the Note to Article XVI of the GATT.
8   The monthly magazine *International Taxation* (KOKUSAI ZEIMU) reports that, from the inception of its transfer pricing enforcement in 1987 through June 1994, the NTA has undertaken "about 60" transfer pricing investigations, which resulted in about ¥120bn of adjustments to taxable income. The NTA does not release data breaking these figures down based on the identity of the other country involved or based on the nationality of the multinational enterprise involved. Accordingly, this writer's suspicion that virtually all cases to date have involved other developed countries and non-Japanese multinational enterprises is based solely on the reports of specific cases that, from time to time, have been released or leaked to the news media (sometimes by the enterprises under investigation) and other anecdotal evidence.
9   GATT Council decision of December 8, 1981, cited at GATT, *Analytical Index, 6th Edition* (Geneva, 1993), p. 425. See also Footnote 59 to the Agreement on Subsidies and Countervailing Measures (one of the multilateral trade agreements annexed to the Agreement Establishing the World Trade Organisation).
10 Unfortunately, this writer has not figured out how to extrapolate these statistics for corporations capitalised at ¥30bn or more to derive an estimate of total usage of tax sparing credits by all Japanese taxpayers. The percentage of domestic manufacturing output that is accounted for by such mammoth, ¥30bn+ corporations is known (it is substantially less than 50%), but there is no basis for assuming that usage of tax sparing credits is proportional to domestic manufacturing output.
11 During the MOF's battle of wills with currency speculators following the Louvre Accord, the Bank of Japan drastically lowered interest rates; and, even when, by the fall of 1987, the domestic economy had improved and asset inflation had emerged, so that it should have been clear that loose money was no longer necessary or appropriate, the BOJ continued to keep rates low (in part because of concern inspired by the New York stock market crash of October 1987), and it continued to pursue this policy into 1989. This, in a nutshell, is what caused the Bubble of 1987–1990.
12 Propensity to save (household savings divided by household disposable income) was 14.7% in 1987; in 1993, the most recent year for which statistics are available, it was 14.7%.
13 The Consumption Tax (VAT), enacted in 1988, was hardly the kind of tax policy that the Maekawa Report envisioned.
14 The Trade Policy Review Mechanism (one of the multilateral trade agreements annexed to the Agreement Establishing the World Trade Organisation) provides that the trade policies and practices of every WTO member shall be subject to periodic reviews, the frequency of which shall depend on the member's share of world trade. In the case of Japan, the frequency is to be every two years. As of this writing it is unclear how deeply these reviews (reports on which will be published by the WTO Secretariat) will delve into the subject of Japan's barriers to imports.
15 For detailed information about specific cases, the best sources are the annual reports issued in March of every year by the Office of the Trade and Investment

Ombudsman, located within the Economic Planning Agency, and reports issued from time to time by foreign chambers of commerce in Japan.

16 Except the United States Treasury bond market, where "over-presence" has political value.

17 Article II:2 of the GATT provides, in relevant part, "Nothing [in the tariff bindings] shall prevent any contracting party from imposing at any time on the importation of any product . . . a charge equivalent to an internal tax imposed ... in respect of the like domestic product . . . ." This loophole is the twin of the loophole cited in note 7 above.

18 Report of the GATT Working Party on Border Tax Adjustments (1970), cited at GATT, *Analytical Index, 6th Edition* (Geneva, 1993), p. 135.

19 GATT, *Analytical Index, 6th Edition* (Geneva, 1993), pp. 759–760. But see the Understanding on the Interpretation of Article XXIV of the General Agreement on Tariffs and Trade (one of the multilateral trade agreements annexed to the Agreement Establishing the World Trade Organisation), in which the members of the WTO pledge to rectify both deficiencies.

CHAPTER 3
GOVERNMENT RELATIONS AND THE ADMINISTRATIVE PROCESS: ENGINEERING THE REGULATORY ENVIRONMENT

by John P. Stern

The road into the city centre from a major international airport in North America, Europe, Southeast Asia or even China will be lined with billboards advertising major international brands. Yet while Toshiba, Siemens and General Electric may jostle for highway advertising space in most industrial economies, the road from Tokyo's Narita International Airport is different. For more than 90 minutes, the visitor may travel without seeing a single advertisement for a foreign-brand product. A periodic Japanese government survey has quantified the scarcity of foreign-owned business in Japan: the ratio of sales by all foreign-capital companies (American, European, Asian and other) in Japan to total sales in Japan is a mere 0.9%, and has been falling for the past five years.[1] Thus, for the foreign-owned company, the practice of managing one's relations with the Japanese government, business and society is often an exercise in playing a weak hand well.

In games involving a mixture of skill and chance, it sometimes happens that a player with a weak hand does well against other players, or at least limits his/her losses. In a decade of representing American-owned electronics, telecommunications and software companies in Japan, the author has influenced Japanese legislation, obtained a joint resolution of the Japanese Diet (national legislature), participated in government advisory bodies, served on the board of directors or overseers of Japanese trade associations, worked to develop Japanese national standards, authored a newspaper column in Japanese, appeared on late-night television "talk shows", written a section of a Japanese high school textbook, and spoken to audiences in Japan ranging from housewives to company presidents. In most cases, no foreign organisation had ever achieved such influence, and in all events the foreign business viewpoint was still a novelty. Of course, one must be prepared to accept defeats, unsatisfactory compromises and lingering problems: this is true even in a capital such as Washington, D.C., where the representation before the domestic government of foreign business interests is itself a major industry. Nevertheless, a foreign company with an understanding of the regulatory relations process, it must be emphasised, can demonstrably improve the environment for its business interests in Japan.

THE ROLE OF GOVERNMENT AND THE SOCIAL CONTRACT

The role of government in Japan remains strikingly different from ideas about government prevalent in the post-Reagan United States, the post-Thatcher United Kingdom, or even in contemporary Australia. Japan's history, culture and postwar economic success have combined to create an ethos that is increasingly difficult for many English-speaking foreigners to accept, but that remains highly attractive to economic reformers in Asia.

It is not uncommon to encounter the feeling among the generation who entered Japan's military during the Second World War that Japan was defeated because it lacked access to key natural resources or because the enemy had superior technology. The "lessons" of the past are reflected in the present. To take one instance, if one looks at Japan's energy policy, one finds that Japan goes to great lengths to obtain petroleum resources, such as crude oil, natural gas and LNG, from a wide spectrum of countries around the world, rather than only from the cheapest vendor. This policy insulates Japan against the vagaries of Middle East politics, allows Japan to bargain down prices through its ability to switch energy suppliers, and makes the country independent of any attempt by a latter-day President Roosevelt to embargo oil to Japan. The group of engineers who developed Japan's semiconductor production equipment industry under guidance of the Ministry of International Trade and Industry sing WWII Japanese military songs when they have their annual reunion:[2] they have succeeded in giving Japan technology as good as its (largely American) rivals. For the wartime generation of Japanese men, Japan's national security requires that it has technology at least as good as that of foreign countries, and a supply of natural resources that is not subject to interdiction by the actions of foreign countries. As Japan continues to enjoy a half-century of peace and prosperity, the younger generation of Japanese civil servant may personally be uninfluenced by the Second World War, but he/she works in a system created by those who were haunted by the idea of avoiding a second defeat due to dependence on foreign technology and supplies.

The Allied Occupation flooded Japan with U.S. ideas of government and society. Some of those ideas, such as universal female suffrage, continue to promote democratisation in Japan much as their proponents envisioned. Other U.S. ideas were quickly domesticated: Japanese antitrust law was introduced with the assumption that it would grow following the U.S. model, but it has never developed the private right of action or treble damages that are key to U.S. antitrust enforcement. The U.S. Occupation created a judiciary whose independence was guaranteed, but was unable to recreate the historical struggles that made the U.S. judiciary not only independent, but also one of the three co-equal powers of government. As a result, the Japanese judiciary is honest and generally apolitical. Unfortunately, it is sometimes so independent as to be aloof, with little interest in business issues, a sense of monetary damages that reflect prices and wages of a past generation, and a pace of adjudication so slow as to make the final decision often moot. It is a common but dangerous mistake for foreigners to conclude that a Japanese organisation, law or institution with a name or formal role similar to that of a U.S. institution functions in the same way as its U.S. progenitor. In some cases, the Japanese institution created during the Allied Occupation may actually be negative toward U.S.-owned business interests in contemporary Japan.

From the Occupation to the 1964 Tokyo Olympics, Japan was a relatively poor country. In 1960, Japan had a per capita GNP of only $477, barely 20% that of the United States. Fast forward to 1990, and Japan's per capita GNP exceeded that of the United States, and had multiplied nearly fifty-fold.[3] The Council of Competitiveness, a Washington think-tank, found that Japan's standard of living showed 77% real growth between 1973 and 1993, compared to only 29% real growth for the American standard of living.[4] Japanese life expectancy is among the highest in the world, and its crime rate per person is among the lowest in the world. Japanese unemployment is low, Japanese tourist spending is high, and Japanese companies are among the largest in the world. A city block that lay in ashes in 1945 may now be among the most expensive pieces of real estate in the world. Foreign critics of Japanese economic practices overlook the massive and objective gains in the Japanese standard of living that those practices engendered. The European who lectures Japan on its "rabbit hutch" level of housing, and who then returns to double-digit unemployment in Europe, and the American who lectures Japan on its lack of consumerism, and then returns to a double-digit murder rate in the U.S., are frequent visitors to Japan. Neither understand that a population, be it Japanese, American or European, that is prosperous and safe, is unlikely to feel that its government is in need of revolutionary reform.

The Japanese social contract for the last 30 years has been simple: so long as the Japanese standard of living, evidenced by health and disposable income, continues to rise, the government will be given considerable leeway in economic, trade and foreign policy. This license to run the country is granted by Japanese even if it means a lesser level of individual rights that one might insist upon in much of the Anglo-American legal system. Historically, the Japanese have never experienced the Anglo-American legal system, and in the view of many Japanese, a small, secure house is a better social bargain than a large one that cannot be paid for lack of job security or that cannot be defended against rampant crime. The government relations advisor to foreign interests can argue, for example, that an existing Japanese policy will not serve Japan's goals in the future because the world has changed, or can argue that an existing Japanese policy harms one group of Japanese interests that now deserve government support. It must always be remembered, though, that the average Japanese central government official is proud of the success of Japan's economic system, feels that its success has vindicated his/her ministry's actions, and is increasingly intolerant of lectures on foreign economic systems that he/she feels have failed to equal Japan's record.

INDUSTRIAL POLICY

Much of what has been written about Japanese industrial policy in the last decade has actually been a discussion about the kind of economic policies the United States, the EC or Australia should pursue, as opposed to the kinds of policies Japan actually pursues. In these foreign discussions, Japanese "industrial policy" is typically attacked as inimical to free trade, and an oppressive exercise in "picking winners and losers."

The author has met very few Japanese career or elected government officials who privately believe in "free trade", if "free trade" means that a foreign company with a comparative advantage in a certain commercial sector should be allowed to gain market share in Japan at the expense of less competitive domestic firms. To the average Japanese government official, the free-market policies of post-Reagan America or post-Thatcher Britain are more a warning than an example. U.S. and British government officials are privately viewed as at best foolish, and at worst grossly negligent, for allowing foreign-capital companies to dominate significant areas of their respective economies. True, Japanese regulators may believe that Japan needs the cutting-edge telecommunications technology, or the lucrative insurance market, or the innovative airline industry that deregulation can bring. In common with bureaucracies everywhere, of course, Japanese regulators fear the diminution of their authority implied by deregulation. Even beyond self-interest, though, Japanese government officials believe that a free market economy brings with it unacceptable social and economic upheaval, in which productive citizens are suddenly rendered jobless, and companies that were mainstays of the local economy one day are bankrupt the next. Public opinion surveys regularly show that the average Japanese citizen is also reluctant to allow more competitive foreign products into the domestic market if the result is unemployment for their fellow Japanese. Thus, Japanese government officials believe that their role is to stand between their economy and free market forces as a buffer and a filter for the winds of change. Change cannot be postponed inevitably, but many Japanese government officials feel that change can be managed and measured out in controlled doses.

Japanese industrial policy has never been an exercise in "picking winners and losers" and for this reason Japan has created competitive industries without the continuing state subsidies of France's policy of "national champions." Rather, Japanese industrial policy is about reducing the risk to Japanese business of uncertainty in markets. "Industrial policy" may run the gamut from study missions, to joint research, industry-wide standards-making, government subsidies, the creation of new industry associations, laws empowering ministries to restructure markets, and operating as a quasi-receiver for dying industries. Some industrial policies have been strikingly successful: Japan went from a net importer of semiconductors to a major exporter after 1979 as a result of Japanese government policies promoting a domestic semiconductor industry. Some industrial policies have been a failure: the billions of dollars poured into the Japanese aviation industry have yet to produce a Japanese jet plane competitive in world markets. Some industrial policies have been a trade-off: although lacking both basic materials and cheap electric power, Japan created an aluminium industry. However, because Japanese aluminium is among the most expensive in the world, Japanese customers for aluminium such as the can and automobile industries have been rendered less competitive. These customer industries are increasingly obtaining raw and finished aluminium products overseas and importing them into Japan, making the domestic aluminium industry in turn less stable. More recently, some Japanese industrial policies have been industrial mercy killing. The Japanese cement industry, for example, was competitive on world markets in past decades but can no longer hope to take significant market share from Taiwanese, Korean or Brazilian competitors. As a result, the Ministry of International Trade and Industry has been assisting in liquidating major portions of the domestic cement industry in the past few years.[5]

Often, actions by a government ministry in the name of "industrial policy" are those which the private sector itself agrees are necessary, but which it cannot pursue itself due to inter-company rivalry.

The attitude of Japanese industry toward industrial policies is ambiguous. Like their regulators, Japanese companies do not like to be dependent on foreign sources, and traditionally have wished to understand and control every technology key to their industry. But many larger Japanese companies often resemble teen-age boys and girls, loudly insisting on their independence but returning home for money and comfort. Government officials, in turn, are occasionally quoted in the Japanese press as deriding the notion that industries under their jurisdiction have the maturity to succeed in world markets without government guidance.

Readers should beware of periodic statements in the English-language press that Japanese officials, while once active in guiding industrial growth, are now too "weak" to influence the sectors under their charge. This expression of self-deprecation would be odd coming from the mouth of a bureaucrat anywhere, and should be viewed with suspicion. The statement's purpose is to convince foreign governments that there is no point in demanding action from Japanese regulators regarding Japanese industry exclusionary behaviour, because the bureaucrats are powerless to order change. The Japanese press never describes the major central ministries as "weak": the canard is confined to a gullible U.S. and EC, not Japanese, audience.

Industrial policies in Japan are not necessarily anti-foreign. In many cases, Japanese industrial policies are neutral regarding the source of capital of the Japanese corporation benefitting from the policy. For example, the Japanese research and development tax credit and depreciation systems can make it much less expensive for a company to develop certain technologies in Japan.[6] The Japan Development Bank maintains a system of low-interest, long-term, fixed-rate loans for regional and industrial development that has been repeatedly tapped by foreign-owned companies, even though its primary focus is assisting Japanese-owned companies. Where industrial policies involve generating consensus on standards or testing, even foreign-owned firms may prefer Japan to the anarchy of overseas markets. Certain pre-competitive technologies that are the focus of Japanese industrial policies, such as micromachines, may indeed best be addressed by research consortia rather than the laboratories of individual profit-making companies. Often Japanese industrial policy results in the generous funding of research into topics that in the United States are left to the meagre budgets of the private sector: the creation of a high-efficiency battery for electric automobiles and the technical problems of managing a power grid for the necessary battery charging stations, for example. The mission of the government relations advisor to foreign-owned companies, however, is to prevent Japanese industrial policies affecting his/her clients' industry from degenerating into protectionist policies.

MOTIVATING THE REGULATOR

The government relations professional working for a U.S. company will quickly discover that the principal restrictions on his/her activity are generated by corporate headquarters. Certain U.S. laws, such as the Foreign Corrupt Practices Act, can be interpreted in an excessively cautious fashion that prevents some activity. In fact, the U.S. Foreign Corrupt Practices Act is not a bar to either the ethical or the successful management of government relations in Japan. Some U.S. multinational corporations are hypersensitive to contacts with foreign governments, and ban individual contact with Japanese legislators. Unfortunately, group or indirect contact with Japanese legislators is almost always ineffective in promoting the company's interest against competitors.

Japan does not regulate "lobbyists" per se, perhaps because very few Japanese choose a career as an independent lobbyist. Most of the visitors to Japanese government offices seeking understanding of their company's position are company employees in the *shogai bu* (External Affairs Department), or in the operating division directly affected by regulation. The Japanese regulation of the legal profession is described elsewhere in this book.

Japan's Campaign Funds Regulation Law flatly forbids an elected official from accepting funds from "a foreigner, a foreign juristic person, or other organisations where the majority of members are foreigners or foreign juristic persons".[7] At first reading, it would seem that Japan's law, with its ban on contributions by Japanese corporations the majority of whose shareholders are foreign persons or organisations[8] is stricter than comparable U.S. statutes that allow campaign contributions by Japanese subsidiaries in the U.S. to candidates for U.S. national office. In practice, the Campaign Funds Regulation Law is less severe than it appears.

Nothing prevents an individual Japanese citizen, who happens to be an executive of a foreign-owned company, from making a campaign contribution.

Money may be the "mother's milk of politics" in Japan as well as elsewhere, but it is unlikely to be a useful means of improving relations with politicians in Japan. The Lockheed bribery scandal of the mid-1970s, in which the late Prime Minister Kakuei Tanaka was found to have taken funds ultimately traced to a foreign corporation, led to political oblivion for all who received the bribe. Since then, no Japanese politician wishes to allow even the appearance of impropriety with foreign companies. In addition, the scale of fund-raising is so vast in Japan as to be beyond the means of most U.S. and EC firms. The author attended a party in honour of then Prime Minister Noboru Takeshita, for example, in which US$81 million in campaign contributions was reportedly collected in the space of two hours. In contrast, an incumbent candidate for President of the United States would be considered very well funded if he were to raise US$81 million for re-election after four years in office.

While funding scandals involving elected officials and Japanese (not foreign) contributors are common in Japan, bribery cases involving officials are rare. In more than a decade, the author recalls only three prosecutions for bribery against central government career public servants subject to the National Civil Servants Law.[9] This law is enforced much more strictly by the prosecutor's office than is the law relating to political contributions, and judges often make an example of punishment of corrupt civil servants.

In the elite ministries, career officials are typically indignant at the suggestion that their pursuit of Japan's national interest could be tainted by personal material considerations. The author was present one day when a *kacho* (director)-level central ministry official was visited by a new salesman (a Japanese citizen) for a Japanese-owned office supply company. The hapless salesman proceeded to offer the official a small towel, a box of tissues and a roll of cellophane food wrap. These are typical gifts offered for a new account by Japanese banks, small businesses and even the post office. The retail value is less than US$10, and few in Japanese society view this type of gift as worth enough to influence the recipient's actions. Nevertheless, the government official broke off his conversation with the author and told the salesman: "I don't know you. I don't accept gifts. Get out." Financial favours for civil servants may be a common business practice in other parts of Asia, but they are a fatal mistake in dealing with Japanese government officials.

What coin does one use to obtain information, if the exchange of money is forbidden? There are a variety of reasons why a member of the Japanese government might wish to meet with a representative of foreign-owned interests in Japan. In creating policies for Japan, officials routinely survey practices and experiences in other countries. The level of research is astonishing: in the course of discussing a change in the cellular telephone regime in Japan, the Ministry of Posts and Telecommunications studied telephone rates and fees in 44 countries. Japan's modern history has attuned it to the need to learn from foreign (typically Western) experience. In addition, a willingness to learn from the successes and failures of others is one of the great strengths of the Japanese character, as well as being a component of good government everywhere. The foreign-capital company in Japan is a key source of information on markets, technologies, trends and social issues for Japanese regulators. Assistance in visiting overseas sites where an innovative regime or technology is practiced is always appreciated, and many foreign firms host a visit to their headquarters or factory as part of the itinerary. Information about foreign practices is appreciated by government officials striving to create rational policies for Japan that avoid problems encountered overseas. At the less heroic end of the spectrum, bureaucrats everywhere seek to avoid controversy, and representatives of foreign-capital companies can be useful barometers of whether contemplated regulation will inadvertently lead to an international trade dispute. The author has frequently assisted in molding Japanese administrative measures so that they can accomplish their goal without inadvertently burdening non-Japanese firms.

Regulators use advisory panels to obtain a variety of views on a subject of regulatory interest, and to obtain broad support for their proposals. Each ministry has a number of formal statutory advisory committees called Study Councils *(shingikai)* that are open to Japanese citizens with knowledge of the regulatory area; a few Study Councils have Japanese members who are executives of foreign-capital companies in Japan. More common are the scores of unofficial advisory bodies and study groups created by senior officials in a ministry. These groups are conducted entirely in Japanese, but are open by invitation without regard to nationality. It should be the goal of every foreign-capital company in Japan to participate in government advisory panels affecting its business. The panels are also a useful source of high-level industry contacts and regularly provide an education on worldwide industry trends and technologies.

The civil service is peopled by officials who typically have been with their ministry or agency since graduation from a university. In contrast, Japanese politicians come from all walks of life: it is rare for a politician, not the son of a politician, to have been a Diet member all his life. Thus, the representative of foreign semiconductor interests in Japan may find, for example, that at least one Diet member was a salesman for a distributor of American semiconductor products before entering politics. Several Diet members hold degrees in electrical engineering. Such people are interested in what a representative of American electronics interests might have to say about the world electronics industry because they are interested in the subject matter.

There are many Diet members who have lived or studied overseas, often on a Fulbright scholarship. It is common for central government agencies to send relatively young officials overseas for a posting to an international organisation, or an advanced degree at a famous foreign university. These members of the Japanese government often retain an interest in things foreign, and a desire to trade information with knowledgeable representatives of foreign interests. There is a parliamentary exchange program with the legislators of virtually every one of Japan's trading partners.

Curiosity is often enough to motivate a government official to meet with a representative of foreign interests. The author has been told many times by Diet members that they had never been briefed by a Japanese-speaking foreigner, and that curiosity represented a major reason for scheduling the initial meeting. Many civil servants have never been visited by a Japanese-speaking foreigner either. Once the initial curiosity has been sated, whether one is invited again depends on the facts and arguments one presents, of course, not on one's nationality.

Behind the job title is a person, and Japanese government officials share the same emotions as people everywhere. It may happen that one can engage a certain official on his/her favourite hobby, or his/her favourite sport, or his/her favourite Italian restaurant. At times, a skillful practitioner can benefit from a desire by an elected official to put officials "in their place" when the politician felt that the bureaucrat was disrespectful. There are internal rivalries and personal feuds in Japanese organisations, as there are everywhere.

The representative of foreign-capital interests must be alert to being used as a pawn in domestic disputes. A bureaucrat may seek to convince a reluctant Japanese industry to follow a certain industrial policy by allowing a foreign company, for a time, to compete vigorously with the domestic industry. The idea is to allow the foreign firm to harry the Japanese firms into seeking the sanctuary of government guidance, at which point the foreign firm's privileges are often curtailed. When two ministries are engaged in battles of jurisdiction over an issue, one ministry may seek to use a foreign firm as a critic of the rival ministry. Foreign interests can be effective in obtaining an agency's budget request from politicians in the face of resistance from rival ministries and the Ministry of Finance. For example, the author successfully intervened to maintain the budget for a program providing beneficial financing for foreign interests by pointing out to the Finance Minister (a politician) that the program, if undiminished, was scheduled to finance key foreign investment in his electoral district. An allegation that foreign interests favour or do not favour a certain policy is an often-used arrow in the quiver of politicians, regulators, reporters and other Japanese advocates. The concern over foreign opinion may at times be genuine, and at other times it is merely a rhetorical trick for promoting the speaker's agenda. The representative of foreign interests should not automatically reject the role of a tool. As in paddling a kayak through rapid waters, sometimes the safest path is to steer close to the rocks, and sometimes the safest path is to avoid them altogether.

PLAYERS ON THE BUSINESS STAGE

Regulation of the Japanese business environment often appears faceless and monolithic to outside observers. This is due in large part to the fact that very little useful information is ever translated from the Japanese. In addition, in the Orient, it is common not to reveal any more information to outsiders than what one thinks the outsiders will be pleased to hear. Members of the Japanese government are rarely under any legal obligation to reveal pending rule-making that will affect a foreign company's interests. There is typically no right of notice that one's interests are at stake and no right to an opportunity to be heard before a regulation is promulgated. As a result, the average foreign company is often oblivious to government forces shaping its destiny. Unfortunately, in a high-cost, competitive environment such as Japan, sleepwalking is not a viable corporate strategy. The representative of foreign interests needs to understand the powers and uses of the key players on the Japanese business stage.

OFFICIALS

Foreign newspaper editors, academics, legislators and other malleable opinion leaders who visit Japan are regularly paraded before a series of English-speaking Japanese, all of whom inform the foreigners that in Japan, the civil service runs the country. Yet if one visits the office of a key Diet member shortly after New Year's Day, one will find a 15 centimeter-high stack of calling cards from civil servants at the Bureau Chief and Vice Minister level, begging the Diet member's continuing favour in the New Year. One of the secrets in Japan best kept from foreign-owned companies is that key elected politicians have enormous power over the bureaucracy.

It is certainly true that on a day-to-day basis the civil servant runs the Japanese government. Political appointees are limited to the Minister/Agency Chief and the Parliamentary Vice Minister. Civil service is traditionally the nation's highest calling. In the major central ministries, all career, non-technical officials will have graduated from an elite university and scored at the top of a national examination before joining a ministry or agency directly after completing university studies. Japanese central ministry officials are paid at a level that seems to be competitive with the private sector initially, less competitive in early mid-career, and competitive again for ages 45–59[10]. However, the person who enters government service is not motivated by money, but rather, at least at the elite ministries, by the opportunity to work for Japan's future. Indeed, on the rare occasions when a civil servant quits, the typical complaint is not the salary, but that the job was not the higher calling the employee hoped for, merely bureaucratic infighting and needless generation of documents.

It may come as a shock to read that while the typical Japanese central ministry civil servant works for the good of Japan, he/she does not necessarily view himself as working for the good of Japanese business. Businessmen are privately viewed by many Japanese government officials as a necessary evil, the means by which a resource-poor island nation became rich. This does not imply, however, that businessmen can be trusted to think of anything more noble than their own short-term financial interests. The latest Western management consultant may have replaced Confucius as required reading in many ministries, but the Confucian view that merchants are an unruly, selfish social segment is by no means dead. Many of the civil servants in elite ministries would be insulted by the notion that they operated for the benefit of individual Japanese companies, or even for the benefit of a certain Japanese industry: they work for Japan.

Many civil servants view Japanese politicians as opportunists and dilettantes interested only in campaign contributions. These same civil servants, however, are careful not to express this view in public, and immediately and courteously answer telephone calls from a Diet member. Nevertheless, most ministries have a folklore tradition of famous gaffes committed by uninformed and unprepared politicians who suddenly were placed in the Minister's seat. Of course, one can hear similar stories from the career civil service in most world capitals.

For the first 10–15 years, promotion in the civil service is largely based on entering class: a satisfactory employee is moved up the ranks in lock step with other employees who entered the ministry during the same year. Thereafter, competition begins for the most influential posts. Since the identity of the individual who holds a key post can be a matter of great concern to Japanese companies with business before a ministry, there are several periodicals devoted to following the careers of promising individuals. If one visits the book stores in the basements of the major ministries, one will find, in addition to the magazines following the fortunes of movie stars and business tycoons, publications such as *Gekkan Kankai* ("Monthly Bureaucrat World"), that are devoted to "handicapping" the horses racing for a certain prestigious ministry post. Patronage from a powerful Diet member is necessary in most ministries to rise to the Director General or higher level, which is one of the reasons civil servants make a pilgrimage to legislator's offices.

Post-ministry employment is a major force in understanding some civil service actions. This topic will be covered in more detail in the section on Japanese industry associations.

LEGISLATORS

In many Western countries, national legislators and national civil servants check and balance each other to control the national agenda. Even in countries in which the civil service is firmly in control, politicians fancy themselves to be influential. In Japan, in contrast, the author had the startling experience of testifying before a Diet panel on deregulation, only to be told by a politician that "the civil service has done a good job of managing Japan, and we Diet members lack the ability to do better". Not all of this Diet member's colleagues might agree with him: some Diet members are genuine experts in such fields as telecommunications policy, either through extensive study or as a result of previous employment by the Ministry of Posts and Telecommunications. Still, for most of the postwar era, the Japanese public, the Japanese civil service and the Diet members themselves have been satisfied with a system in which civil servants not only run the country on a daily basis, but also draft laws and set industrial and financial policy. Although the Cabinet does have an impartial official who checks the drafting of legislation, the Diet does not have professional staff members who create legislation, and the modest allotment for secretaries given to Diet members is usually exhausted on secretaries fulfilling constituent-service and fundraising, not legislative, functions. Even the handful of legislators who have non-Japanese as secretaries do not use them to compare pending Japanese legislation to foreign prototypes. Legislation submitted by individual Diet members is not rare, but such individual member bills are almost never passed. Formal hearings on policy matters in which advocates from the private sector can appear before the Diet as witnesses to champion given policies are rare. The full text of legislation is not routinely available before it becomes law, although a general outline of pending legislation typically appears in the trade press once the draft has been sent to the Diet. During the era when the Liberal Democratic Party (LDP) had a majority of both houses of the Diet, it was common for non-LDP members to be denied a copy of the full text of legislation before they were asked to vote on it, on the LDP-inspired theory that non-LDP votes were irrelevant anyway.

Despite these characteristics, the Diet is key to the success of career officials' plans in more ways than personal career advancement. To illustrate, it will be useful to follow the typical path of new legislation in Japan.

At some point in time, a ministry may decide that it should consider a new law dealing with a certain industry or technology. It may reach this decision as a result of study of overseas markets and domestic trends, or as a result of the deliberations of a private-sector advisory panel, or as a result of the urging of a few senior business leaders, or because a rival ministry is preparing to encroach into the sector and the ministry wants to clarify its authority at the highest level. The ministry will draft a law to accomplish its purpose. The law will be circulated to a small group of affected interests for initial review. It is common for Japanese laws to state as little as is necessary to understand the subject of the legislation, with the actual details being determined after the legislation passes and authorised by an article delegating to the ministry the authority to promulgate implementing regulations. Once the ministry is confident that the legislation makes sense to key private-sector interests, the draft legislation is brought to a small group of Diet members interested in the ministry's work. Prior to July 1993, when the LDP lost its Diet majority, that group was typically the LDP's party study bureau for the ministry or issue concerned. Since the head of the standing, bipartisan Diet committee in charge of the ministry concerned was also, prior to July 1993, always an LDP member, the head of the relevant Diet committee was informed simultaneously when the majority party was briefed. If the politicians in the ministry's *zoku* ("tribe", a band of politicians in charge of issues involving a certain ministry) are supportive of the law, the law will then be placed on the Cabinet's agenda for formal approval.

Cabinet members in Japan are simultaneously both elected politicians, and heads of the various ministries and agencies of the government. In general, Cabinet members usually follow the directions of their career ministry staff in voting, but occasionally override those recommendations when they conflict with their personal political interests. This happens because, with the exception of the Prime Minister, most Cabinet members are still hoping to become Prime Minister some day, and none of them wish to be associated with politically damaging legislation. Conflicts over jurisdiction between ministries are resolved at the Cabinet level if not before: the tradition is that any Cabinet member can veto the submission to the Diet of pending legislation. In practice, the major reason for such a veto is inter-ministry jurisdictional conflict. In order to avoid such a veto, the submitting ministry will try to mollify other affected ministries well before the Cabinet vote, and will in addition try to seek as much political support for the legislation as possible among non-Cabinet Diet members .

A ministry's budget is also ultimately in the hands of Diet members. Between August and October of a typical year, each ministry will begin to put together its desired budget for the next fiscal year. During this period, some of the more aggressive ministries will float "trial balloon" ideas for budget allocations, to determine Japanese industry and political support for the ministry's new ideas. Many of these "trial balloons" are never funded, but this period is valuable for frank discussions with ministry officials concerning the ministry's future interests. Around October, a ministry begins to negotiate for approval of its final budget with the Ministry of Finance. The Ministry of Finance desires to avoid overspending of the national budget and duplication of effort among ministries, in addition to pursuing fiscal policies that vary with the economic cycle. It is notable that in recent years, the Ministry of Finance has refused to fund many "industrial policy" projects in which the government would fund action that industry was likely to take on its own, with private funds. The Ministry of Finance has also forced ministries to take joint jurisdiction of projects, or abandon them altogether, rather than fund each ministry in competition with another.

During the budget process, civil servants commute to the offices and homes of Diet members. Once convinced, Diet members are able to pressure the Ministry of Finance because the Diet (initially the House of Representatives) must approve the budget prepared by the Ministry of Finance. Companies and localities in a Diet member's district that will benefit from a national budget allocation are recruited by the ministry to exhort the Diet member to support the ministry's budget request.

Readers who follow Japanese politics will want to know how the process described above has changed since the Liberal Democratic Party lost its long-standing majority of both Houses of the Diet in July 1993. The answer is that the situation has become more difficult for the civil service and slightly more favourable toward the representative of foreign-capital interests. In order to assure political support and passage, the civil service must now brief not only members of the LDP, but also members of other key parties. Some of these new party members were LDP members for most of their political lives; the cynical would say that they are the same personalities with a new party label. Their views are well known. However, there are other legislators who are now relevant to building consensus who were ignored by the civil service in the past, but now must be consulted. Having been ignored for so long, these politicians are now wary of over-reliance on the civil service, and often welcome the fresh perspective brought by a representative of foreign-capital interests. In sum, the more politicians who must be consulted by a ministry, the more ears available to the foreign-capital company.

In theory, after the legislation has been submitted by the government to the Diet, there should be a period of uncertainty as to whether the legislation will pass, as rival political factions debate the merits of the new law. In more than a decade, the author has seen budget bills delayed, and has seen bills with broad social implications, such as a national retail consumption tax, fail to pass. He has never seen, however, a government-submitted bill regulating an industry or a technology fail to pass. To the extent that a foreign-capital company is concerned about pending Japanese legislation, the time to address those concerns is before the draft reaches the Cabinet approval meeting.

THE PRIME MINISTER

In Japan's parliamentary system, as in the English system, the party with the majority of seats in the House of Representatives names the Prime Minister. The Prime Minister serves until he is unable to retain the allegiance of a majority of seats, or less frequently, until he is statutorily required to call an election. Here the similarity to the English system ends: although powerful Japanese Prime Ministers that genuinely drive economic reform, like the late Kakuei Tanaka, have been known, recent Prime Ministers have been much less dynamic. The powers of a Japanese Prime Minister are far less than those of an American President who is elected for a fixed term and names the country's top 3000 bureaucrats from the list of his political allies. In contrast, Japanese bureaucrats have been known to comment that "Prime Ministers come and go" but that the bureaucracy will still be in authority after the next election.

The Prime Minister is unlikely to be the right person for a foreign interest to approach regarding the Japanese regulatory climate. The Prime Minister, indeed, is unlikely to be approachable at all: at the summit of Japanese politics, he no longer needs to cater to his constituents, further his career or fight battles with other ministries. Only the heads of the largest foreign companies are likely to obtain access to the Prime Minister. Accordingly, foreign companies that believe that they must address the Prime Minister have two choices. Either they must have their message carried by their own head of state, ambassador or minister, or they must establish a friendship with a promising legislator at a stage early enough to gain entrance once the formerly obscure individual becomes Prime Minister.

PRIVATE CORPORATIONS

Japanese corporations owned by private investors appear to the businessman in a wide variety of roles: customer, competitor, supplier, subcontractor, distributor, licensee, investor, etc. To the government relations professional, however, Japanese corporations are either supportive of, opposed to, or neutral about a change in the regulatory environment affecting foreign-owned business.

All Japanese corporations are not created equal in terms of government influence. In most years surveyed, for example, the construction, banking and real estate industries have been the leaders in political contributions to Diet members; in contrast, the Japanese electronics industry typically represents less than 10% of political contributions.[11] Within a given industry, larger companies are almost always more influential at the ministries, if only because they have the staff needed to monitor administrative actions. Certain ministries, in turn, are known to be more or less solicitous of the opinions of smaller companies. At the Diet level, though, a relatively small company may happen to have great influence with a powerful legislator. The foreign-owned company in Japan will usually be at a disadvantage against better-known and larger Japanese firms in the industry. Most foreign companies, even world-famous ones, are unknown in much of rural Japan. Traditionally it is rural Japan that re-elects its representatives until they have the seniority needed to control key Diet positions. A Japanese telecommunications giant that employs Japanese voters in nearly every Diet district is likely to gain a more earnest hearing from a politician than the foreign-owned company that employs people only within a 50-km radius of downtown Tokyo. The personalities of industry executives play a role as well: a gregarious, outspoken, well-connected Japanese company executive can be more influential on industry policy than the plodding head of a rival Japanese firm 10 times the size.

For every demand of a foreign government, or market-expanding proposal of a foreign company, there is a sector of Japanese industry that stands to benefit. Regrettably, if one expects the Japanese industry or companies that benefit publicly to support the foreign position, one will be disappointed: nearly every Japanese organisation will shy away from public support of a foreign company against a domestic one. However, privately, Japanese allies can be helpful in locating and convincing Japanese decision-makers. They also afford the foreign business interest the ability to argue persuasively that the desired change is not a stark battle between native and foreign interests. Rather, the argument can be made that desired change will allow even more Japanese interests to prosper than before, with the relevant Japanese interests appearing at appropriate times to form an approving chorus.

To find a striking example, one has only to look at the flourishing Tokyo shops of an internationally famous fast-food hamburger chain with headquarters in the United States. This chain does not sell hamburgers made of domestically-produced Japanese beef: it could not afford to, because Japanese beef can cost hundreds of U.S. dollars per kilogram. Predictably, Japanese domestic beef interests vocally opposed the import of the cheaper foreign beef patties that were the basis of an inexpensive fast-food hamburger. Many U.S. companies would have abandoned the general Japanese market at this point; indeed, the chief U.S. rival to the company in question until very recently limited its market in Japan to U.S. military bases. However, this successful company gathered together all the Japanese interests that would benefit from a nationwide chain of uniform hamburger shops: the farmers who produced the milk for milkshakes; the bakers who produced the hamburger buns; the paper companies and printers who produced the cups, napkins, wrapping materials and boxes for millions of hamburgers; the suppliers of sugar, salt, and cooking oil; the advertising firms and trucking firms that served the chain; even the real estate agents who located the shops were enlisted to form a powerful counter-lobby to the Japanese beef interests. The company even formed its own Japanese hamburger trade association to create a forum for group action. The Japanese operation of this U.S.-based hamburger chain is now ubiquitous.

The successful introduction of new products or technologies to the Japanese market does not end with the creation of a coalition or the approval of a new store, product or service. One's Japanese competitors, faced with the relatively rare defeat at the hands of foreign-based interests, can nimbly shift gears and ram their own identical store, product or service into the breach created by the lobbying of foreign-capital companies. To be truly successful, the foreign-based company must not only create a broad-based revolution in an industry, it must also make sure that once the revolution succeeds, its own family takes over the throne. Time and time again, foreign governments have pressured Japan to open its markets to foreign companies, only to find that once the doors are open, the foreign companies are trampled by hordes of Japanese companies moving faster into the new business opportunity.

PUBLIC CORPORATIONS

Japan has approximately 100 corporations or entities that are public corporations, i.e., a majority or all of their stock is owned by the Japanese government. In some sectors, these public corporations face limited competition, and therefore may be open to business relations with competitive foreign companies. In most areas public corporations have an effective monopoly. As a result, these corporations are uninfluenced by normal business considerations, and their staff rarely has any business experience, or any experience with foreign interests. Since the Japanese government has acknowledged many of the public corporations as quasi-governmental organizations, remedies for problems with public corporations may be available through bilateral or multilateral trade treaties. In recent years, some public corporations have become sensitive to adverse publicity because they wish eventually to sell their stock to private Japanese investors, or because they wish to avoid being pilloried as ripe targets for deregulation and dissolution. The traditional public corporation, though, is virtually impervious to market forces: the Japan Tobacco and Salt Public Corporation, for example, is the lineal descendant of the feudal government's tobacco and salt monopoly. The feudal government was toppled in 1867, but the Japan Tobacco and Salt Public Corporation did not lose its monopoly until 1985, and did not have non-government shareholders until 1994.

INDUSTRY ASSOCIATIONS

The role of the thousands of Japanese industry associations in shaping markets and industries in Japan has only recently become the focus of English-language scholarship.[12] Japanese non-profit associations can be allies to the foreign-capital company, sources of information for the foreign-capital company, or barriers to market access.

Perhaps the best-known Japanese industry association overseas is the *Keidanren* (Japan Federation of Economic Organisations). This pan-industry chamber of commerce, under MITI jurisdiction, was originally composed of industries such as steel, electric power and shipbuilding that were the locomotive of Japan's economic recovery after the Second World War. The *Keidanren* then evolved into the organisation that channelled campaign contributions from large, established corporations to key Liberal Democratic Party members. With the evaporation of the LDP's majority in the Diet, and the consequent decline in the effectiveness for Japanese industry of political contributions, the *Keidanren* seems most active in the production of foreign-language public relations materials and the promotion of overseas lobbying activities. It has suffered notable failures in its inability to effect *Keidanren* policies on further competition in Japan's telecommunications market or deregulation of the Japanese economy in general. The *Keidanren,* unlike rival pan-industry organisations, has never had a self-made business tycoon or company founder as its head: the Chairman of the *Keidanren* has always been the employee of a company founded before he joined. On a given issue, such as procurement from overseas foreign suppliers, the *Keidanren* will typically produce a statement defensive of Japanese industry, but laced with vague promises of future change, while the rival *Keizai Doyu Kai* (Japan Association of Corporate Executives) will flatly acknowledge that to improve their image abroad, Japanese companies need to purchase more from local non-Japanese suppliers. In short, the advocate of foreign interests in Japan is likely to find that among the major pan-industry groups, the famous *Keidanren* will be less supportive of change than some of the newer groups such as the *Keizai Doyu Kai*, the *Nikkeiren* (Japan

Federation of Employers' Association) or regional business associations.

In the mature manufacturing industries, it is common for every member of an industry to belong to the single Japanese trade association that is without question in charge of that industry, product or technology. If every Japanese competitor belongs to the same group, it tends to produce a uniform exclusionary posture towards the "outsider" foreign-capital company. In newer manufacturing sectors, or in service industries, though, there is often no single trade association in charge. For example, Japan's software industry is fragmented into associations that represent software in mainframe computers, software in personal computers, software produced by systems integrators, software used in telecommunications networks, and software in consumer electronics. The viewpoint of an association representing developers of personal computer software, which are often smaller companies, is different from the viewpoint of an association representing giant manufacturers of Japanese mainframe computers. The evolution of technology can also drive a wedge between Japanese trade associations: two associations, one representing radios and one representing wired telephones, that 40 years ago had nothing in common, may now compete to control Japan's mobile telephone industry. From the viewpoint of the foreign-capital company attempting to enter a market, the less monolithic the industry associations influencing a market, the more likely a newcomer will be able to compete and prosper.

Traditionally, full membership in a Japanese manufacturing trade association is afforded only to companies that manufacture in Japan: this requirement disqualifies most foreign-owned companies, since few manufacture in Japan. Even when domestic manufacturing is present, the foreign-capital company is often barred from the board of directors, or from committees that discuss trade policy. Nevertheless, at times a foreign company's lack of participation in Japanese industry associations is due to ignorance of the Japanese association's role, unwillingness to pay the US$3000–US$100,000 initiation fees, or an ultimately futile attempt to control the Japan operation's group memberships from Washington, Brussels, or wherever the company's government affairs presence is located. Several important Japanese industry associations have representatives of foreign capital companies on their Board of Directors; the author, a foreigner, has held one such position for a decade.

Regardless of whether full, voting membership is available in a Japanese industry association, membership promotes the foreign-capital company's business in Japan. The association is usually a source of invaluable information on technology trends, standards, pending tax and environmental legislation, and market information on foreign markets. The opportunity to talk to competitors without antitrust liability is essential to maintaining a balanced view of where an industry is going, while the substantial user representation in many manufacturing trade associations is a source of future customers for the foreign-owned firm.

A 1993 Japan Fair Trade Commission survey of participation by 500 foreign-capital firms in Japanese trade associations indicates that 32.4% of foreign firms surveyed were not members of the relevant nonprofit organisation(s) for their industry.[13] Among Japanese nonprofit associations surveyed, 28.7% admitted discriminating against "outsiders",[14] and 72.1% admitted that their quality "seal of approval" was not available to "outsiders".[15] Of those foreign-capital firms that were not members of their industry association in Japan, 55.2% found it difficult to obtain information regarding their industry and customers in related industries, and 38% found it difficult to obtain Japanese government information.

Japanese- and foreign-capital companies alike share a weariness with the continuing proliferation of Japanese industry associations, often with vague or overlapping objectives, each requesting membership dues. The number of Japanese industry associations has mushroomed out of control because they offer bureaucrats a second career after leaving the civil service; they become *amakudari saki*, lit. "a place to which one descends from heaven."

In Japan, Article 34 of the Civil Code[16] provides that nonprofits can only be incorporated after receiving permission from the ministry with jurisdiction over the activities proposed for the new organisation. The Civil Code provides bureaucrats with the spark of life for nonprofit industry groups, and the power to supervise their finances. It is virtually impossible to form an incorporated nonprofit organisation without active promotion by the career civil service.

Japan's National Civil Servants Law provides the motive for injecting the personal interest of the bureaucrat into the establishment of new nonprofit industry groups. The National Civil Servants Law provides that a public servant may not become employed, for a period of two years after leaving public office, without a waiver by the National Personnel Agency[17], by a *for-profit* organisation that was under the jurisdiction of the public servant during a period up to five years prior to termination of public service.[18] This leaves a public servant with two choices while waiting out the statutory two-year ban on starting a second career with a corporation that would be most likely to value the bureaucrat's connections:

pursue a post with a for-profit corporation not directly under the jurisdiction of the public servant prior to the termination of public service, or pursue a post with a non-profit organisation.

Japanese on the average live longer than people in most other countries, but they retire from salaried white-collar occupations earlier: upon leaving a career at 55, the typical Japanese faces more than 20 years of retirement. Ministries are often on the lookout for opportunities to create new nonprofit retirement posts. However, an unfunded nonprofit industry group is of no use in providing a salary or pension[19] to a retired government official. Thus, ministries must consider the financial stability of nonprofit industry groups.

The ideal source of financial stability, of course, is a well-conceived organisation addressing a clear need of a wide variety of potential financial contributors. Unfortunately, the ideas of bureaucrats for post-retirement careers sometimes exceeds the interest of industry in paying for them. The *Keidanren*, for example, has reportedly refused at least nine times, since 1991, to fund ministerial ideas for new nonprofit organisations.[20] Some of the ideas, such as a sports promotion foundation to which industry was asked by the Ministry of Education to contribute ¥10 billion (about US$100 million) seem totally unnecessary. Others, such as an organisation proposed by the Ministry of Transport to place facilities for the handicapped in railroad stations, would have performed quasi-governmental functions that would not normally be funded by a ¥2 billion industry contribution.[21] In addition, none of the requests for funding new organisations were accompanied by promises to sunset organisations that had outlived their usefulness.

An unfortunate consequence of *amakudari saki* is an increase in regulations impeding market entry. This occurs because ministries will often give favoured nonprofit groups a monopoly on quasi-government functions such as certifications, standards and approvals. The income that the nonprofit group obtains from certification and approval fees, or from member companies that join to obtain closely-guarded information about standards, funds the personnel costs of the organisation. Nonprofit industry groups with quasi-governmental monopolies are common in U.S.-Japan trade disputes. Wherever a Japanese nonprofit group stands as a toll collector for market access by foreign-capital companies, the potential for international trade friction is high.

The author has experienced many international arguments over Japanese testing and certification associations, ranging from wired telecommunications customer premises equipment (1984) to software quality (1995). The representative of foreign interests can call on extensive precedent to argue that no single organisation should have a monopoly on mandatory testing and certification, that foreign test results, certifications and approvals be recognised in Japan, and that Japan should follow international norms rather than create its own unique technical standards. Unfortunately, persuasion does not always work in convincing an otherwise redundant Japanese nonprofit group to give up its sole source of revenue, and resort to Japanese and foreign government assistance is often necessary.

THE JAPANESE MASS MEDIA

In many parts of the English-speaking world, newspaper reporters picture themselves as critics of the established order and defenders of the disenfranchised. In Japan, ordinary reporters for the major newspapers travel in chauffeur-driven limousines with their newspaper's flag fluttering from an ornamental flagpole: reporters are bulwarks of the established order. The attention of the Japanese mass media can be one of the most powerful tools wielded by a representative of foreign-capital interests, but it is also one of the most difficult to use with precision.

The Japanese media, like the Japanese public, tends to be satisfied with Japan's achievements, and bewildered by foreign criticism, but it is not monolithic. The major split within the Japanese mass media is between newspapers, and other forms of media (chiefly magazines, broadcast media and books). The major newspapers' reporters are members of an institution called the "press club" *(kisha club)*.[22] Each major source of news, such as the Ministry of Finance, the *Keidanren*, or the Diet, will have its own press club. Only members of the press club can cover news at that institution without harassment and perhaps physical attack by newspaper reporters belonging to the press club. None of the foreign news media are full members of any Japanese press club, although a token representative of foreign media recently has been given the right to listen to Japanese press club briefings without asking questions. Conversely, members of a given press club are not allowed to cover any news except that originating in their club, for the two-year term of their membership in the press club.

As a result of the press club system, only a small group of reporters have constant access to news from a specific government or industry organisation. If they anger a news source in their assigned organisation, the news source may refuse to talk to them in the future. This would result in rival newspapers having exclusive access to the news source, and the reporter's being unable to file stories as detailed as his/her rivals. Since the reporter is unable to cover news other than that from his/her press club during a two-year period, angering a government news source jeopardises the reporter's career. In contrast, because many major magazines and television stations are denied access to the press club system, they often begin with some measure of hostility to newspapers' coverage of issues.

There are a number of reasons why a foreign-capital organisation might wish to talk to the Japanese mass media. The exchange of information with individual Japanese reporters who are knowledgeable about the inner workings and personalities of a ministry can be valuable. Most foreign-capital companies in Japan suffer from low name recognition, so positive reporting on a company's technology, products or people can translate into increased business opportunities. The author has frequently experienced Japanese business interest in U.S.-brand computer or telecommunications products as a result of the previous day's favourable treatment in Japanese mass-circulation daily newspapers.

Public criticism of the Japanese practice of blocking market access to a foreign-capital company is risky: if successful, it can destroy the market barrier, but if unsuccessful, it can destroy the critic. One cannot assume that pledges of "off the record" comments will be honoured: even if the source is not printed in the newspaper, the reporter may reveal the source to the foreign company's opposition. Of course, for television or radio appearances, comments "off the record" are usually not an option.

The representative of foreign-capital interests needs to be able to pick the most desirable avenue for publicity. A reporter from the Ministry of Transport press club, for example, would be a poor choice for a foreign-owned airline to use to criticise high Japanese airport landing fees. The reporter will most likely not print the criticism, and will trade information about the foreign-capital company with Ministry of Transport sources for an exclusive story. The Washington, London or Paris office of the same Japanese newspaper might be a better venue to discuss grievances, since the foreign offices of Japanese newspapers exist in part to transmit information about what foreigners think of Japan. A magazine like *Bungei Shunju* that has a reputation for exposing government inefficiency, or a privately-owned television network that panders to popular indignation, might be more receptive to an argument that bureaucrats have raised landing fees to an unacceptable level where it is adversely impacting Japan's growth as a regional air hub, or the ability of the average Japanese to travel.

Television appearances are effective if the representative of foreign-capital interests speaks Japanese very well (or is a native Japanese) and understands the strengths and limitations of television reporting. Translations from foreign languages appearing on Japanese television are frequently inaccurate, and the delay creates a wall between the speaker and effective communication. Television advertising in Japan is often unavailable to the foreign-owned firm, either due to Japanese business practices or cost. A foreign firm appearing on Japanese nationwide television has reached 20–40 million people with its message. Televised criticism of a Japanese regulatory practice brings an instant response: either massive retribution from the regulator, a modification of the practice, or both.

THE FOREIGN MASS MEDIA

Several hundred foreign publications maintain reporters in Tokyo. Publicity in the foreign publications is useful primarily for the home-country audience of shareholders, customers, politicians and regulators, but Japan constantly monitors the foreign press. A foreign-based organisation whose Japan business appears in the home country press of a major trading partner will become familiar to key Japanese regulators. Some U.S.-capital companies in Japan, for example, have cultivated the image of "successful in Japan" in the U.S. press, and claim to have obtained business in Japan as a "reward" that was denied to their publicly dissatisfied rivals.

The major U.S. newspapers people their Tokyo bureaus with individuals who rotate every few years, and who rarely understand the Japanese language or culture well enough to develop news stories independent of what the Japanese press is reporting. English-speaking reporters for European publications, particularly British publications, often have more lengthy experience in Japan and develop their own views. Perhaps more surprising is that much coverage of Japan in the U.S. is often dictated by editors in New York or Washington: this is why articles about Japan in the American press cover the same hoary topics of the "Westernising" Japanese youth, the "changing" Japanese economy, the "revolving door" Japanese Prime Minister race, and the "disappearing" Kyoto geisha. Some reporters for U.S. industry or technical publications have extensive experience in Japan and can supply useful information, but the typical reporter without Japan experience is useful largely as a means of reaching the home audience.

Reporters for U.S. publications tend to be cynical about U.S.

72

business efforts in Japan. This appears to be due largely to insufficient efforts by the average U.S.-capital company in Japan to create and defend a positive image among the Tokyo-based news media. In contrast, the major Japanese companies devote startling amounts of manpower, resources and money to influencing their image in the American press. Money does not guarantee a positive press, but abdicating the public relations function in Japan often promotes an unsatisfactory press.

THE AVERAGE CITIZEN

The average Japanese citizen does not live in cosmopolitan Tokyo, does not know anybody who works for a foreign-owned company, does not use any foreign-brand products, and is basically content with Japan's postwar economy. In the last five general (House of Representatives) elections in Japan, public opinion polls found "trade friction" or "foreign opinion about Japan" to be a minor concern of the electorate, well below "the faltering economy", "campaign funding reform" and other domestic concerns. Traditionally, the average Japanese resisted paying lower prices for foreign goods if that meant beggaring their highly-paid Japanese neighbour, but the prolonged recession of 1991–1995 has made virtually every Japanese think of their own pocketbook first. As a result, a well-conceived plan to appeal to Japanese public opinion can be successful, particularly if one can demonstrate savings or convenience for the Japanese consumer. The consumer movement in Japan is stillborn, though, so one should not expect organised private individual support for a pro-consumer public relations posture.

FOREIGN GOVERNMENTS

Japan does not throw bait after fish that it has already caught. As a result, the foreign governments and foreign business groups that are able to influence the Japanese government on trade issues are those that are not yet beholden to Japan for trade or investment. This principle explains why the nations of Asia are largely ineffective in clamouring for an increase in their manufactured exports to Japan: those nations depend on Japan for technology, components and investment. From 1985–1987, when the European Community was suspected of building a "Fortress Europe" that would be closed to Japanese and other foreign-owned companies, Japan catered to the market access requests of EC-based companies. EC telecommunications, avionics, semiconductor and satellite equipment companies suddenly received the level of attention from Japanese regulators that had previously been reserved only for U.S.-based companies. "Fortress Europe" crumbled after 1987 due to internal factionalism, the transformation of the U.K. into a staging ground for Japanese exports to the Continent, and attacks on EC trade barriers by the United States that resulted in windfall benefits for Japanese exporters. EC companies that attained prominence with the Japanese government at the high-water mark of EC influence are still consulted, but the Japanese cater less to EC business interests in Japan than it did a decade ago.

The United States has historically been the foreign government with the most influence in contemporary Japan. This is due in part to U.S. military influence on modern Japanese history, but this factor is becoming less important as memories of the Second World War and the Cold War fade away. The United States remains Japan's largest single-country market and its primary source of new business ideas. Although Japanese capital is a prominent factor in U.S. financial policy and the U.S. economy is totally dependent on Japan for a variety of industrial and consumer goods, the United States is unpredictable enough that at least the older generation of Japanese regulators believes that Japan needs to placate U.S. interests from time to time. The younger generation of Japanese regulators often believes that U.S. interests can be ignored with little more than lip service because the United States government is too impatient to pursue any negotiation to a long-term solution.

Scores of U.S.-capital companies have relied upon the U.S. government to promote their regulatory agenda in Japan, with mixed success. It should be noted that the United States has no mid-term or long-term trade or investment policy toward Japan, and each question of whether the U.S. should champion company A, industry B or service C requires a new debate in Washington. U.S. companies without a large Washington office, staffed with former employees of the major trade-related agencies, are at a disadvantage in mobilising American trade policy. Once the U.S. government begins negotiations with Japan on a given topic, the end result can be influenced by upcoming domestic elections, North Korean belligerence, White House personnel changes, or a variety of factors beyond the control of the company or industry nominally driving the negotiations. If, as often happens, the U.S. negotiators accept a less-than-desired compromise from the Japanese side, the company or industry nominally driving the negotiations will come under intense pressure from the U.S.

negotiators publicly to accept a trade agreement that may not adequately further its market interests in Japan. Thus, intervention by the U.S. government in promoting U.S. business interests in Japan can be effective, but requires a well thought-out control strategy on the part of the government affairs professional. Whether the U.S. government will promote the business interests of EC-owned or Canadian-owned companies in the U.S. toward Japan depends on the politics of the Presidential Administration in power.

FOREIGN-JAPANESE BUSINESS DISCUSSION GROUPS

Japan has discovered that Western businessmen do not become angry at people with whom they regularly have pleasant conversations; as a result, there are scores of business discussion groups between Japan and other nations or industries. Typically these groups are populated by relatively unbriefed, inexperienced Western businessmen from the service sector on one side, and the drilled, coordinated and dedicated executives of their Japanese customers on the other side. These business groups are rarely a setting for an agreement by the Japanese side to increase competition in Japan through private sector efforts. The Japanese side usually argues that the foreign companies do not understand the Japanese way of business, or that similar barriers face Japanese companies overseas. If the government relations professional can obtain an expression of concern from the entire foreign delegation, including the largest multinationals, over a given Japanese administrative practice, then the Japanese side may consider modifying the practice.

FOREIGN PUBLIC OPINION

Foreign public opinion in the abstract is of continuing concern only to the diplomats in Japan's Foreign Ministry. The average Japanese government official is no more affected by foreign public opinion than the average foreign government official is affected by Japanese public opinion. Boycotts raise the visibility of an issue, and until recently consisted of foreign boycotts of Japanese products in reaction to alleged environmental or social errors by Japanese representatives. In 1995, however, Japanese consumers began to organise boycotts of French products to protest an issue of concern to the average Japanese: France's continued nuclear testing in the South Pacific.

Still, in most cases foreign public opinion will be relevant primarily in generating support in the home country, as opposed to influencing thought in Japan.

RECURRING ISSUES

ACCESS TO INFORMATION

Few foreign-capital companies in Japan have access to regulatory information affecting their business at the same time, and in the same depth, as their Japanese competition. The regulators' standard advice is that the foreign company should send people regularly to the ministry to "drink tea" with the regulators. Once the regulator and the regulated establish a rapport, the argument continues, the foreign-capital company will receive information without bias or delay.

Assuming for the moment that a given civil servant intends honestly and completely to brief the foreign-capital company on pending regulations to the same extent as he/she would a large Japanese competitor, there are many reasons why regular chats with ministry officials should not be allowed to become the sole means of monitoring the regulatory environment. Within a given ministry, there may be rival departments, or individuals higher placed in the hierarchy, who do not agree with one's principal contact, and who have the power to alter the regulatory environment. Depending on the business sector, several ministries' approval may be needed, or one must consult regulators at the local and provincial, as well as the national level. Finally, the typical Japanese regulator is totally unfamiliar with the thinking of a foreign-capital company and often does not know what is of interest and should be mentioned.

Whether one is dealing with the generous, well-meaning regulator or the regulator who is blind to foreign-capital interests, it is vital that one be thoroughly briefed before one begins to ask for a briefing. "Never ask a question to which you do not already know the answer" is a principle familiar to common-law trial lawyers conducting a cross-examination. Prior to inquiring about pending regulation, for example, the representative of foreign-capital companies in Japan needs to have studied everything publicly available on the issue, and consulted contacts in the Japanese news media, industry and Diet. Otherwise, rather than obtaining a draft of the regulation for comment, the representative of foreign-capital interest may be dismissed with "there is no such pending regulation" or "it is just a proposal". The "proposal", though, can become law the next day.

The author has had a fruitful relationship with a given ministry for more than a decade after a difficult beginning. In a two-person meeting, an official of the ministry repeatedly denied that the ministry had a research program in a given field; after asking the question five times, to make absolutely certain that the official was flatly denying the program, the author produced an eight-page Japanese monograph on the subject, written by the very ministry official in question, published in an obscure journal of a Japanese research association. After a few seconds of shock, the ministry official replied, "Oh . . . that research project" and delivered a 45-minute briefing on the current status. Since that time, the author believes that he has always received the truth from the ministry in response to a precise question.

ADMINISTRATIVE GUIDANCE

The Japanese government counts 10,942 situations in which a ministry or agency has the legal right to require a permit, license or approval as a condition for doing business.[23] More ubiquitous is "administrative guidance", in which a regulator takes an action, or refuses to take an action, or makes a request not directly supported by law. Typical examples are the refusal to accept an application for government review, or a direction to a company to cease a certain action, or a demand that a company clear certain unregulated activities with the government. Administrative guidance is viewed by Japanese legal scholars as necessary to efficient government, but even its supporters recognise abundant potential for abuse.[24] A party injured by abuse of administrative guidance has for years had the right to sue the Japanese government for damages, but such lawsuits may take a decade, during which time the plaintiff is subject to the allegedly illegal administrative guidance and often additional retaliation.[25] More than 30 years after a government advisory panel suggested the idea[26], Japan passed an Administrative Procedure Act[27] that has been in effect since October 1, 1994, a period of time too brief to form an opinion of the Act's effectiveness. However, given the slow pace of judicial decision and the difficulty of obtaining interim injunctions against the administrative body, it seems unlikely that the new Administrative Procedure Act will provide meaningful relief to foreign-capital firms, blocked by administrative guidance, who sought to introduce a product or technology before their Japanese competitors.

The Japan Fair Trade Commission may assist foreign-capital interests to combat certain types of administrative guidance that violate Japan's Antimonopoly Act. The JFTC in June 1994 listed the following kinds of administrative guidance as suspect:

> Guidance requiring new entrants to obtain the consent of existing firms or the trade association in the relevant field of business or to coordinate the conditions for entry with such parties . . .

> Guidance requiring new entrants to join the trade association . . .

> Having the trade association . . . intervene . . . with a view to adjusting supply and demand . . .

> Guidance regarding raising or reducing prices, stating specific figures relating to amount, percentage (range) or the like . . .

> Requiring reports, through trade associations, on matters which are usually considered the trade secrets of individual firms . . .

> Giving guidance to manufacturers, distributors or their respective associations so as to stabilise prices . . .

> Guidance regarding production and sales volumes . . .

> Requiring submission of business plans concerning production and sales volumes, export and import volumes, the construction of new facilities, or the expansion of existing ones . . .[28]

THE NAIL THAT STICKS OUT IS HIT?

The Japanese proverb best known to foreign businessmen is "the nail that sticks out is hit", with its implication that the organisation that is conspicuously out of line invites massive pressure to conform. Nevertheless, a few foreign-capital firms, frustrated by the weakness of other solutions available to them to remedy administrative discrimination in Japan, have in recent years been highly vocal in challenging the status quo. Do those foreign firms that trigger trade negotiations, hold press conferences and circulate trade petitions end up standing tall, or do they suffer the hammer of retaliation? Three case studies illustrate a range of possible methods and outcomes.

U.S. company X is a telecommunications equipment company. It is willing to produce products for the Japanese market, meeting Japanese specifications and quality expectations. X has a short-term, mid-term and long-term business strategy toward Japan that is understood by and supported by its most senior executives. X's operations in Japan are peopled by both Japanese and expatriate (not necessarily American) managers who take direction from company headquarters. X has a large Washington, D.C. office with many employees experienced in trade negotiations. Prior to publicly criticising its fate at the hands of Japanese regulators, X explained its strategy to its Japanese employees and steeled them against the expected controversy. Only a few executives were designated as spokesmen for X, allowing X to maintain a consistent public relations profile.

When company X revealed to the world news media that it had prevailed upon the U.S. government to protest against alleged discrimination by Japanese regulators in the assignment of wireless telephone licenses, it became the subject of a hurricane in Japan. Company X was attacked in the Japanese press as anti-Japanese; a leading Japanese trade association executive commented that X would "never do business again" in Japan. Company employees were reportedly summoned to the accused ministry and berated. Individual Japanese employees of X received late-night telephone calls from a variety of individuals urging X, in not always pleasant terms, to desist. Japanese diplomats warned the U.S. government that this dispute would jeopardise 45 years of security and political relations. Opinion for hire in the United States was mobilised to write editorials denouncing the company as "protectionist" "whining" and a variety of shopworn epithets. Company X remained steadfast in insisting on implementing an extremely detailed, quantified, date-specific purchasing plan for its technology in Japan, and pressed this solution on both Japanese and U.S. government parties to the dispute. Once the dispute was settled on terms satisfactory to X, X instantly moved corporate resources and product into the new market opportunity.

The result of X's high-risk but well-executed confrontation has been an extra $1 billion in Japanese business in the last 3 years, the predicted result. There have been many unpredicted results as well: because the controversy was repeated by the Japanese press and television for months, company X became the wireless telephone company in the Japanese market with the highest consumer brand recognition. In addition, name recognition rocketed among college graduates, resulting in a flood of applicants for jobs at a company that in 1983 had name recognition of under 5% of graduating college students. Finally, the ministry involved is now careful to brief representatives of company X whenever X's interests in wireless telephones might be affected, although the briefing is not always delivered with a smile.

U.S. company Y is another telecommunications equipment company. It has the capability to manufacture products for the Japanese market and to meet Japanese specifications and quality expectations, but the Japanese market is not seen as justifying the expense of a separate product run. Y has no company-wide business strategy toward Japan: each business unit follows its own strategy. Y's operations in Japan are peopled by both Japanese and expatriate managers who take direction from a variety of executives based in business units around the United States. Y has a large Washington, D.C. office with many employees experienced in trade negotiations, but they must work with the same multiple agendas toward Japan as the company as a whole. The company frequently complains to the U.S. government about alleged discriminatory Japanese practices, but has difficulty producing senior executives who are willing to endorse the complaints on behalf of the whole company. The company is rarely willing to acknowledge publicly its complaints. The employees of Y in Japan are not briefed in advance on controversies affecting the company's Japan operations, and usually oppose the U.S. trade negotiations affecting Y.

Although Y is a much larger company than X, and its technology is universally respected in Japan, Y's telecommunications business in Japan has been minor and stagnant. Y is seen as a source of complaints without strategy. In situations where new markets have been opened, Y has been slow to exploit the opportunities, and indeed has abandoned several telecommunications markets after fitful attempts to compete. Y is regularly lectured on the "standing nail" proverb by Japanese regulators, and is rarely seen participating in government regulatory panels. Y is a well-known company in the United States, but its products are virtually unknown to the Japanese consumer and the company is not popular with Japanese college students.

U.S. company Z is the smallest telecommunications equipment company in the group. It is willing to produce products for the Japanese market, meeting Japanese specifications and quality expectations. Z's chairman, based in the U.S., and its regional senior vice president, based in Japan, develop the company's Japan policy. Z's operations in Japan are peopled by both Japanese and expatriate (not necessarily American) managers who take direction from the American president of the Japan operation, who in turn reports to the Tokyo-based senior vice president. Z has a small Washington, D.C. office with junior employees, but its chairman is politically well-connected. Z does not publicly criticise Japanese regulatory barriers, but does publicly acknowledge its close ties to the White House and Congress. It arranges for Cabinet-level U.S. officials to mention its name in meetings with high-level Japanese civil servants. Z is not well known among the Japanese public, but it received orders worth US$300 million in the Japanese market as a result of favourable rulings by the Japanese government concerning Z's selling its product line in Japan.

The author's conclusion is that the foreign-capital company with a government relations strategy that is supported by senior executives, when coupled with a competitive business plan, can succeed in removing regulatory obstacles to sales in Japan. Whether the government relations strategy is public or behind-the-scenes seems less important than whether the strategy is vigorous and played to win.

RECIPROCITY WITH THE EC

The representative of non-EC foreign-capital interests in Japan needs to be alert to the tendency of the EC to impose reciprocity requirements and unique standards. Much of Japan's relations with foreign nations is based on reciprocity, and Japan reacts quickly to EC measures designed to restrict Japanese access, or that incidentally affect Japanese companies but which are really targeted at satisfying EC internal directives. When the EC created "interoperability" requirements for computer data transmission equipment from outside the EC, Japan proposed different "interoperability" requirements for computer data transmission equipment from outside Japan. When Japanese companies had problems obtaining ISO 9000 certification for their software development processes in the EC, Japan reacted by creating its own ISO 9000 certification system for software development processes that would have been a hurdle for non-Japanese companies. U.S. companies that are used to compatibility requirements and software quality processes driven by the market, not the government, are often caught in the cross-fire between Japan and the EC. The author's experience is that Australian, New Zealand, Singapore, Hong Kong and Canadian firms are also frequently victims of regulatory battles between the EC and Japan, but that firms from those countries often have interests identical to that of U.S.-based firms.

UNIQUE STANDARDS AND CERTIFICATION PROGRAMS

An association of Japanese ski makers once proposed that since Japanese snow is "different" from snow in the rest of the world, skis to be used on Japanese slopes would have to be certified by their association. This scheme was thwarted by strong protests from European ski equipment manufacturers, but it illustrates the Japanese tendency to insist on standards unique from the rest of the world. The ski association's idea was a transparent attempt to cap the

Japanese market share of foreign-made ski equipment by restricting entry. In other situations, a unique standard or testing requirement in Japan may be an attempt to provide revenues for an otherwise unnecessary testing organisation. Some unique Japanese standards are motivated by a genuine belief that they are necessary.

Whatever the motivation behind unique Japanese standards, they invariably raise a foreign company's costs of doing business in Japan. Unique Japanese standards are never proposed in ignorance: one may be assured that Japanese standards experts are completely familiar with the foreign standard they propose to replace. Containment and control actions should begin at the earliest stage and escalate quickly, while the proposal is still being discussed by a non-government body such as a Japanese industry association. International standards organisations affected by the measure can be called upon to protest that internationally accepted standards and procedures be used. Provision should be made for automatic acceptance of foreign test results and certifications, so that if the Japanese proposal is successful, the sole arbiters of conformity will not be Japanese certification officials with no international experience. Some large Japanese companies are beginning to see unique Japanese domestic standards as a burden preventing volume production savings on their U.S.-bound and EC-bound product lines, and can be useful behind the scenes in supporting foreign-led efforts.

TIPS FOR THE FOREIGN BUSINESSMAN

Since 96% of the information affecting a foreign-owned business in Japan is never translated from Japanese, the opportunities to mold the regulatory environment are limited for foreign businessmen not fluent in Japanese. The businessman can benefit from briefings by knowledgeable officials of his government in Japan and by employees of foreign agricultural or manufacturing trade associations representing the company's product in Japan. Discussing the business environment with the Japan operations of one's home-country customers and suppliers is usually an excellent source of advice.

The foreign businessman with ongoing but not daily needs for government affairs assistance can choose among a very small number of public relations, consulting or law firms in Japan. These firms are most cost-effective when hired to deal with an immediate, isolated problem but may be expensive when hired to manage a strategy over a multi-year period. In addition, devotion to client confidentiality varies widely: some firms trade client information for regulatory information. A foreign-owned company in Japan with daily regulatory and public relations needs in Japan should have its own in-house staff.

A number of foreign-capital firms with substantial sales in Japan have tried to use in-house Japanese staff to handle their government relations work. In several instances, retired government officials have been hired as liaisons with their former ministries. These efforts have met with limited success. Japanese staff may have personal contacts in a few key ministries, but being Japanese, they are immediately pigeon-holed by age and university graduation so that they can only approach a certain level of government official. Retired government officials are granted much wider access in their former ministry, but are useful chiefly as facilitators when the foreign-owned company and the ministry do not disagree. For example, retired government officials are useful in assisting the foreign-owned company to obtain funding or join a consortium when those decisions are made by their former ministry, but are a liability in approaching a rival ministry. Retired government officials in a foreign-owned company are expected by their former government employer to provide information about the foreign company's activities. Several U.S.-capital firms hired Americans to manage their Japanese government affairs work after finding that during disputes Japanese citizens were unable to withstand the pressure to agree with their government instead of their employer. The foreigner, however, can never develop the school or social ties to regulators possessed by some Japanese.

IN CLOSING

Often multinationals attempt to run their Japanese government relations function with their headquarters government relations staff. Even assuming an individual were present in headquarters with the necessary background, the information needed to follow the Japanese regulatory environment is simply unavailable outside Tokyo. It is also common for a foreign firm to rely upon a Japanese joint-venture partner for liaison with the Japanese government, but this is rarely successful in building within the foreign firm an understanding of industry regulations. It also has the disadvantage of denying to the foreign firm the sources of information available to it as an organisation outside of the traditional Japanese social and economic hierarchies. The most widespread problem is the unwillingness of headquarters to fund a "staff" function, such as external relations, in a high-cost location such as Tokyo, and to insist that the only company personnel located in Tokyo be those whose contribution to sales can be precisely quantified each quarter. In regulated industries such as telecommunications, financial services or health care, one's ability to generate sales is at least as dependent on favourable relations with Japanese regulators as it is on business acumen. Given the pervasive influence of government on the Japanese economy, it will be a rare foreign company that is adequately defending its business interests in Japan without adequate strategy and resources for engineering the regulatory environment.

---

[1] Ministry of International Trade and Industry, *Dai 28 kai gaishikei kigyo doko chosa no gaiyo,* June 30, 1995, p. 4

[2] As televised in *Denshi rikoku* (A Nation Built On Electronics), a six-hour series on the rise of Japan's electronics industry, broadcast in its entirety by NHK on January 13, 1992.

[3] *Asahi Shimbun,* June 14, 1990.

[4] Council on Competitiveness, *Challenges,* July 1994. "Standard of Living" is defined as gross domestic product per person.

[5] See the discussion of restructuring the Japanese cement industry in *Nihon kogyo shimbun,* January 14, 1991 and *Tsusansho koho,* May 7, 1994.

[6] For a more detailed discussion, see Stern,"Technotaxes — Japan's Subtle Competitive Weapon", *Global Competitor,* 1:1 (Winter, 1993).

[7] Campaign Funds Regulation Law, Art. 22-5 (Law No.194 of 1948)

[8] This is the interpretation of the Home Affairs Ministry department in charge of monitoring Japanese campaign contributions, Jijisho senkyo bu, *Shugiinn sosenkyo ni okeru seito/seijidantai seiji katsudo no tebiki* (Tokyo, 1986) p. 124.

[9] National Civil Servants Law (Law No. 120 of 1947).

[10] See the survey of Japanese civil service pay versus Japanese private sector pay in *Nihon keizai shimbun,* February 7, 1994. Japanese civil servants are now among the highest paid civil servants in the world in U.S. dollar terms, *Nihon keizai shimbun,* December 31, 1994.

[11] See, e.g., the *Nihon keizai shimbun,* September 8, 1989, and September 14, 1990.

[12] See, Stern, "Between Bureaucrat and Buyer: The Role of Japanese Nonprofit Industry Groups in Braking Market Forces" in The Mansfield Center for Pacific Affairs and The Pacific Basin Institute, eds., *Reshaping the Marketplace: Deregulation in Japan (Kanryotachi No Taikoku,* Kodansha, March 1996); Procassini, *Competitors in Alliance* (Westport, CT: 1995); Lynn and McKeown, *Organizing Business: Trade Associations in America and Japan* (Washington, 1988).

[13] JFTC Study Group on Trade Associations, *Jigyosha dantai no katsudo to dokusen kinshiho jo no sho mondai* (Business Groups Activities and Antimonopoly Law Problems, "JFTC Business Groups Study") March 1993 p. 75.

[14] Ibid, p. 16.

[15] Ibid, p. 17. More than 12% of companies polled replied that their business would be "difficult" or "impossible" without the quality mark.

[16] Law No. 89 of 1897.

[17] *Jinji In.*

[18] National Civil Servants Law, Article 103.

[19] Japanese pensions tend to be a lump-sum payment based on length of service, rather than a funded annuity. As a result, Japanese civil servants may retire with a pension that is insufficient to sustain them for even five years, let alone twenty. Therefore, senior bureaucrats desire to retire to second careers in which they can quickly multiply their pensions, which in some cases are lump sum payments exceeding ¥30 million (over US$300,000 at current exchange rates) after a few years of service. One of the complaints of labour unions is that these payments deplete financial resources available for other employees of the organization, Seifu kankei hojin rodo kumiai rengo, *Seiroren amakudari hakusho* ("Amakudari White Paper of the Government Employees' Unions"), (Tokyo: 1992), pp. 172–223 .

[20] *Nihon keizai shimbun,* May 20, 1994. These frequent requests are addressed by the long-standing "Department of Contributions" *(Shakai koken bu)* of the Keidanren.

[21] *Ibid.*

[22] Not to confused with the Foreign Correspondents Club of Japan, a private club, or the Japan Press Center, run by the Ministry of Foreign Affairs.

[23] Somucho, *Kyoninka-to no toitsuteki haaku no kekka ni tsuite* ("A Comprehensive View Of Permits And The Like"), December 1992.

[24] For example, the Japanese Government Printing Office offers a guide on the proper use of administrative guidance, meant for civil servants and written by a former member of the Cabinet Legislative Bureau, Ichio Yamanouchi, *Komuin no tame no gyosei shido ron* ("A Discussion Of Administrative Guidance For The Civil Servant"), Tokyo: 1986. Much of the book is devoted to exhorting the civil servant not to abuse administrative guidance.

[25] In the "Condor Derringer" case, a plaintiff was wrongly directed by the National Police Agency to stop manufacturing a toy derringer pistol. After a legal battle that stretched from 1963 to 1976, the plaintiff was awarded damages, but in the meantime the plaintiff company had to dissolve, and the plaintiff's managing director was improperly detained on suspicion of violating Japanese laws controlling weapons manufacture. See Yoshizaki, *Gyosei shido to kokka baisho seikyu — Condor Derringer jiken* ("Administrative Guidance And Government Liability: The Condor Derringer Incident"), *Juristo* 642 (1976).

[26] The Japan Times, October 1, 1994.

[27] Law No. 88 of 1993.

[28] "The Antimonopoly Act Guidelines Concerning Administrative Guidance", *FTC/ Japan Views* No. 20, (March 1995), pp. 12–17.

PART II
PREPARING TO DO
BUSINESS IN JAPAN

CHAPTER 4

CONTRACT LAW AND THE JAPANESE NEGOTIATION PROCESS

by Noboru Kashiwagi and E. Anthony Zaloom

A JAPANESE PERSPECTIVE

The basic principles of the Japanese law of contract are provided for in the Civil Code promulgated in 1898. The Civil Code was modelled after the then German Civil Code with the strong influence from the French Civil Code. After several amendments, the Japanese law of contract still follows the civil code system.

Contract is defined as a judicial act to join two opposing wills. Contracts will be created by offer and acceptance (Civ. C. 521 to 528). In case an offer provides for a period within which acceptance shall be made, the offer becomes irrevocable. If the offerer does not receive acceptance within that period the offer becomes ineffective (Civ. C. 521). In case there is a distance between offerer and offeree, the contract will be entered into when the offeree despatches acceptance (Civ. C. 526 [1]). If the offeree accepts with new condition(s) or modification(s) then this is construed as a rejection of the offer and as a counter offer to the offerer (Civ. C. 528).

There is no generally applicable statute of frauds requiring that contracts be in writing. In certain exceptional cases, the law may impose an obligation on a party to a consumer contract to deliver a document setting forth conditions of the transaction. (For example, see Installment Sales Contract Act (*Kappu Hanbai Ho,* Law No. 159 of 1961 Sec. 4) The Account Law (*Kaikei Ho)* Sec. 29-8 requires the Government to make a written contract when it awards a contract to government contractors.

The Civil Code provides expressly for 13 types of contracts but other types of contract may exist. These 13 types of contracts are: gift (*zoyo),* sales (*baibai),* exchange (*kokan),* loan for consumption (*shohi taishaku)*[1], loan for use (*shiyo taishaku)*[2], lease (*chintaishaku)*[3], employment (*koyo),* contract for work (*ukeoi),* mandate (*inin),* bailment (*kitaku),* partnership (*kumiai)* and life annuity (*shusin teikikin).* Some of these types of contract are either obsolete, eg. life annuity, or otherwise regulated under specific laws such as employment which is regulated under labour laws. Recently, many new types of contracts which do not fall squarely within the above 13 types of contracts have emerged. These include franchise agreements, swap agreements and financial leases.

In cases where a party has a right to cancel a contract under the contract or law, it may do so by giving notice to the other party. A typical case in which a party has the right to cancel a contract under the Civil Code is when the other party wilfully defaults or neglects to perform his/her obligation. If one party delays in performing his/her obligation, the other party may terminate the contract if the former still fails to perform after the latter requests performance granting further reasonable time (Civ. C. 541). Also if the obligation of one party becomes impossible to perform for a reason attributable to the obligor, then the other party may also cancel the contract (Civ. C. 543).

COMMERCIAL CODE

The provisions of the Commercial Code have precedence over commercial trade practices. Commercial trade practices have precedence over provisions of the Civil Code (Com. C. 1). The Japanese Commercial Code set forth the following:

(1)   General rules to be found in most commercial codes including application of the Commercial Code, definition of merchants, commercial registration, trade name, books of account, trade employee including general manager, commercial agents

(2)   Companies and corporations, including corporations (*kabushiki kaisha*) and closed corporations (*yugen kaisha*)

(3)   Definitions of commercial acts and special provisions relating to agency, mandate, offer and acceptance, joint and several obligation, legal rate for claims arising from commercial acts (6 percent per annum), lien between merchants and statute of limitations

(4)   Special provisions concerning sales between merchants

(5)   Open account (*kogo keisan*)

(6)   Undisclosed associations (*tokumei kumia*)

(7)   Brokerage (*nakadachi eigyo*)

(8)   Transportation agent transactions (*unso toriatukai eigyo*)

(9)   Commission agent transactions, or consignment (*toiya eigyo*)

(10) Transportation

(11) Bailment by merchants

(12) Insurance

(13) Maritime Law

FREEDOM OF CONTRACT

The Japanese law of contract recognises the principle of freedom of contract. It is understood that the principle of freedom of contract includes the freedom of entering into or not entering into a contract, freedom of selection of contracting party, freedom of determination of contents of a contract and freedom of form of contract. However, in order to protect the weak, there are many provisions to restrict the freedom of contract. For example, utility companies do not have freedom to select the other party to a utility supply contract – the consumer. The terms and conditions of supply to consumers of utilities are regulated and utilities must be supplied to all qualified consumers. Some provisions of lease contracts of houses and land for houses are regulated to protect tenants. As society becomes more and more complex and the need to protect consumers becomes greater, more regulations and restrictions on the freedom of contracts are enacted, while obsolete or inefficient regulations are removed.

RELATIONAL CONTRACTS

The Japanese law of contract is designed to regulate discrete contracts, that is, according to classical theory, contracts standing alone. Accordingly most judges and law professors are construing and applying the Civil Code in accordance with the traditional classical theory of contract law.

However, it should be pointed out that the Japanese rely more on human relationships than the law or legal rights and obligations.[4] The key element of the human relationship which the Japanese sees in the contractual relations is trust (*"shinrai kankei"*).[5] The most important thing for Japanese business people is to earn the trust of the other party. A favourite Japanese fable refers to an ambitious businessman who persistently tries to impress a big shot by waiting at the gate of his house every morning or giving free service liberally.[6] The common feature of this kind of story is to emphasise that you cannot spend too much energy and time in order to earn the trust of potential customers.

In such a world, relational contract theory seems appropriate in many cases. Therefore among young scholars the relational contract theory advocated by Ian Macneil, Stewart Macaulay and others in the United States is gaining strength.[7]

THE DECISION MAKING PROCESS WITHIN JAPANESE BIG CORPORATIONS AND ITS EFFECTS ON THE JAPANESE NEGOTIATION STYLE

BOTTOM-UP AND TOP-DOWN

It is frequently said that the decision making system of Japanese corporations is bottom-up.[8] However, in small corporations where owners, founders or families of founders decide everything, the decisions are made top-down. In the case of big corporations where executives are promoted from among employees and none has dominant control, corporate decision making systems may seem to be bottom-up.[9]

Within such big corporations, they adopt a complicated decision making process, characterised by unanimous decision making, sharing of information, a large number of participants and a final *ringi* (or approval) procedure.[10]

CORE ORGANISATION OF DECISION MAKING

First, information which may lead to a sizeable transaction may be received at any level of the hierarchy of a corporate organisation. All such information will ultimately be referred to a business department. Business departments will study the viability of the matter. This department will be the core organisation for the promotion of possible business opportunities, subject to some variance in accordance with the size of the business opportunity. All information concerning the business will thereafter flow to this department. If it concludes that it is worth pursuing the matter, staff of the business department will formulate a basic strategy to promote the project. The evaluation and the strategy will be reported to the executive in charge of the matter for his approval and the executive will give instructions and suggestions from time to time. These executives have substantial power to determine basic policy matters and may be able to veto the project. But they are rarely concerned with details. Reports to the executives are made very frequently as the project develops.

COMMENTS AND OPINIONS OF PEOPLE CONCERNED

Then, staff of the Department will start getting the opinions of other departments concerned, such as the legal department, the financing department, the accounting department, the credit department, the planning department and so on. In this way the staff members will get basic policy instructions from managers and executives in charge of the various departments. The business department will seek informal opinions from government agencies which regulate the industry and whose approval is necessary for consummation of the project, and from banks who may grant the necessary finance. After completion of this preliminary work, the business department will formulate terms and conditions to be proposed to the other party.

SELECTION AND AUTHORITY OF NEGOTIATORS

In most cases, the chief negotiator will be the department manager or a section manager in the responsible department. Other negotiation team members will be his/her assistant staff members from other departments concerned such as accounting department, legal department, or planning department as the case may be. Other members are usually of the same rank or of junior rank.

The chief negotiator will not be chosen because of his/her ability as a negotiator.[11] Top executives themselves rarely conduct business negotiation.

The authority of the Japanese negotiator is not clear.[12] No clear mandate or instruction is given to the negotiator. Since no one in a large Japanese corporation can make decisions by himself but must obtain the consent from various groups, even an executive does not have the authority to bind the corporation without clearance of an internal decision making procedure called *ringi*. However the negotiator will have learned from previous experience to what extent he/she can make commitments or in what situation he/she has to obtain consent of the relevant departments and organisations. Actual authority depends on the extent to which the negotiator can persuade and obtain consent of relevant departments and organisations. If the negotiator is capable, and has foresight and persuasive powers, his/her actual authority is considerable. If the negotiator's persuasive skill is poor, his/her actual authority becomes comparatively small.[13]

NEGOTIATION THROUGH CONSENSUS

After commencement of the negotiation, the negotiator has to report the progress of the negotiation in detail to all the departments and organisations concerned and then seek their comments. Those whose comments were not sought may feel neglected and object to the project.

Almost always, unanimous consents are necessary. If the negotiator wants to deviate from the scenario which was previously discussed, either the negotiator must get prior clearance from such departments and organisations or must be confident that he/she can later get consent from them. This is the reason why the negotiators of Japanese big corporations in foreign countries send lengthy telexes and faxes to headquarters every evening. Thanks to time differences and the efforts of supporting staff members at headquarters, negotiators abroad can obtain opinions and comments of executives, other departments and organisations by the next morning. This constant effort to obtain consent and approval from all people concerned requires enormous energy and time. During this process, objections not supported by the majority will be forced to be withdrawn. To get consent of all people concerned using various skills is called "*nemawashi.*"[14]

RINGI AS A RITUAL

When negotiation comes to the final stage, the terms and conditions agreed by the negotiators should also have been approved by all people concerned as above. Then the general manager of the business department will prepare a circulation proposal of the transaction called a "*ringi-sho*" or proposal paper. It will be circulated to all departments concerned within the corporation. Heads of the relevant departments will put their seals on the covering page of the *ringi-sho* as an indication of approval. They should have at that stage no particular objection to the proposal because they have received periodic reports and have already conveyed their opinions and comments to the negotiators. After obtaining all necessary approvals, the *ringi-sho* will be sent to the executive in charge of the matter for approval. Again, the executive will put his/her seal on the *ringi-sho* thus ending the ritual. Sometimes a number of seals will be put on the covering page of *ringi-sho*.

BOTTOM UP DECISION MAKING?

It is misleading to say that decision making in Japanese big corporations is bottom up. Details of a business plan are formulated at the department level or section level in accordance with the size of the project. But executives and top management determine basic policies and are the most influential persons in the formation of the project. On the other hand, it is true that other people also have a substantial influence on the project. It may be more properly expressed as "group decision making."

EFFECTS OF *RINGI* DECISION MAKING ON JAPANESE NEGOTIATION STYLE

LENGTHY NEGOTIATIONS[15]

Since the negotiators have to persuade a large number of people, decision making takes time. Therefore, big corporations are not good at takeovers and other businesses which require quick decisions.

The Japanese negotiators are always conducting two way negotiations; one with the opposite party to the transaction and another internal one with people in relevant departments and organisations.

Unanimous decision making in Japanese corporations delays negotiations considerably. This difficulty is offset by the fact that if a substantial majority approves a proposal it becomes very difficult to raise objections because of tacit pressure to follow the majority.

QUICK IMPLEMENTATION

At the performance stage of contracts, implementation by Japanese corporations is said to be quick because all people concerned know the details of the project and they approved the contract. As noted above, until the final stage all people concerned will approve or be forced to approve the proposal. It is impossible to raise objections at the performance stage.[16]

RELATIVE INFLEXIBILITY

Because of the number of people whom the Japanese negotiator must persuade and the enormous amount of energy expended, the negotiator cannot change the basic structure or policy of the proposed transaction quickly. It is just like a big ship which cannot turn quickly. It follows that if counsel to a Japanese corporation, or the other side in the negotiations, comes up with an excellent idea in the middle of the negotiation stage which may save tax or other transactional costs considerably but may require a fundamental change of transactional structure, the negotiator would not accept the idea even though he/she fully understands its merits.[17] It would require another round of persuasion which takes too much energy and time.

SIMPLE NEGOTIATION TACTICS

Japanese negotiators may not freely use negotiation tactics like bluff or threat because they have to answer to too many people and departments. The Japanese negotiators' first offer would not be far more than what they expect because overly aggressive proposals may be considered greedy. Usually they do not have alternatives, because discussion and review of alternatives in the other relevant departments and organisations need further time and energy. Thus it invites other departments and organisations to determine the best proposal and to concentrate on pursuing that best proposal. A writer commented that the Japanese negotiator starts with quite a unilateral proposal and gives in little by little. This is known in Japan as the "banana vendor's way" and is disclaimed.[18]

PREFERENCE FOR SIMPLE LEGAL STRUCTURES

The Japanese do not like a complicated or sophisticated legal structure for transactions. Such structures may seem technical and may easily be interpreted by judges, government officials and scholars as a means of evasion of tax or other regulations. Also a complicated legal structure would hinder the persuasion process.[19]

PREPARING FOR AND NEGOTIATING WITH THE JAPANESE

Foreigners notice these characteristics of Japanese negotiation styles;

GROUPISM AND GROUP DECISION MAKING

The Japanese consider it very important to belong.[20] They make efforts to form a cohesive organisation to negotiate,[21] and have solid commitment to positions agreed in the organisation.[22] They consider "negotiator" an important rank.[23] Because they are afraid of being blamed within the group, they are timid in taking risks,[24] afraid of fixing responsibility,[25] and frequently refer to superiors or head office.[26] Because they have to obtain consensus, there will be no quick answer.[27]

EMPHASIS ON THE HUMAN RELATIONSHIP

Some commentators emphasise the importance of good human relationships[28] for the Japanese. They have a penchant for sound human relations[29] and make efforts to establish relations based upon mutual trust.[30] As a corollary, the Japanese will try to avoid confrontations which are detrimental to good relationships,[31] and will spend time at pre-negotiation trust building, where social conversations begin with general issues and the lack of the logic of a plan,[32] with nobody stating clearly his position to avoid confrontation.[33] They prefer to make overall agreements first,[34] choosing short contracts as a guide to building relationships.[35] They conclude contracts only with trustworthy parties[36] and seek to obtain the understanding (*rikai*) of the other party by showing sincerity (*seii*).[37]

For the Japanese, the contract is the symbol of entering into a transactional relationship based upon mutual trust. The most important thing in the negotiation is to show sincerity and trustworthiness. Negotiation skill and strategy is disdained as contradictory to sincerity[38] and it is believed that negotiation skill may not be taught.[39] Arguments become defensive[40] if the parties feel threatened or victimised by aggressive tactics.[41] The Japanese like simple non-innovative solutions.[42] Since they do not believe that negotiation skill is important, they put less emphasis on the quality of the negotiator.[43] They are hesitant to reveal details of the proposal[44] and make successive small concessions.[45] They do not specify objects of negotiation but flexibly adjust the objectives in accordance with the overall situation of the negotiation.[46]

SOME CAUTIONS IN NEGOTIATION WITH THE JAPANESE

Americans and Koreans frequently start with a big request which they hope to, but do not realistically expect to obtain from the Japanese company.[47] This attitude may lead the Japanese to believe that the other party does not have enough sincerity — thus the Japanese will shy away from the beginning without entering into negotiation.

Showing a strong desire to win — like Americans[48] — or showing anger — feigned or real[49] — also will have a detrimental effect on business relations because the Japanese will view parties that exhibit such traits as untrustworthy.

Threats are the last thing to use in negotiation with the Japanese. If the negotiation is the last one with the particular Japanese party such as the negotiation of fundamental dispute resolution and the foreign party would never deal with the Japanese party again, threats may work. Because the Japanese are not used to such negotiation styles, the "threat" strategy against the Japanese was once advocated.[50]

In contrast to the Japanese negotiator who will try to build up a long lasting human relationship based upon mutual trust, American lawyers do the opposite. American lawyers from the big law firms try to maximise the benefit from the deal for which they are hired to negotiate, whether by threatening, showing anger or starting from a big request. The Japanese once succumbed to such tactics because they dislike acrimonious adversary relations and prefer to find a mutually satisfactory solution through cooperative and friendly relations. These American tactics may be appropriate for negotiation of one-off discrete contracts. However, the experience of bitter negotiation will be shared by the great many Japanese involved in the negotiation process and the party who plays hard ball is unlikely to find a second welcome.

AN OUTSIDER'S PERSPECTIVE

Primarily from his perspective as one who rose to a senior position within Japan's most prestigious general trading company, Professor Kashiwagi has provided together with his discussion of contract principles an excellent description of the process by which Japanese businesses reach decisions and negotiate about contracts.

Japanese companies often fail in international contract negotiations. One common cause for this — perhaps surprisingly — is the very simple one of language. Another is the process that the first part of this chapter describes. As so aptly stated by one of Japan's leading sociologists, "the goals of the organisation tend be deflected by the every day procedure of group life."[5] The heavy inertia and inward-looking nature of Japanese decision making often makes it easier for Japanese negotiators to seriously antagonise the other side or even abandon a project rather than go back to the numerous parts of their own organisation to rebuild a consensus.

True, this inertia is sometimes a source of strength in negotiations. It makes the Japanese side seemingly impervious to the other side's arguments. It takes a while for Western negotiators to realise that using "logic" to "score points" in large negotiation sessions, as if one were engaged in a debate, has almost nothing to do with the outcome. Thus it is that the Japanese side sometimes does very well by simply exhausting their Western counterparts, which accepts the Japanese position or something close to it just to "get it over with."

More often, however, the inertia and inflexibility is bad for everyone. Sometimes there is no deal when there could have been one, or a deal is done but with a lot of unnecessary hard feelings. And even a deal with no hard feelings could often have been a much better one for both the Japanese and the other side but for the ways in which Japanese organisations reach decisions.

Two examples may give the reader some idea of the pressures which the Japanese decision making process puts on individual Japanese negotiators. In the first example, the Japanese negotiator suffered the consequences of going out on a limb during the process. In the second, another such negotiator managed to save himself, but at a high cost to his organisation.

Example No. 1. A Japanese company once teamed up with an American one (the "American partner") to bid in an auction for the purchase of another American company (the "target"). Since the American partner had the best "feel" for what would likely win the auction, it was delegated the authority, limited by a ceiling of $100 million, to submit the two companies' bid by a Friday 5 PM deadline. By Wednesday, however, the American partner had apparently reliable information that it might take as much as $110 million to win the auction, an amount it still considered a reasonable price for the target. The American partner communicated this to the Japanese company, and the man there responsible for communicating with the Americans took upon himself the difficult task of securing a new consensus within the Japanese company that even $110 million was indeed a reasonable price. After much effort in such a small period of time he did so, and by early Friday afternoon the American partner had full authority to bid up to $110 million. But by that time the American partner was getting a new feel for the situation. It now understood that the original authorized amount was more than enough, submitted a bid for $90 million — and won the auction. When the American partner went to the Japanese representative, however, with the "good news" that the target had been successfully purchased for much less than might have been bid, it was greatly surprised by his reaction.

As the American partner's responsible executives later expressed it, "we thought we'd be heroes for getting the target so cheap." Instead the Japanese representative and most of his company were furious. They had received "false" information about the value of the company and had been forced to push their decision making machinery to the limit for "no good reason." The American partner was forced to write a letter of apology. The Japanese representative's position within his company was very difficult for a long time afterward for his role in this "mistake."

Example No. 2. A Japanese bank in the United States was once negotiating with an American party about the fee that it would receive for issuing a standby letter of credit in a very large amount.

Time was very short, and the bank's U.S. representatives were asked in a meeting on Tuesday whether they could be in touch with their Tokyo head office and communicate a final price by Thursday evening. In that same meeting, on prompting, the American party reluctantly admitted that it had been willing to have the letter of credit issued by another bank for 5/8% of its principal amount, but that the other bank had withdrawn at the last moment; hence the tight time schedule. Clearly, then, 5/8% was an effective floor for negotiation of the rate.

Unfortunately for the Japanese bank, however, its representative present at the meeting, a Japanese national, failed to hear this rate because of his language handicap. He therefore proceeded to obtain Tokyo's consensus on this issue based on his own general understanding of local market rates for such transactions. The result: by Thursday morning Tokyo had authorised him to price the transaction at 3/8%, a rate which would yield the Japanese bank $2,000,000 less fee income over the life of the letter of credit. At that point, however, the Japanese bank's American representatives told their Japanese colleague of what he had missed in the Tuesday meeting. He was indeed surprised. But after talking the matter over with one or two of his counterparts in Tokyo he finalised the bank's decision. To the amazement of all of the Americans involved he fixed the pricing at 3/8%. Thus it was that he and those working closely with him avoided any responsibility for having made the "mistake" of reporting back to Tokyo an inaccurate estimate of local rates.

The behaviour of these two individuals is actually quite rational when considered within the constraints of the Japanese decision making process. That process makes inevitable a heavy emphasis on amassing from the outside raw data for processing by the decision making apparatus and the faithful communication of the group's decision to the other side. The Japanese negotiator's job is therefore not to be interactive with the other side, nor to provide insights or conclusions to his company. Negotiators are not penalised for failing to have a crucial insight or make the right decision. Such insights and decisions are supposed to result from group deliberation. On the other hand they are penalised for making a mistake in gathering data, for supporting a position that later turns out to be incorrect, or for not following the usual procedure for touching base with everyone.

The Western negotiator who appreciates his Japanese counterparts as only intermediaries and gateways to a long and complicated process within the Japanese organisation will often do much better for both his own organisation and the Japanese as well. He also should do the following:

As soon as possible communicate to the Japanese negotiators any information that needs to be widely disseminated within their organisation, which means *any* important or potentially important information. He should also make absolutely sure, by gentle cross examination or otherwise, that the Japanese negotiators understand it. Seemingly fluent English often masks a relatively low level of comprehension.

Make the Japanese negotiators understand if any of the information is subject to uncertainty. The Japanese hate surprises, and with good reason. Their organisations often react to them not so much by trying to cope with the new situations they create as by worrying about why there was a surprise and who is to blame for it. This weakness is greatly mitigated if the organisation knows beforehand that certain information is subject to revision.

If possible track the consensus process within the Japanese organisation so as to see early if it is going off in the wrong direction because of a misconception or some other reason. Sometimes this can be done through the Japanese negotiator. Other times it is done through alternative channels that the American negotiator has into the Japanese organisation.

Avoid wasting time in "debate" with Japanese negotiators. Find out from them why their organisation is taking the wrong direction and then give them information that will tend to change the direction, monitoring the process as much as you can.

Above all, remember that the Japanese are not irrational. It's only the way they organise for decision making that makes it sometimes seem that way. Understanding why their behaviour is rational is the first step to understanding how to work with them to achieve better agreements for both of you.

---

1   A loan for consumption contract will be established when a party receives money or other assets from the other party, promising to return same kind of things of same quantity and of same quality. (Civ. C. 587)

2   Loan for use contract will be established when a party receives thing(s) from the other party, promising the return of the same after the use without payment of consideration.

3   Chintaishaku contact will be established when a party promises the other party to allow use of thing(s) and the other party promises to pay money therefor. Civ. C. 601

4   Koichiro Fujikura, *Comparison of Legal Culture,* Kokusai Masatsu 3 (Nihon Hyoron-sha 1989); Tomoyuki Ota, *Role of Contracts in the Procedure of Exchange,* Id. 204 wrote that the advice to Americans negotiating with the Japanese written in the United States generally points out the importance of human relationship to the Japanese in the business negotiation. It is not defined what "human relationship" means but it seems to indicate comfortable social relationship or understanding of the other party's way of thinking.

5   Ryuho Shimizu, *Nihon no "Shinrai Torikiki"*, Nihon Keizai Shinbun, Oct. 30, Oct. 31, Nov. 1, Nov. 2, Nov. 3 and Nov. 4, 1990; Robert T. Moran and Richard G. Stripp, *Kokusai Business Kosho-jutsu,* 185 (Keiso Shobo 1994)

6   Robert M. March, *The Japanese Negotiator,* 17 (Kodansha 1988)

7   Takashi Uchida, *Keiyaku no Saisei,* Kobundo 1990; Takashi Uchida, *Gendai Keiyakuho no Aratana Tenkai to Ippan Jyoko,* 514 NBL 6, 515 NBL 13, 516 NBL 22, 517 NBL 32, 518 NBL 26

8   Moran & Stripp, supra note 5, at 198

9   It is important to distinguish Japanese big corporations managed by executives who are former employees and other corporations which are ruled by owners, founders, family of founders, corporate raiders or other dictator type management. It seems that the decision making process of these latter corporations is top down and their negotiation style does not differ much from those of other people of other cultures.

10 Naoto Sasaki, *Management and Industrial Structure in Japan, 2nd ed.,* Pergamon Press (1990) 60; Elliot J. Hahn, *Japanese Business Law and The Legal System,* in Law and Investment In Japan 212 (Yukio Yanagida, Daniel H. Foote, Edward Stokes Johnson, Jr., J. Mark Ramseyer and Hugh T. Scogin, Jr. 1995); It seems that this style of decision making began within Tokugawa clans, see Yoshio Hirai, *Hoseisakugaku 2nd. ed.,* 27 (Yuhikaku 1995)

11 In contrast, in the United States, the negotiator seems to be selected putting large emphasis upon the ability as a negotiator. See Moran and Stripp, *Kokusai Business Koshojutsu,* 145: In Japan, selection of negotiator is almost automatic. Chief negotiator will be selected taking into consideration the rank of person within a line of people who are in charge of the transaction within business division or department.

12 E. Anthony Zaloom, *Obstacles to the Effective Rendering of Professional Advice to Japanese Companies,* in Law and Investment in Japan (Yukio Yanagida, Daniel H. Foote, Edward Storks Johnson, Jr. , J. Mark Ramseyer and Hugh T. Scogin, Jr.,1994) 215

13 Mark H. McCaumack, *The Terrible Truth about Lawyer,* Beech Tree Books (1987) 114

14 Importance of *nemawashi* is vividly written in *"Nemawashi Bunkani Genkai",* Nihon Keizai Shinbun Jan. 3, 1993 Morning, 1

15 Mitsunori Takahashi ed., *Beikoki no Kosho Senryaku,* 105 (Chuo Keizai-sha 1994)

16 Moran & Stripp, supra note 5 at 189

17 Zaloom, supra note 12, at 216

18 John L. Graham and Yoshihiro Sano, *Smart Bargaining-Doing Business with the Japanese,* 23 (Ballinger Pub. Co. 1984)

19 Zaloom, supra note 12, at 218

20 This tendency is called Groupism. Moran & Stripp supra note 5, at 184

21 R. March, supra note 6 at 209

22 R. March, supra note 6, at 209

23 Moran & Stripp, supra note 5, at 183

24 Moran & Stripp, supra note 5, at 189

25 Zaloom, supra note 12, at 218

26 R. March, supra note 6, at 211; Graham & Sano, supra note 18, at 12

27 Hahn, supra note 10, at 213

28 Moran & Stripp, supra note 5 at 183, 185, 188

29 R. March, supra note 1, at 210

30 Graham & Sano, supra note 18, at 13

31 Nobuo Kanayama, *Hikaku Bunka no Omosirosa,* 237 (Taishukan Shoten 1989)

32 R. March, supra note 6, at 210: also in Spain, Moran and Stripp, supra note 5, at

289

[33] Moran & Stripp, supra note 5, at 182

[34] R. March, supra note 6, at 210

[35] Moran & Stripp, supra note 5, at 190

[36] Kanayama, supra note 31, at 236

[37] Id. 236

[38] R.March, supra note 6, at 208

[39] Kanayama, supra note 31, at 236

[40] R. March, supra note 6, at 208

[41] Id. 211

[42] Zaloom, supra note 12, at 218

[43] R. March, supra note 6, at 210

[44] Kanayama, supra note 31, at 236

[45] Id. 236

[46] Id. 237

[47] R. March, supra note 6, at 9; Moran and Stripp, supra note 5, at 217

[48] R. March, supra note 6, at 9, 211

[49] Edward and White, *The Lawyer as Negotiator*, (West Pub. 1977) cited in Takeshi Kojima, ed. *Ho Kosho-gaku Nyumon*, 175 (Shoji Homu Kenkyukai 1991)

[50] *"EC no Kyotu Senryaku, Nihonjin ni Takabishani"*, Nihon Keizai Shinbun Dec. 26, 1981 (Morning Ed.)

CHAPTER 5

FOREIGN DIRECT INVESTMENT IN JAPAN
by Christopher P. Wells

There are three primary forms for the establishment of a business presence in Japan. These forms may be ranked in order of legal and regulatory complexity as follows:

1. Representative Office;
2. Branch Office;
3. Subsidiary Corporation (which may take various forms).

A variety of other forms of organisations exist under Japanese law which may be used in specialised circumstances where minimum capital investment, operational control or tax treatment are issues. For example, a *yugen kaisha* is sometimes used to operate a close or family corporation which avoids the higher capital cost of a *kabushiki kaisha* (¥10 million versus ¥3 million for a *yugen kaisha*), need have only annual shareholder and director meetings and requires only a single representative director. These features have made the *yugen kaisha* the favourite form of business for investment bankers seeking special purpose vehicle companies for financial transactions.

Similarly, in certain specialised investment situations where there is a need for full tax pass through status (including the ability to take losses and credit taxes paid in other jurisdictions) the *nin-i kumiai* (civil code partnership) is sometimes used. As in other jurisdictions, the trade-off for such benefits is the possibility of unlimited liability using the partnership form. A discussion of the features and circumstances for use of these alternative forms of business is beyond the scope of this chapter. The discussion herein focusses on the forms most often used by foreign individuals or corporate groups to establish a business presence in Japan.

Set forth immediately below is a general discussion of each of the forms of establishment listed above. A detailed discussion of each form follows in Section III. In addition, Attachment 1 presents a comparison of these forms and provides an overview of their characteristics.

OVERVIEW OF FORMS OF BUSINESS PRESENCE

REPRESENTATIVE OFFICE ACTIVITIES

The activities of a representative office in Japan are limited; it may not engage in transactions or do business in Japan. There are no published legal guidelines on what constitutes "doing business in Japan." In practice, however, a representative office may not execute contracts, engage in transactions, provide services, or, in general, conduct any revenue generating activity in Japan.

JAPANESE TAX CONSEQUENCES

So long as a representative office does not engage in the activities described above, it is not subject to Japanese corporate income taxes.

PROCEDURE FOR ESTABLISHMENT

A representative office is the simplest form of a presence that a foreign corporation may establish in Japan. There are no Japanese governmental approval, registration, filing or reporting requirements to establish and maintain a representative office.

BRANCH OFFICE ACTIVITIES

A Japan branch office may conduct any lawful activity specified in its branch registry or any activity reasonably incidental thereto.

JAPANESE TAX CONSEQUENCES

Typically, a Japan branch office is a taxable entity (although this need not be so) and is subject to Japanese corporate national income tax at the rate of 37.5 percent (additional tax may be assessed by prefectural and local government depending on the location which could increase the effective rate of tax to approximately 55 percent).

PROCEDURE FOR ESTABLISHMENT

The procedure for establishing a Japan branch office by a foreign entity is not difficult and requires the filing of (i) a branch registration application with the relevant legal affairs bureau having jurisdiction over the location of the proposed branch office; and (ii) a simple notice and certain related documents with the Ministry of Finance (MOF) through The Bank of Japan. The Bank of Japan may request that the notice also be filed with other agencies that may have jurisdiction over the activities of the proposed branch office.

SUBSIDIARY CORPORATION ACTIVITIES

There are four possible forms in which companies may be incorporated in Japan: *Gomei Kaisha* (partnership company), *Goshi Kaisha* (limited partnership company), *Yugen Kaisha* (limited liability company) and *Kabushiki Kaisha* (stock company). The Kabushiki Kaisha (a "Stock Corporation") is, however, the most common form of company in Japan. Accordingly, foreign investors (engaged in commercial operations as contrasted with mere investment) almost always establish their Japanese subsidiaries as a Stock Corporation and the discussion herein is limited to a consideration of such form.

A subsidiary in the form of a Stock Corporation may conduct any lawful activity specified in its corporate registry or reasonably incidental activity. In contrast to the branch office form of operation (in which the head office has full exposure to credit risk and similar claims related to its activities in Japan), the liability of shareholders of a Stock Corporation is limited to the amount of their capital contributions. A Stock Corporation is managed by a Board of Directors which meets periodically and is represented by one or more representative directors who are elected from among the members of the Board of Directors elected periodically by shareholders.

JAPANESE TAX CONSEQUENCES

The taxation of corporations in Japan is quite complex and can be significantly different than that which applies in the context of a branch (although the financial impact may be similar). Corporate earnings are subject to national, prefectural and local taxes. The aggregate rate of taxation for most corporations with respect to these three sets of taxes taken in combination is approximately 55%. Stamp taxes, securities transactions taxes and consumption taxes also will apply to the activities of such corporations in connection with their business activities.

The creditability of Japanese taxes against taxes paid in other countries may depend on the existence of a double income tax treaty with the foreign country and the rules of the foreign jurisdiction with respect to creditable foreign taxes, consolidation of returns, limitation of credits to dividends paid, etc. Japan maintains double income and estate taxation treaties with a large number of countries. In the absence of a double taxation treaty reducing the withholding tax rate (to an amount not less than 5 percent and generally 10 percent), corporate dividends paid abroad will be subject to withholding taxes in Japan at the domestic rate of 20 percent. Similarly, interest paid abroad will be subject to interest withholding tax at the rate of 20 percent unless reduced by treaty (at present to not less than 10 percent). Interest paid to a parent or other affiliate may be disallowed if certain earnings stripping tests are not met.

PROCEDURES FOR ESTABLISHMENT

To establish a Stock Corporation in Japan, there must be one or more promoters, who may be either natural or juridical persons. Two methods for establishing a Stock Corporation are available: Private Subscription Establishment and Public Offering Establishment. In connection with the formation of a Stock Corporation, a company name search will be made, the Articles of Incorporation will be prepared and notarised, decisions will be made as to the classes and issue price of shares, promoters, initial directors and statutory auditors will be selected, certain matters will be registered and documents filed with the relevant legal affairs bureau, and corporate accounts established. In order to register the corporation (and thereby obtain official recognition of its existence), funds representing the contributed capital of the corporation must be placed on deposit with a Japanese bank which certifies their existence and availability in connection with the registration process.

In general, shortly after formation, a first meeting of directors will be held to elect the representative directors of the corporation. Unlike in other jurisdictions, because of fiduciary and ethical considerations, it is not customary for a lawyer or accountant to act as the representative director of a corporation in formation, although it is customary for them (and/or members of relevant firm's staff) to act as promoters and, subject to various regulatory and ethical considerations, directors after formation.

JAPAN PRESENCE

REPRESENTATIVE OFFICE IN JAPAN

A Japan representative office is an extension of a foreign corporation's head office; it is not an entity separate from the foreign corporation. Except for certain limited fields of business (e.g., banking and securities businesses where a separate registration filing may be required), there are no Japanese governmental formalities required for a foreign corporation to establish and maintain a representative office in Japan, provided the representative office does not engage in commercial transactions or conduct a business in Japan.

ACTIVITIES

There are no guidelines or judicial precedents as to what constitutes "doing business" in Japan. Legal authorities, however, generally agree that a Japan representative office may not conduct any revenue generating activities, such as negotiating and implementing transactions and executing contracts. A representative office in Japan may conduct on behalf of its head office activities that do not generate revenues, such as market research, collection and distribution of information, advertising and publicity and, in general, other activities of a "liaison" nature (i.e., non-revenue generating).

If a head office directly conducts business in Japan (and not through its representative office), consideration must be given as to whether the Japan representative office may receive payments on behalf of the head office in respect of these activities. No guidelines or judicial precedents exist as to whether a Japan representative office may receive such payments. While it may be argued that the receipt of such payments is a liaison activity (i.e., not a revenue-generating activity and therefore permissible for a representative office), it is possible that the receipt of such payments by a representative office may cause Japanese authorities to examine whether the representative office itself is doing business or engaging in transactions in Japan and therefore should be registered (and/or taxed). To avoid any such inquiry and the risk of Japanese tax liability (if the inquiry results in a determination that the representative office is doing business or engaging in transactions)[1], it may be advisable for the representative office not to receive such payments on behalf of its head office.

The head office of a Japan representative office may freely remit operating funds to or for creditors of the representative office through any foreign exchange bank licensed and authorised under the Japanese Foreign Exchange and Foreign Trade Control Law (the "FEL")[2] unless the MOF imposes a separate license requirement (the absence of any such requirement should be checked on a case-by- case basis). Under existing provisions of the FEL, a license for such a remittance may be required in certain circumstances, including if the remittance would cause a drastic change in Japan's balance of international payments or foreign currency exchange rates or would adversely affect money markets.

JAPANESE TAX CONSEQUENCES

So long as a representative office does not conduct a business or engage in commercial transactions in Japan, it should not be subject to Japanese corporate income taxes. However, many operations established as "representative offices" in Japan over time come to engage in activities which are primarily commercial in nature (i.e., they are undertaken with the primary purpose of obtaining an economic benefit for a foreign enterprise) and thereby attract the attention of Japanese tax authorities. In order to maintain a non-taxable status, careful attention must be paid over time to the scope of activities undertaken by the representative in Japan and the staff of the representative office.

As noted below, as soon as a representative office of a foreign corporation is determined to be conducting a business in Japan on a continuous basis (i.e., is engaged in profit-making activities) it must register a branch office in Japan. Such branch office will, in general (although non-taxable status may be preserved by careful supervision of activities), constitute a taxable presence in Japan and all business conducted in Japan by the foreign entity could become subject to taxation. Thus, conducting activities beyond the scope of activities allowed to a representatives office (i.e., non-revenue generating activities) could result both in a violation of the commercial code (the failure to register a branch in Japan as discussed below) and serious tax consequences to the foreign head office (exposure of all business conducted by such entity with respect to taxation in Japan).

Careful planning is therefore essential when considering the establishment of a representative office. In particular, personnel of the representative office in Japan must be oriented carefully as to the activities in which they will be permitted to engage and also as to how they are to represent themselves to foreign parties (including the use of titles on business cards and correspondence, avoidance of the preparation, negotiation or execution of any agreements or understandings of a commercial character, etc.). While Japanese tax authorities have not in the past focussed closely on the occasional violation of these rules (because of resource and other constraints), in most cases prudence and compliance with head office directives must be followed carefully by the staff of the representative office in Japan.

PROCEDURE FOR ESTABLISHMENT

The lack of any formal establishment and/or registration in Japan frequently results in difficulties for the foreign business in securing office space, opening bank accounts and obtaining services and living accommodations for the person selected to act as the "Representative in Japan" of the relevant business. Many major landlords in Tokyo and other Japanese cities insist on being provided with a copy of the corporate registration of the proposed tenant (or employer of the proposed tenant) before agreeing to lease property to the tenant. Similarly, lessors of computer and office equipment prefer to deal with an entity legally established in Japan. These problems can, in most circumstances, be overcome, but only after tedious explanations and considerable aggravation (although recent economic changes in Japan have reduced such problems considerably).

BRANCH OFFICE

Like a representative office, a Japan branch office of a foreign corporation is an extension of the foreign corporation's head office; it is not an entity separate from the foreign corporation. A Japan branch office is a taxable entity and subject to Japanese corporate income taxes (although, in certain instances, a licensed branch too may escape taxation by carefully limiting its activities).

ACTIVITIES

The general rule governing a foreign corporation's activities in Japan is that a foreign corporation engaging in transactions or doing business in Japan on a continuous basis must register a place of business in Japan (a "branch office") and register a representative resident in Japan (who need not be a Japanese citizen) with the relevant Japanese authorities.[4]

Any lawful activity may be conducted by the Japan branch office on behalf of its head office. Any remittance between such head office and its Japan branch office (whether inward to Japan or outward from Japan) may be made freely through any foreign exchange bank licensed and authorised under the FEL unless, as discussed above, the MOF exercises its authority to impose a license requirement or similar restriction on such remittances. Loans and other remittances not made through an authorised foreign exchange bank may be subject to reporting and/or approval requirements through filings made with the MOF through The Bank of Japan under the FEL.

JAPANESE TAX CONSEQUENCES

A Japan branch office is subject to Japanese corporate income taxes at the rate of 37.5% with respect to its income originating from sources in Japan.[5] In addition, a branch office will be subject to prefectural and local taxes where its office is registered. The rate of prefectural and local taxes will vary depending on the place of registration; however, the overall tax burden will approximate the aggregate tax rate applicable to corporations of around 52%. Like corporations, branch offices also are subject to payment of enterprise taxes which are assessed on the basis of the prior year's business volume. Business activities undertaken by the branch office may incur transaction taxes of various types including stamp taxes, securities transaction taxes and interest withholding taxes. As a resident of Japan, a branch will file national, prefectural, local and enterprise tax returns in respect of its operations.

CORPORATION TAX

The Corporation Tax is generally computed at a rate of 37.5 percent (plus a Special Corporation Tax at a rate of 2.5 percent) on all earnings. However, for small corporations capitalised at ¥100 million or less, the first ¥8 million of income will be subject to tax at a rate of 28%.

A Japan branch office which is subject to tax, i.e. a branch office engaged in commercial activities in Japan, is subject to the Corporation Tax at the same rates as indicated above, including the lower rate applicable to the first ¥8,000,000 income of foreign companies capitalised at ¥100,000,000 or less. The Corporation Tax on a branch office, however, is computed on the basis of Japan source income only, whereas the general Corporation Tax is based on worldwide income. This factor has resulted in many foreign corporations wishing to do business in Japan to elect to do business in branch, rather than corporate, form.

In order to determine the appropriate Japanese tax rate in respect of a Japan branch office, the capitalisation of the foreign corporation must be employed and expressed in yen as of the end of each fiscal year by converting the paid-in capital of the foreign corporation to Japanese yen at the exchange rate prevailing on the last business day of such fiscal year.

INHABITANTS TAX

Both the Prefectural and the Municipal Inhabitants Taxes consist of

(i) a corporate levy portion calculated as a standard percentage of the Corporation Tax amount, and (ii) a per capita levy calculated on the basis of the capitalisation and size of the corporation.

PER CAPITA LEVY

The per capita levy portion of inhabitants taxes is payable regardless of profit or loss. At the prefecture level, the per capita levy is calculated on the basis of the capitalisation of the foreign corporation as a whole (not just the capital employed at the Japan branch). At the municipal level, however, the size element, namely the number of employees, is determined by reference to the number of employees within the relevant municipality only, not by reference to the subsidiary or foreign corporation as a whole. These rules apply both to the Japanese branches of foreign corporations and to Japanese corporations which have multiple branches within Japan. In the case of branches of foreign corporations, the rules for the Prefectural Inhabitants Tax may result in the use of a capitalisation figure much greater than the value of the assets actually used in a Japanese branch operation. On the other hand, if the foreign corporation has incorporated a Japanese subsidiary, these per capita levies would be calculated solely by reference to the capitalisation and size of the Japanese subsidiary.

The standard rates for the per capita levy portion of the annual Prefectural and Municipal Inhabitants Tax are as follows:

PREFECTURAL INHABITANTS TAX

Capital amount (including capital reserves)	Standard tax amount
¥10,000,000 or less	¥20,000
over ¥10,000,000 but not over ¥100,000,000	¥50,000
over ¥100,000,000 but not over ¥1,000,000,000	¥130,000
over ¥1,000,000,000 but not over ¥5,000,000,000	¥540,000
over ¥5,000,000,000	¥800,000

MUNICIPAL INHABITANTS TAX

Capital amount (Including capital reserves)	Number of employees	Standard tax amount
¥10,000,000[1] or less	50 or less	¥50,000
	over 50	¥120,000
over ¥10,000,000 but not over ¥100,000,000	50 or less	¥130,000
	over 50	¥150,000
over ¥100,000,000 but not over ¥1,000,000,000	50 or less	¥160,000
	over 50	¥400,000
over ¥1,000,000,000 but not over ¥5,000,000,000	50 or less	¥410,000
	over 50	¥1,750,000
more than ¥5,000,000,000	50 or less	¥410,000
	over 50	¥3,000,000

Note 1: Municipal Inhabitants Tax may be adjusted by the local municipal government up to a maximum levy of 120 percent of the rates quoted above.

As can be seen from a review of the above table, a small Japanese branch operation of a very large foreign corporation could very well incur a substantially higher per capita tax levy than would be the case if the same operation were conducted through a Japanese subsidiary.

CORPORATE LEVY

The amount of the corporate levy is determined by applying the Prefectual and Municipal tax rates against the amount of Corporation Tax payable by the branch. The following standard rates may vary slightly depending on the location of the relevant operations in Japan. For example, Tokyo (which is treated as a prefecture for administrative and tax purposes) applies the maximum combined rate of 20.7% for corporations capitalised at over ¥100 million or having a Corporation Tax liability of over ¥10 million.

	Standard Rate	Maximum Rate
Prefectural tax rate:	5.0%	6.0%
Municipal tax rate:	12.3%	14.7%
Tokyo Metropolitan Tax:	17.3%	20.7%

The corporate levy is treated as an expense for the purpose of calculating taxable income under the Corporation Tax. Accordingly, the effective total tax burden (i.e., Corporation Tax, Inhabitant Tax and Corporate Levy) is approximately 55% of taxable income.

PROCEDURE FOR ESTABLISHMENT

The establishment by a foreign corporation of a Japan branch office is governed by the Commercial Code, the FEL and various other laws and subordinate regulations. The procedure to establish a Japan branch office requires the filing by the foreign corporation of a notice (the "Notice") with the MOF through The Bank of Japan, (which has been delegated the authority by the MOF to process and review the Notice).[6] Such Notice may be required to be filed before or after the registration of the branch office with the commercial registration office (see discussion below) depending upon the nature of business to be conducted. The Notice requires disclosure of, among other things, information concerning the foreign corporation's business and the proposed branch office's business.

The foreign corporation establishing the Japan branch office is required under the Commercial Code to register the Japan branch office with the commercial registration office (the "Commercial Registration Office") of the local Legal Affairs Bureau (*Homukyoku*) of the Ministry of Justice for the jurisdiction in which the Japan branch office will be located.[7] The Commercial Code also requires the foreign corporation to appoint a representative resident in Japan and register an address in Japan for the branch office (which may be the representative's personal address).[8]

The resident representative need not be a Japanese citizen. The process for registration of a branch office normally takes approximately two weeks. Once the registration is effected, the branch office may commence its activities.

BRANCH ACTIVITIES

Any lawful activity (i.e., legally permissible and not separately registered) may be conducted by the Japan branch office on behalf of its head office. Any remittance between such head office and its Japan branch office (whether inward to Japan or outward from Japan) may be made freely through any foreign exchange bank licensed and authorised under the FEL unless, as discussed above, the MOF exercises its authority to impose a license requirement for such remittances. Loans and other remittances not made through an authorised foreign exchange bank may be subject to reporting and/or approval requirements through filings made with the MOF through The Bank of Japan under the FEL.

JAPANESE TAX CONSEQUENCES

Japanese corporations are taxed in Japan on the basis of their worldwide income rather than only their Japan source income as is the case with a branch office. A discussion of all of the varieties of taxes, duties and other assessments which are applicable to Japanese corporations is beyond the scope of this discussion. However, set forth below is a summary of the principal taxes applicable to Japanese corporations.

CORPORATION TAX

The Corporation Tax is generally computed for capital of more than ¥100 million at a rate of 37.5 percent on all earnings. However, for small corporations capitalised at ¥100 million or less, the first ¥8 million of income will be subject to tax at a rate of 28 percent.

INHABITANTS TAX

Both the Prefectural and the Municipal Inhabitants Taxes consist of (i) a corporate levy portion calculated as a standard percentage of the Corporation Tax amount, and (ii) a per capita levy calculated on the basis of the capitalization and size of the corporation. Inhabitants taxes are not deductible for the purpose of computing the taxable income for the corporation tax.[ii]

PER CAPITA LEVY

The per capita levy portion of these taxes is payable regardless of profit or loss. At the prefecture level, the per capita levy is calculated on the basis of the capitalization of the corporation. At the municipal level, however, the size element, namely the number of employees, is determined by reference to the number employed within the relevant municipality only, not by reference to the corporation as a whole (i.e., where the corporation has operations in other municipalities).

The standard rates for the per capita levy portion of the annual Prefectural and Municipal Inhabitants Tax are as follows:

PREFECTURAL INHABITANTS TAX

Capital amount (including capital reserves)	Standard tax amount
¥10,000,000 or less	¥20,000
over ¥10,000,000 but not over ¥100,000,000	¥50,000
over ¥100,000,000 but not over ¥1,000,000,000	¥130,000
over ¥1,000,000,000 but not over ¥5,000,000,000	¥540,000
over ¥5,000,000,000	¥800,000

MUNICIPAL INHABITANTS TAX

Capital amount (Including capital reserves)	Number of employees	Standard tax amount
¥10,000,000 or less	50 or less	¥50,000
	over 50	¥120,000
over ¥10,000,000 but not over ¥100,000,000	50 or less	¥130,000
	over 50	¥150,000
over ¥100,000,000 but not over ¥1,000,000,000	50 or less	¥160,000
	over 50	¥400,000
over ¥1,000,000,000 but not over ¥5,000,000,000	50 or less	¥410,000
	over 50	¥1,750,000
more than ¥5,000,000,000	50 or less	¥410,000
	exceeding 50	¥3,000,000

CORPORATE LEVY

The amount of corporate levy is determined by applying the Prefectual and Municipal tax rates against the amount of Corporation

Tax payable. The following standard rates may vary slightly depending on the location of the Japan operations. For example, Tokyo applies the maximum combined rate of 20.7 percent for corporations capitalised at over ¥100 million or having a Corporation Tax liability of over ¥10 million.

	Standard Rate	Maximum Rate
Prefectural tax rate:	5.0%	6.0%
Municipal tax rate:	12.3%	14.7%
Tokyo Metropolitan Tax:	17.3%	20.7%

The corporate levy is treated as an expense for the purpose of calculating taxable income under the Corporation Tax. Accordingly, the effective total tax burden (i.e. Corporation Tax, Inhabitant Tax and Corporate Levy) is approximately 55 percent of taxable income.

ENTERPRISE TAX

In addition to the corporation tax and the inhabitants tax, a corporation is also subject to the imposition of enterprise taxes. The tax base for computing the enterprise tax is the taxable profits, computed in the same manner as for the corporation tax. The enterprise tax is deductible for the purpose of computing the taxable income on which the enterprise tax is based. The taxable income of a corporation is taxed at the following rates.

Taxable Income	Rate
¥350 m or less	6%
Over ¥350 m up to ¥700 m or less	9%
Over ¥700 m	12%

However, corporations that maintain offices or factories in three or more prefectures and whose capital equals or exceeds ¥10,000,000 are taxed at a flat rate of 12% of taxable income. Also, these tax rates may differ depending on the financial circumstances of the local tax body, but in no event can the rate be greater than 110% of the basic rate.

TYPES OF CORPORATIONS

There are four possible forms in which companies may be incorporated in Japan: *Gomei Kaisha* (partnership company), *Goshi Kaisha* (limited partnership company), *Yugen Kaisha* (limited liability company) and *Kabushiki Kaisha* (stock company). The "Stock

Corporation" is, however, the most common form of company in Japan. Accordingly, foreign investors almost always establish a Japanese subsidiary in the form of a Stock Corporation. In contrast to branches, the liability of shareholders of a Stock Corporation is limited to the amount of their capital contributions.

As the most commonly accepted form of business entity in Japan, the Stock Corporation provides a familiar framework for limiting liability and maintaining control. It is the most appropriate form for large corporations, the other forms being used primarily for small businesses. The availability of limited stockholder liability is the most significant feature which favours the use of a Stock Corporation over a branch.

FORMATION OF A STOCK CORPORATION

To establish a Stock Corporation in Japan, there must be one or more promoters, who may be either natural or juridical persons. Promoters serve a function similar to the incorporators required in many Anglo-American jurisdictions and perform the acts necessary to the establishment of a Stock Corporation and the issuance of its shares.

Two methods for establishing a Stock Corporation are available; Private Subscription Establishment (*Hokki Setsuritsu*), where all the shares to be initially issued are subscribed for by the promoters, and Public Offering Establishment (*Boshu Setsuritsu*), where subscribers other than the promoters subscribe for the remainder of the shares subscribed by the promoters. These two methods are described in greater detail below. In general, however, the formation steps for both methods of formation of a Stock Corporation are as follows:

(a) **Execution of Articles of Incorporation.** All the promoters execute the Articles of Incorporation, which may contain provisions similar to "by-laws" of Anglo-American practice. There is no separate document called "by-laws" under the Commercial Code (although some corporations adopt "Board Regulations" which may serve a similar function).

(b) **Notarisation of Articles of Incorporation.** The Articles of Incorporation must be notarised by a Japanese notary public. The promoters may apply for notarisation by proxy.

(c) **Subscription of Shares.** All the promoters must subscribe to at least one share each, with the remaining new shares, if any, being subscribed in writing by subscriber(s). Where a wholly-owned subsidiary is involved, it is common practice for a single promoter to subscribe to a single share with the remaining shares being subscribed by the parent company. After formation, the promoter transfers the single share to the parent making the Stock Corporation a wholly-owned subsidiary.

(d) **Making of Contributions.** The promoters must have all the contributions paid to the account of the new company at a designated bank (licensed as an authorised foreign exchange bank in Japan) which is listed in the application forms for subscription. No installment subscription is permitted in Japan. A company cannot be established before the payment of subscription money. After the subscription money is paid, the bank issues a certificate that the subscription money has been deposited. Without this certificate, an application for registration of incorporation of a company will not be accepted by the commercial registration office.

(e) **Organisational Meeting.** After all the contributions are made, the organisational meeting of the promoters and subscribers, who are the original shareholders, is convened and the directors and auditor(s) are elected.

(f) **Meeting of Board of Directors.** The meeting of the board of directors is convened after the organisational meeting, and the representative director is elected by resolution of the members of the board of directors.

(g) **Registration of Formation.** The registration of formation is made by the representative director at the Commercial Registration Office of the Legal Affairs Bureau having jurisdiction over the company's principal place of business.

(h) **Effectiveness of Establishment.** A company is incorporated and acquires its legal status upon registration. The registration becomes effective upon the filing of the application, the Articles of Incorporation and other documents with the Commercial Registration Office.

PRIVATE SUBSCRIPTION ESTABLISHMENT

COMPANY NAME SEARCH

A company name search is undertaken to confirm that no other company in the jurisdictional area of the relevant local Commercial Registration Office has registered or reserved the same or similar name as the proposed Stock Corporation. The promoters may reserve the name of the proposed Stock Corporation at the relevant Commercial Registration Office to preclude other companies from using such company name for one year. A name may not be adopted if there is a similar tradename already registered in the same administrative district (in the case of Tokyo, the relevant jurisdiction is the "ward" or "*ku*" and in other cities, "city" or "*shi*") for use in a similar business. Potential name conflicts should be checked before starting the incorporation procedure. A party may reserve the proposed corporate name one year from the date of application, subject to the payment of a deposit with the Commercial Registration Office.

It is also advisable to consult with the Commercial Registration Office at an early stage concerning the proposed "business objectives" of the company to be incorporated since the Commercial Registration Office may reject the registration of "business objectives" on the ground of vagueness or other reasons. Foreign parties should be aware that standardised "business objectives" exist for a wide variety of industries and that it is often wise (in order to avoid delays and aggravation) to conform to "form". "Short form" articles (used in many United States jurisdictions) are not acceptable in Japan and the proposed business objectives must be specified in detail. On the other hand, registration authorities do not like applicants to "reinvent the wheel" and prefer to see descriptions which follow established precedents even if they describe a broader scope of operations than is really intended. Amending corporate descriptions to expand the scope of a company's operations is a routine procedure.

PREPARATION AND NOTARISATION OF ARTICLES OF INCORPORATION

Articles of Incorporation must be prepared and signed by the promoters and notarised by a Japanese notary public who belongs to the relevant local Commercial Registration Office. The notary confirms that (i) the document complies with all aspects of relevant laws, and (ii) that it has been duly executed by the promoters. One or more of the promoters, or their agent, must appear before the notary public and furnish the notary with all of the promoters' seal certificates issued by the relevant municipal offices for natural person promoters and certificates showing the authority and power of their representatives for company promoters. The Articles of Incorporation of a Stock Corporation function as a combination of the Articles of Incorporation and by-laws used in the United States and must include the following items:

(i)   The business purposes of the Stock Corporation;

(ii)   The name of the Stock Corporation;

(iii)   The authorised number of shares (the number of authorised shares can be up to four times the number of outstanding shares);

(iv)   The par value of the Stock Corporation's stock, if the Stock Corporation issues par value shares (the company may issue shares with or without par value; however, it is very rare that shares without par value are issued in Japan);

(v)   The number of shares to be issued by the Stock Corporation upon establishment for each of the par value shares and the non-par value shares (the minimum amount of capital for a Stock Corporation is ¥10 million);

(vi)   The location of the principal office of the Stock Corporation (the registered corporate office may be located at the home or company address of any of the parties concerned, while the actual business office may be established in another place);

(vii)   The manner by which the Stock Corporation gives public notices (the "Publication Manner"; normally, public notices are made on the official gazette "*Kampo*"); and

(viii) The full name and address of each promoter.

In addition, if one or more of the promoters proposes to make a contribution in kind, the Articles of Incorporation must include: (i) the name of such promoter, (ii) the asset to be contributed, (iii) the value of the asset, and (iv) the class and number of shares to be issued for such contribution in kind.

MATTERS RELATING TO SHARES TO BE ISSUED UPON ESTABLISHMENT

The promoters must determine the following matters relating to the shares which will be issued upon establishment of the Stock Corporation (these items may be included in the Articles of Incorporation).

(i)   The class of shares (preferred or subordinate in terms of distribution of profits or liquidation assets), and the numbers of shares for each class, if the Articles of Incorporation provide for the issuance of such class of shares;

(ii) The issue price of shares (which must be ¥50,000 or more per share); the issue price of shares cannot be less than the par value; and

(iii) The amount of the issue price not to be credited to stated capital (such amount may not exceed one-half of the issue price and must be credited to capital surplus reserve).[10]

SUBSCRIPTION FOR SHARES BY PROMOTERS

Each promoter must subscribe for at least one share of the initially issued shares by a written share subscription instrument, which must include the number of shares to be subscribed for and the price thereof. Such price must be the issue price or more.

The promoters must designate a bank in Japan which is in charge of receiving payment for the shares from each promoter (the "Designated Bank"). A certificate of payment is issued by the Designated Bank and filed at the Commercial Registration Office at the time of the registration. The Commercial Code requires a minimum stated capital of ¥10,000,000.

Payment for shares may be made by contribution in kind. In such case, a court valuation of the contributed property is generally required.

A shareholder can freely transfer his/her shares. However, the company may stipulate in the Articles of Incorporation that transfers shall be subject to the approval of the Board of Directors. If the Board of Directors does not give its approval, the Board must designate another transferee and, under certain circumstances, the company may purchase such shares.

ELECTION OF INITIAL DIRECTORS AND STATUTORY AUDITORS

After the promoters subscribe for all the shares, they must, without delay, elect the initial directors and statutory auditors. The directors and statutory auditors so elected must investigate whether all the shares to be issued have been subscribed for by the promoters and whether any proposed in-kind contribution has been made. The directors also must hold the first meeting of the board of directors and elect one or more representative directors.

COMMERCIAL REGISTRATION

The representative directors must register the Stock Corporation's establishment at the relevant local Commercial Registration Office within two weeks from the completion of the above-mentioned investigation by the directors and statutory auditors. At the same time, a representative director's seal will be registered.

MATTERS FOR REGISTRATION

The following matters must be registered (this list is similar to, but narrower than, the items to be included in a company's articles of incorporation):

(i) The business purposes of the Stock Corporation;

(ii) The name of the Stock Corporation;

(iii) The authorised number of shares;

(iv) The par value of shares, if the Stock Corporation issues par value shares;

(v) The manner of publication;

(vi) The location of the principal office and branches;

(vii) The number of preferred or subordinate shares, if applicable;

(viii) If share transfers are restricted, a statement to that effect;

(ix) The number of outstanding shares;

(x) The amount of stated capital;

(xi) The full names of the directors and statutory auditors;

(xii) The full names and addresses of the representative directors; and

(xiii) If two or more representative directors jointly represent the company, a statement to that effect.

DOCUMENTS TO BE SUBMITTED

At the time of the filing for registration, the following documents must be submitted:

(i) The Articles of Incorporation;

(ii) The certificates of subscriptions for shares;

(iii) Any promoters' resolutions on matters relating to shares issued upon establishment;

(iv) A report of the directors and statutory auditors concerning the investigation of the establishment of the company;

(v)   A written document concerning the election of directors and statutory auditors by the promoters;

(vi) Written acceptances of office by the new directors, representative directors and statutory auditors;

(vii) A certificate of receipt of issue price for the subscribed shares provided by the Designated Bank; and

(viii) A power of attorney authorising registration by the person filing the application therefor (typically a registration clerk (*shihoshoshi*) specialising in registration office matters handles such filings).

Although the company is considered to have been established as of the date of its registration, approval of the registration (and issuance of the official commercial register (*tokibotohon*), usually requires 10-14 days.

OPENING OF THE STOCK CORPORATION'S BANK ACCOUNT

After completion of the registration, the Stock Corporation's representative director must deliver a certified copy of the registration to the Designated Bank, together with a certificate of the seal impression of the Stock Corporation's representative director. The representative director can then open an account on behalf of the Stock Corporation and the Designated Bank will transfer the capital funds deposited by shareholders and promoters during the establishment of the company held by the Designated Bank to the new account (the "Payment Date").

PROCEDURE OF PUBLIC OFFERING ESTABLISHMENT

COMPANY NAME SEARCH

The procedures for this requirement in a public offering establishment are the same as described above.

PREPARATION AND NOTARISATION OF ARTICLES OF INCORPORATION

The procedures for this requirement in a public offering establishment are the same as described above.

DETERMINATION ON MATTERS RELATING TO SHARES TO BE ISSUED UPON ESTABLISHMENT

The procedures for this requirement in a public offering establishment are the same as described above.

SUBSCRIPTION OF SHARES BY PROMOTERS AND SUBSCRIBERS

In the case of a Public Offering Establishment, the promoters will solicit subscribers of the shares which are not subscribed for by the promoters. The promoters may either solicit unspecified subscribers from the public or give certain persons options to subscribe for such shares.

A person who wishes to subscribe for shares must complete an application form provided by the promoters. The application form must include the following information:

(i)   The notarisation date of the Articles of Incorporation and the name of the notary public;

(ii) The name and business purposes of the Stock Corporation;

(iii) The authorised number of shares;

(iv) The par value, if the shares are par value shares;

(v)   The number of shares to be issued for each type and class at the time of establishment;

(vi) The location of the principal office of the Stock Corporation;

(vii) The publication manner;

(viii) Certain items included in the Articles of Incorporation;

(ix) Restrictions on transfer of shares, if applicable;

(x)   The amount not to be credited to stated capital;

(xi) The number of shares for each type and class which was subscribed for by the promoters and its price; and

(xii) The Designated Bank.

Subscribers other than promoters may not make a contribution in kind. In practice, subscribers must pay the purchase price for shares at the time of the application as an advance payment to the Designated Bank. The Designated Bank transfers the money received to the Stock Corporation's account on the Payment Date.

ORGANISATIONAL MEETING

The promoters must convene an organisational meeting. At this meeting, the promoters report on matters related to the establishment of the Stock Corporation and directors and statutory auditors are elected. To pass resolutions at an organisational meeting, the vote of at least two-thirds of the subscribers (including promoters) who are present, and who represent majority ownership of the total number of shares subscribed for, is necessary.

The directors and statutory auditors so elected must investigate whether all the shares to be issued have been subscribed for by the promoters and subscribers and whether any proposed in-kind contribution has been concluded. The directors must hold the first meeting of the board of directors and elect one or more representative directors.

COMMERCIAL REGISTRATION

The procedures for this requirement in a public offering establishment are the same as described above, except that the minutes of the organisational general meeting must be submitted instead of written documentation electing directors and statutory auditors by the promoters.

OPENING OF THE STOCK CORPORATION'S BANK ACCOUNT

The procedures for this requirement in a public offering establishment are the same as described above.

LIMITATIONS ON DISTRIBUTIONS OF CORPORATE PROFITS

Under Article 290 of the Commercial Code, a Stock Corporation may distribute its profits as dividends only to the extent that the amount of the net assets on the Stock Corporation's balance sheet exceeds the sum of the following amounts:

(a) The Stock Corporation's stated capital; and
(b) The larger of (i) the sum of the capital surplus reserve and the earned surplus reserve plus the amount to be added to the earned surplus reserve in respect of the relevant business year; or (ii) the sum of start-up expenses and R&D expenses recorded as assets on the balance sheet.

Net assets means total assets less total liabilities, as shown on the balance sheet. Under the Commercial Code, the Board of Directors must declare at least the greater of (i) 50 percent of the funds received in consideration for issuance of shares or (ii) par value or, in case of non-par value shares, ¥50,000 per share, as stated capital. The remainder of the funds received is treated as capital surplus reserve.

At least 10 percent of the amount disbursed as dividends for each business year must be set aside as an earned surplus reserve until such time as the aggregate earned surplus reserve reaches 25 percent of stated capital.

Start-up expenses and R&D expenses may be treated as assets on the balance sheet. Start-up expenses must be amortised within five years after commencement of business and R&D expenses within five years after the expenses were incurred.

CAPITAL REDUCTIONS

Under Article 375 of the Commercial Code, a special resolution of a general meeting of the shareholders is required to effect a capital reduction. A special resolution requires a two-thirds majority of votes present.[11] The quorum for a general meeting of shareholders is a majority of the outstanding shares.

In addition, to protect creditors of the Stock Corporation, the Stock Corporation must, within two weeks after the resolution, give notice of the proposed capital reduction publicly and to each known creditor.[12] If there are any objections from creditors, the Stock Corporation must satisfy the creditors by repayment or by providing sufficient security.

These procedures apply regardless of whether the proposed capital reduction would be accompanied by distribution of the Stock Corporation's assets or not.

Apart from a capital reduction, a Stock Corporation is not in principle permitted to acquire its own shares.[13]

CORPORATE GOVERNANCE

A Stock Corporation has four corporate organs:

(i)   The General Meeting of Shareholders;

(ii) The Board of Directors;

(iii) The Representative Director(s); and

(iv) The Statutory Auditor(s).[14]

The shareholders, acting in a general meeting, are the highest organ and possesses the power to vote on matters of fundamental concern to the company. The Board of Directors, which consists of directors appointed at the general meeting of shareholders, decides the affairs of the Stock Corporation. The representative director(s), who are appointed from the members of the Board of Directors by resolution, administer the affairs of the company and represent the company in accordance with the resolutions of the Board of Directors. The auditor(s) are appointed by the general meeting of shareholders and audit the accounts of the company or the execution of the duties of the directors. The auditor need not have any professional qualification (e.g., be a CPA or hold an accounting degree). The directors and auditors are often referred to as the "officers" of the Stock Corporation, although the nuance of that term is different than in Anglo-American practice. The offices of secretary and treasurer, which may exist in corporations established under the laws of the United States and other countries, does not exist in a Japanese Stock Corporation.

SHAREHOLDER'S MEETINGS

The ordinary general meeting of shareholders must be convened once a year at a fixed time. A shareholder who holds, either alone or with other shareholders, shares representing not less than three per cent of the total number of the issued shares continuously for at least the previous six months may demand that the company convene an extraordinary general meeting. A meeting may be attended by proxy.

The Commercial Code provides that a company shall hold its shareholders meeting in the place of its registered principal office; therefore, even a joint venture Stock Corporation formed between a Japanese and foreign company as shareholders may not hold a shareholders meeting outside Japan. The general meeting may pass resolutions only on matters provided for in the Commercial Code or the Articles of Incorporation.

ACTIVITIES AND RESPONSIBILITIES OF DIRECTORS

NUMBER, TERM AND RESIDENCE

The number of directors of a Stock Corporation must be three or more. The term of office of directors may not be more than two years. The directors may resign or be removed from office by a resolution of the general meeting of shareholders at any time with or without cause. Reappointment is possible with the approval of a general meeting of shareholders. A non-resident of Japan may be appointed as director. The change and reappointment of directors must be registered at the Commercial Registration Office. Individual directors normally have no formal power to represent the company.

LIABILITY OF DIRECTOR

In case a director acts negligently or in bad faith in the performance of his/her duties as director, the director will be liable to the Stock Corporation. If the director acts with gross negligence or bad faith, he/she may be liable to third parties as well as to the Stock Corporation. Otherwise, the director will not be liable for the acts of the company.

A director is required to perform his/her duties faithfully on behalf of the Stock Corporation and also must conduct the business entrusted to the director with the standard care of a "good manager". These obligations mean that a director must act for the benefit of a Stock Corporation at all times. A director may not act only for the benefit of the shareholder who designates him to be a director of the Stock Corporation. A director is liable for any damage to the Stock Corporation when the director acting on behalf of the Company violates any relevant laws or the Articles of Incorporation. Therefore, if the Stock Corporation suffers damage due to the director's not complying with such obligations, the director is liable in damages to the Stock Corporation.

BOARD MEETINGS

A meeting of the Board of Directors may be convened by any director, unless otherwise set forth in the Articles of Incorporation. However, it is usual for the Articles of Incorporation to stipulate that the meeting shall be convened by the representative director. The meeting must be attended by the directors in person. Such meetings may be held outside Japan. The Commercial Code provides one week as the notice period for the convocation of a directors' meeting, although this notice period may be shortened by the Articles of Incorporation. In the case of a joint venture between a Japanese and a foreign company, the period should be sufficiently long to secure the attendance of foreign directors, if necessary. The meeting may be conducted either in Japanese or English with the help of interpreters. The minutes may be prepared both in Japanese and English. However, minutes prepared only in English are not permissible.

The Board of Directors must meet not less than once every three months. It has the power to determine all important business matters of the company except those matters which the Commercial Code stipulates must be approved by the shareholders. However, the Articles of Incorporation of a company may make other issues subject to the approval of the shareholders.

Under the Commercial Code, a majority of directors must attend board meetings and the majority of directors present must vote affirmatively in order to resolve a matter on behalf of the Stock Corporation. These conditions can be made more stringent by the Articles of Incorporation. As would be expected in a joint venture Stock Corporation between a Japanese and a foreign corporation, issues are typically handled between the joint venture partners initially by way of correspondence and then ratified at directors' meetings.

BOARD ACTIONS

The directors may act by simple majority. However, many Stock Corporations require that certain important issues require approval by more than a majority of the board. The issues selected to require super-majority approval will be stated as requiring such approval in the Articles of Incorporation of the Stock Corporation. The Articles of Incorporation may provide that all or certain specific issues are subject to the unanimous approval of the Board of Directors, or the approval of, for example, a two-thirds majority.

DIRECTORS AND REPRESENTATIVE DIRECTORS

There may be several representative directors, and unless otherwise stipulated in the Articles of Incorporation, each representative director may represent the company. At least one representative director must be a resident in Japan. The representative director is always a member of the Board of Directors. If he/she loses the office of director, he/she automatically loses his/her position as representative director. He/she may be removed from his/her representative directorship at any time by the Board of Directors, in which case he/she may remain as a director.

All appointments and changes of directors and statutory auditors must be registered with the relevant legal affairs bureau. The position of the president (a title which has no significance under the Commercial Code but great significance in practice) of a company is almost always occupied by the representative director, and the vice-president(s) are sometimes representative director(s).

In the case of a large Japanese company, the management would typically consist of more than 20 directors who are members of the Board of Directors. They are ranked in the following order: (1) president, (2) vice-presidents, (3) senior managing directors (*senmu torishimari-yaku*), (4) junior managing directors (*jomu torishimari-yaku*) and directors without a special title (*torishimari-yaku*). Typically, certain high-ranking directors have the power to represent the company as representative directors.

RELATIONSHIP WITH TITLES OF CORPORATE OFFICERS

The Commercial Code does not require the use of any title, including Chairman, President or Vice-President, and there is no concept of an "officer" under Japanese law. References to President and Vice-President are to directors of the Company and are based on their relative seniority. The President and any Vice-President are senior to any Senior Managing Director, etc. Although there is no difference between directors under the Commercial Code, the Articles of Incorporation of a Japanese company may (although it typically does not) specify such distinctions with respect to the delegation to take action similar to that which corporate officers in an Anglo-American company are authorised to take.

In a large Japanese company, the typical Board of Directors includes one Chairman (*kaicho*), one President (*shacho*), a few Vice-Presidents (*fuku-shacho*) and a certain number of Senior Managing Directors (*senmu torishimari-yaku*), Junior Managing Directors (*jomu torishimari-yaku*) and untitled Directors (*torishimari-yaku*). In Japan, the word "managing director" usually means a director who is ranked between vice-presidents and non-managing directors. The typical Japanese Board of Directors of a large listed company exceeds 20 directors who are generally ranked in the manner noted above. Typically, the Chairman, the President and the Vice-Presidents are all Representative Directors. In certain companies, Senior Managing Directors and Junior Managing Directors are also Representative Directors. The Boards of Directors of all but the largest foreign corporations in Japan do not make such detailed distinctions in rank. In general, foreign corporations distinguish between directors and representative directors and adopt "corporate" titles as the exigencies of the conduct of business demand.

As mentioned above, there is no legal difference between any of the directors except for the difference between representative directors and non-representative directors. The titles used are typically based on seniority and are significant only to the extent that such seniority is respected.

BOARD COMMITTEES

There are several important items upon which the Board of Directors may not delegate its decision making power. However the board of directors may delegate to a representative director or an executive committee the authority to implement and decide details with respect to such important items, after it approves the general framework for implementation of such item.

In Japanese large companies, it is a common practice that a Board of Directors delegates virtually all decision-making powers to a management committee (*jomu-kai*), which is usually constituted of managing directors and more senior directors, including the president. The management committee decides all important matters and representative directors, other directors or other employees conduct the company's business in accordance with decisions made by the management committee. These decisions are nominally approved later by the board of directors (usually unanimously) only to meet Commercial Code requirements. Post-fact approval or ratification by the board of directors is permitted under the Japanese law and upon ratification, transactions in question are deemed to have been effective from the date of their commencement. It should be noted that this decision making system works only if no antagonistic relationship exits among directors. However, harmony (*wa*) is pursued and valued in a typical Japanese corporation (including Japanese subsidiaries of foreign corporate groups) and is the norm.

ROLE OF STATUTORY AUDITORS

Duties of and requirements regarding statutory auditors vary depending on the size of the company. Japanese companies are required to have one or more statutory auditors (*kansa-yaku*), but in the case of large corporations (corporations with stated capital of ¥500 million or more or liabilities of ¥20 billion or more), three or more statutory auditors (one of whom must have no other corporate affiliation in the last five years) elected at shareholders meetings. Statutory auditors supervise the activities of directors.

In principle, a statutory auditor's term of office is three years. To secure his/her independence, an auditor may not at the same time be a director, a manager or any other employee of the company or its affiliated companies. The appointment and change of auditors must be registered with the Commercial Registration Office.

The auditor is entitled to supervise the management of the company by the Board of Directors, and for this purpose, the auditor may ask the directors and other employees for reports of business of the Stock Corporation, otherwise investigate the business, assets and liabilities of the Stock Corporation, and take other procedures required under the Commercial Code. In the case of large corporations, the auditor's duties focus on the company's management other than accounting matters since independent accountants are required to be appointed in addition to statutory auditors.

If a statutory auditor acts negligently or in bad faith in the performance of his duties, he will be liable to the Stock Corporation. If he acts in gross negligence or bad faith, he may be liable to third parties as well. Otherwise, he will not be liable for the acts of the Stock Corporation.

SPECIAL CONSIDERATIONS WITH RESPECT TO JOINT VENTURES

If a foreign company wants to share the risks and benefits of doing business in Japan with Japanese partners, it may incorporate a joint venture company. Typically, the parties begin by negotiating a joint venture agreement ("JV Agreement") which stipulates the basic relationship between the parties and the formation, organisation and management of the joint venture company ("JV Company").

GENERAL CONSIDERATIONS

There are relatively few legal requirements concerning the contents of a JV Agreement under Japanese law. The JV Company is formed pursuant to its Articles of Incorporation, which state its basic business objectives and corporation governance conditions, and provide for the rights and duties of the shareholders, who are the joint venture partners ("JV Partners"). The relationship among the JV Partners is regulated, in different ways, by both the JV Agreement and the Articles of Incorporation. The JV Agreement regulates the relationship of the JV Partners as contracting parties and is governed by contract law under the Civil Code. The Articles of Incorporation state the manner of corporate governance, regulate the relationship among the JV Partners as shareholders, and are interpreted in accordance with the relevant provisions of the Commercial Code. Japanese contract law permits broad freedom of contractual self-determination to the parties, while the Commercial Code must be enforced regardless of the will of the parties.

It is usual for an English draft of Articles of Incorporation to be attached to the JV Agreement as an exhibit. However, the original of the Articles of Incorporation must be written in Japanese and reviewed as such by the notary public and, to the extent relating to the "business objectives" of the company, by the registration office. Consequently, when the JV Company is actually incorporated, a Japanese version must be prepared from the English draft (assuming the original draft was in English) and presented to the notary public and the registration office for their review.

DIRECTORS AND JOINT REPRESENTATIVE DIRECTORS

There is no legal or other requirement that the Japanese partner of a joint venture Stock Corporation be represented by a majority on the Board of Directors. In the case of a joint venture between a Japanese and a foreign corporation, it is a general practice that the directors are elected from both partners in proportion to their respective capital contributions, and some directors from the non-Japanese partner may be non-residents. Indeed, all directors appointed by the foreign partner may be non-residents. However, it is common practice that the foreign partner have at least one resident director who will check up on the daily operation of the JV Company.

Under the Commercial Code, a Stock Corporation must appoint one or more representative directors from among directors of the company.[15] At least one representative director must be resident. Where two or more representative directors are appointed, usually each representative director alone has an authority to act on behalf of the Stock Corporation. However, the Stock Corporation may provide in its Articles of Incorporation that the representative directors act jointly on behalf of the company.[16] In this case, the Stock Corporation's action must be conducted only through joint representation by the representative directors specified in the Articles of Incorporation. In Japan, joint ventures often adopt this system in order to protect each venturer's interest. It should be noted that this joint representation cannot be argued against claims of a bona fide third party claimant without notice unless it is registered with the competent Legal Affairs Bureau.[17]

SELECTION OF A NAME

The JV Company may freely choose its corporate name, although it

134

must contain the words *Kabushiki Kaisha*. However, English or other foreign languages may not be used for the formal or registered corporate name. The JV Company may have an English (or any other language) name for use in its actual business activities. Further, it is permissible to adopt the corporate name or tradename of the foreign partner as a part of the corporate name of the JV Company, if it is written in Japanese.

DILUTION CONSIDERATIONS

Under the Commercial Code, the Board of Directors is entitled to issue new shares from time to time within the limits of the authorised number provided for in the Articles of Incorporation; any change to this number is subject to the approval of the shareholders. Unless otherwise set forth in the Articles of Incorporation or unless the Articles require the Board's approval to transfer of shares, the Board of Directors is entitled to issue new shares to any party, regardless of the views of the shareholders, as long as the price is fair. In order to secure the rights of the JV Partners to new shares, it is advisable to stipulate in the Articles of Incorporation that "the shareholders of the Company shall have preemptive rights to all new shares of stock to be issued by the JV Company." Preemptive rights so created are enforceable by one shareholder against the JV Company and other shareholders under the Commercial Code.

FOREIGN EXCHANGE LAW AND SECURITIES LAW CONSIDERATIONS

In order to form a JV Company, the foreign party is required to file a prior or post facto (depending on the field of business to be conducted) notification to the Ministry of Finance and the minister in charge of the industry involved[18]. This notification is submitted through The Bank of Japan. In the event prior notification is required, the foreign party may not acquire the shares of the JV Company until 30 days have passed after said notification. However, this period may be shortened by the appropriate ministers (i.e., the Minster of Finance or the Minister of the Ministry with regulatory supervision over the concerned industry) or their subsidiary organs (shortening of the period is not unusual in current practice). The ministers have the right to review the notification during the 30-day period after filing and order alteration or suspension of the proposed investment where the investment is considered to have an adverse effect on national security or on the Japanese economy. Such a determination is extremely rare. In the event post-facto notification is required, the filing must be made within 15 days after the incorporation of the joint venture company.

In addition, if the capital to be raised upon the incorporation is ¥500 million or more, a prior notification must be filed with the Minister of Finance under the Securities Exchange Law (Law No. 25 of 1948).

Under the Antimonopoly Law (Law No. 54 of 1947) the JV Agreement must also be reported to the Fair Trade Commission by the Japanese party within 30 days from execution so that the JFTC can investigate the transaction.[19] The JFTC may order the parties to amend any provisions which it finds violate the Law or may issue an invalidation order respecting the offending provision. There is a broad exemption from such reporting requirement available when the Japanese partner falls within certain defined mid-sized or small companies.

CHART FOR COMPARISON OF FORMS OF A JAPAN PRESENCE

Forms for a Japan Presence	Representative Office	Branch Office	Subsidiary (Kabushiki Kaisha)
Characteristics	An extension of the head office of the foreign corporation and not separate entity from the foreign corporation.	An extension of the head office of the foreign corporation and not separate entity from the foreign corporation.	A separate legal entity from the foreign corporation.
Activities	May not engage in transactions **or** do business in Japan. May conduct activities of a non-revenue generating nature such as marketing and market research, collecting and distributing information, advertising and promotion and in general acting as a liaison for the head office of the foreign corporation.	Any lawful activities.	Any lawful activities.
Japanese Tax Consequences	Not subject to corporate income taxes as long as it does not engage in transactions or do business in Japan.	Subject to income tax rate of 37.5 percent with respect to its income originating from sources in Japan.	Subject to income tax rate of 37.5 percent with respect to its world-wide income.
Procedure for Establishment	No governmental approval, registration, filing or reporting requirements to establish and maintain a representative office.	Notification to the MOF and relevant Ministries through the Bank of Japan is required. Registration with the Legal Affairs Bureau is required. The whole process for establishment of a branch office takes less than one month.	Notification to the MOF and relevant ministries through the BOJ is required to subscribe for newly issued shares of the subsidiary. Minimum capitalisation of ¥10 million is required. Registration with the Legal Affairs Bureau is required. Notification to the Securities Bureau of the MOF is required if the initial capitalisation is ¥500 million or more. The whole process for establishment of a *Kabushiki Kaisha* takes one to two months.

1 See supra Note 1.
2 Law No. 228 of 1949, as amended.
3 FEL, Art. 21, paras. 2(1)–(3)
4 The Commercial Code of Japan, Law No. 48 of 1899, as amended (the "Comm. Code"), Art. 479.
5 Corporate Tax Act, Law No. 34 of 1965, as amended (the "CTA"), Art. 143, para. 1.
6 FEL, Art. 26, para. 2(5).
7 Comm. Code, Art. 479, para. 2.
8 Comm. Code, Art. 479, para. 1.
9 Comm. Code, Art. 479.
10 See discussion below.
11 Comm. Code Art. 343.
12 Comm. Code Arts. 376 (2) and 100.
13 Comm. Code Art. 210. Recent amendments to Comm. Code have expanded the scope of exceptions to this principle, however, a Stock Corporation is still prohibited from freely purchasing its own shares.
14 In the case of a large corporation (corporation with stated capital of ¥500 million or more or liabilities of ¥20 billion or more), a board of statutory auditors must be formed.
15 Art. 261(1) of the Comm. Code.
16 Art. 261(2) of the Comm. Code.
17 Arts. 188(2)-9 and 12 of the Comm. Code
18 Art. 26 of the FEL.
19 Art. 6 of the Law.

NOTES
i A foreign corporation that engages in transactions or does business in Japan on a continuous basis is subject to Japanese corporate income taxes and must, among other things, register a place of business (a "branch office") in Japan with the relevant Japanese governmental authorities.
ii CTL art. 38(2)(iii).

CHAPTER 6

FINANCING DIRECT INVESTMENTS AND OPERATIONS IN JAPAN
by Robert F. Grondine

GENERAL BACKGROUND ON CORPORATE FINANCE IN JAPAN: THE WORLD'S LAST GREAT PLAIN VANILLA MARKET

During the Summer of 1995 I received an interesting telephone call from one of my law firm's partners in Hong Kong seeking advice in relation to a global asset-backed secured financing in which she was representing the lenders on a major loan to an international company. The security for the loan was to consist in part of shares in the group's major subsidiaries around the world, as well as mortgages and other direct security over assets in many countries. The loan security structure adopted a global security trustee approach for ease of enforcement and uniformity. However, the partner had been severely surprised when the borrower's local legal counsel in Japan advised her that such structures were of questionable validity in Japan. Not only that, but they had precious little positive advice as to available alternative approaches of proven efficacy in Japan. She opened her questions with the explanation that her surprise derived primarily from the prevailing international image of Japan as one of the world's three leading international capital markets, which of course logically should mean that Japan's financial markets are highly developed and sophisticated.

The above myth is unfortunately shared by many business people throughout the world. In reality Japan represents probably the greatest anomaly in the international finance markets. The country has built the greatest international monetary reserves and holds perhaps the highest levels of average individual savings per capita in the world, yet the banking, financial and capital markets within Japan are probably the most rigid and underdeveloped of any major OECD country. In sum, Japan is the world's largest and perhaps last great plain vanilla finance market.

Until 1990 the total sum of lender credit analysis in Japan could be contained in a short succinct phrase, "Do you own real estate?" If the answer to that question was yes, then any Japanese bank would have been happy to lend you money. If the answer was no, then the only possible alternative in virtually all cases was for you to find someone else who had real estate which they were willing to put forward as security to act as your guarantor. Period. End of story.

This single minded rigidity in lending policies was of course exacerbated by the Japanese securities markets, which had also been of a similarly single minded rigidity in allowing only the largest companies with proven track records of profitability to become publicly listed companies in Japan. The system had no sympathy for the growth and encouragement of venture businesses, which by definition start with no assets and substantial start-up losses from research and development costs. Although a brief spurt in the creation of venture capital investment funds occurred in the mid-1980s (with a large element of foreign money invested), essentially there exists no significant native Japanese venture capital industry. When one considers the venture capital industry in the United States and the role it has played in fostering the growth of significant American computer, software and biotechnology companies, the comparison to Japan is stark.

Japanese banks do not lend against cash flow and do not have the expertise to analyse and evaluate cash flow for this purpose. Nor do Japanese banks lend against assets other than real estate. Japan has no equivalent of the Uniform Commercial Code in the United States, which allows lenders to finance all kinds of equipment, account receivables, intangibles and other assets through a public notice system with a high degree of comfort and protection by the American legal system. Due in large part to the high cost of commencing Japanese bankruptcy or insolvency proceedings in the Japanese court system, which laws require the posting of cash bonds sufficient to cover all expected costs (including receiver and legal fees) of the proceedings at the time of applying for the commencement of any such bankruptcy proceedings, major bankruptcy proceedings continue to be relatively rare in Japan. Only larger companies with substantial asset bases can afford such proceedings. Bankruptcies of small- to medium-sized companies virtually never go through formal legal proceedings due to this high cash bond requirement. Thus the number of successful restructurings or corporate rehabilitations through formal bankruptcy or other such insolvency proceedings in Japan represents only a tiny fraction of total Japanese bankruptcies or business failures. Most bankruptcies in Japan are "de facto" bankruptcies (*jijitsujo tosan*) where the maxim "here today, gone tomorrow" proves literally and devastatingly true. In these circumstances a failing company's employees and creditors literally pick the company's bones dry over night and all assets disappear without a trace. The swirling of the vultures becomes so fierce and effective that subsequent legal procedures become a waste of money. In this environment, access to inside information, rapid action and nerves of steel win the day, not effective loan documentation.

At the same time, the Japanese banking system has a truly effective warning device in relation to the bankruptcy of Japanese borrowers. All drafts, promissory notes and cheques (cheques are seldom used by businesses or individuals in Japan) must be cleared through the central Bank Clearing House. This institution is jointly owned by the major Japanese banks and other financial institutions. If any issuer of such an instrument dishonours payment, such fact is immediately published in official newspapers, putting everyone in Japan on notice that this company is in serious financial danger. If that same company then dishonours a second instrument, all of its banking privileges are cancelled by all of the member institutions of the Bank Clearing House and this fact is immediately published. This action of course has the immediate and total effect of forcing the company to cease all business activity. Everyone in Japan is aware of this effect, meaning that any company which dishonours any such instrument for a second time is instantly "dead on arrival." This is the signal for a company to be stripped clean, if indeed it had not already been stripped by the employees and other major creditors with inside information of the impending second dishonour.

The above background presents a very gloomy and daunting picture for a banker. You might even say that given that surrounding environment, it is no wonder that Japanese bankers have historically lent only against real estate, where the system for recording mortgages is effective (but with some significant cost and enforcement disadvantages compared to other countries) and the collateral cannot be stolen out from under the lender's nose. Some of Japan's leading legal scholars from the law faculties of Tokyo University and Kyoto University have been studying the American Uniform Commercial Code for years and recommending adoption of a similar public disclosure and notice system in Japan in order to cure these stark problems in the Japanese finance system. That process has not progressed very far at all.

In 1994–95 there has been some publicity for a few tentative attempts to lend against intellectual property rights as collateral, particularly trademarks, copyrights and patents. These possibilities have actually existed for many years, but were not utilised due to high fees for registration of such security rights in addition to the overwhelming preference for real estate to be used as collateral.

Another overwhelming characteristic of Japanese financing for small- and medium-sized businesses has been the virtually uniform requirement for personal guarantees from the company's major shareholders and management (which after all tend to be one and the same). This requirement for personal guarantees has frustrated many foreign companies who are not used to suffering this requirement in their home countries, or perhaps have outgrown that requirement in their home country and do not wish to suffer it again in Japan.

The purpose of this admittedly gloomy introduction is to enforce a realistic view on the non-Japanese reader who may be considering the issue of how to finance new or increased operations in Japan. Except at the very highest levels, Japanese finance is brutally simple and unforgiving. There are very few options to consider at the stage of entering the market. The remainder of this chapter will go through those alternatives briefly.

Given the current crisis in Japanese financial institutions due to accumulation of bad real estate loans in the aftermath of the collapse of the "bubble" economy (discussed in Chapter 1), Japanese banks and other financial institutions appear ever more reluctant to engage in any lending to any borrower except sterling corporate credits. Those companies for the most part remain very profitable and have been reducing their bank borrowings consistently in recent years. Thus even though Japanese banks are looking for new opportunities to lend, they remain ever more risk averse and their sole rule of credit analysis in the past (namely the existence of real estate) has proven unreliable. You need tremendous patience and perseverance to achieve your financing goals in Japan. You must be prepared for problems and be flexible.

FINANCING FOR SOLO MARKET ENTRY

BANKING RELATIONSHIPS

Within the Japanese domestic finance system, in the past the key relationship of any company was always with its "main bank." As the company grew it would foster and maintain a very close relationship with one bank no matter how many other banks with which it might have lesser dealings. This main bank would be its primary lender and provide various levels of service to support the company. In return the companies would provide the main bank with high levels of continuing information disclosure. In many cases retiring employees of the main bank would become senior finance officers of the customer company, in a mutually beneficial effort to increase the level of financial expertise in the company and provide the bank with greater information and influence over its borrowers.

During the period from the 1950s through the mid-1980s when Japanese companies held a comparatively high level of debt, this main bank relationship exerted a very high degree of influence over the management and policies of Japanese companies. Since about 1985, however, this system has been in decline. Japanese business people (particularly in the manufacturing sector) have been relying less on debt and have sought to escape the sometimes heavy control exerted by the main bank. The increasingly competitive environment among banks in Japan has caused them to begin to compete to take away the clientele of other banks, also leading to a further breakdown in this main bank system. In the past if a company sought financing from a bank which was not its main bank, the first impression at this new bank would very likely have been that the company must be in severe trouble because its main bank would not lend for the particular project. Now this occurrence has become relatively common and the new bank will often welcome this opportunity to develop a new customer at the expense of its rivals. Without regard to any existing main bank relationships, the major Japanese city banks will visit new companies on cold calls and solicit new business.

This development bodes well for foreign companies. Not having "grown up" in Japan, the foreign companies never felt comfortable with the main bank system until they had been in Japan for a very long time with substantial operations and Japanese personnel of their own. After all, from the perspective of a parochial Japanese lending institution, the tendency was for them to see only the very small Japanese operations of the foreign company, even when the foreign company was a giant outside Japan. Major Japanese banks have seemed more open in the past two years to offering finance opportunities to foreign companies than has been true in the past.

In opening accounts with Japanese banks, and even with the Japan branches of foreign banks, you will be surprised by the level of uniformity in bank documents. For a country where supposedly not much stock is placed in legal documents, the Japan Bankers Association has taken the lead in developing detailed standard forms of documentation for Japanese banks over the past 30 years. When seeking to open a new bank account at any bank in Japan, the company will be required to execute a standard form Bank Transactions Agreement. These forms are very comprehensive and unilaterally favourable to the banks. They are effectively non-negotiable, since every bank knows that every other bank has a similar form. The banks have other standardised forms which go along with this basic agreement, covering foreign exchange transactions, discounting of trade bills and other specific matters.

What are likely to be the most immediate financing needs of foreign companies commencing operations in Japan? Foreign companies setting up wholly owned operations in Japan will obviously need banking facilities for a broad range of purposes, but the most predictable are office and facilities set-up and trade financing.

In renting office space in Japan the commercial real estate market had been totally dominated for most of the last 50 years by severe scarcity, and thus represented a landlord's market. At the peak of this market in 1990-91, landlords could command security deposits for prime (and far less than prime) commercial office space in the range of 24-30 months' rent. These security deposits were placed with the landlord, did not bear interest and did not have to be segregated from the landlord's general funds. (Indeed, the primary use of such funds was to finance the landlords' next building construction. This causes concern among tenants as to whether their security deposits can ever be recovered, particularly in the current 1995–96 depressed Japanese real estate climate.) Once you have found and secured the office space itself, the next step would obviously be to build it out and furnish it. In securing warehouse space and any other space for operations in Japan, the driving factor has been the extremely high cost of land in Japan. Most real estate price surveys have consistently shown Tokyo and Osaka as the two most expensive cities for real estate in the world by a factor of at least two for the past 10 years. Even with the significant reductions in Japanese real estate values in the past two years, the differential above other major world centres remains stark.

Thus at the outset of operations in Japan, a foreign company needs to borrow money from the bank to pay for the security deposit and office renovation. Fortunately, as a result of the bursting of the "bubble" economy in 1991, commercial office space in Tokyo and other major cities has come down about 60% in price from the peak and a vacancy rate of 10–15% has developed. That rate compares with a vacancy rate of less than 1% in 1990! This dramatic shift has changed the Tokyo real estate market to a tenants' market in 1994–95, with a significant reduction in the requirements for office lease security deposits. At the same time the continuing difficulties in the Japanese real estate markets have made tenants more aware of the credit risk they run in relation to unseggregated security deposit funds. As a result, rent, security deposits and all other aspects of the commercial tenant relationship have become open to negotiation. It is possible to reduce and in some cases eliminate security deposits, to obtain six month rent holidays and other benefits which represent true reductions in cost. Commercial space savings in the outlying areas of Japan (in the case of Tokyo, Atsugi, Kawasaki, Yokohama, for instance) can be very significant, but for some businesses, must be weighed against the commercial necessity of central location in the business districts of Tokyo or Osaka. These efforts at cost control and reduction should be viewed as an integral part of the "financing" strategy for any foreign company commencing new operations in Japan.

The last major area of early financing needs is trade receivables. Japanese commercial custom on payment terms for sales of goods will generally be for payment by promissory note on 90 to 180 days credit. As a result of this predominant pattern, one of the major financing functions with your bank in Japan will be the discounting of these trade account receivable notes for operational cash flow. Japanese banks commonly lend under their standard form documentation against such promissory note trade receivables on a discounted basis.

PARENT GUARANTEES

As indicated above, Japan has historically relied heavily on a near universal requirement that major shareholders and senior management of small businesses provide personal guarantees for loans extended to their companies. While this phenomenon may also be true in many other countries to some degree, our experience in Japan has been that the level of this requirement in Japan is broader and continues in place longer in respect of any particular company than may be true certainly in the United States and probably in the major European countries as well.

Especially in any situation involving a newly incorporated Japanese subsidiary corporation or branch operation, regardless of how well the foreign parent may consider the new operation to be capitalised the Japanese banks will require the foreign parent to provide a full corporate guarantee before they would consider any lending to the new operation. The Japanese banks are also likely to suggest that the new company maintain certain deposit balances with the bank in return for such loans. Even though any formal demand by a bank in Japan for a customer to place and maintain such "compensating balances" is a violation of the Japanese Antimonopoly Law, the practice has persisted. If the foreign parent company will take the approach of accepting promptly any request for a parent guarantee, then that affords the best opportunity to draw the line against any further collateral requirements for such start-up loans in funding the new operations.

Where the foreign parent company is itself relatively small or in a country with which Japanese banks are not familiar or comfortable, such guarantee from the parent company will almost certainly not suffice. In this case the only alternatives become the offering of bank letters of credit from the foreign company's "main bank" in its home country. Alternatively, it is possible for the Japanese head of the company's operation in Japan to provide collateral to a personal guaranty by offering a mortgage over personal real estate to the Japanese bank. This latter approach has obvious and distinct disadvantages in making the company captive to its Japanese managers. You simply cannot fire someone who is the primary source of credit support for critical bank financing, no matter how bad or even destructive that person's performance may be.

There is one Japanese governmental program under the auspices of the Japan Small Business Corporation which can assist in providing guarantees to small Japanese and foreign businesses to assist them in obtaining bank financing at these initial stages. This agency (the Small Business Guarantee Agency or *Hosho Kyokai*) will issue a guarantee to third party lenders and accept the personal guarantees (possibly with real estate as collateral) of the Japanese management and the foreign parent company in some case.

In approaching the Japanese market, foreign investors need to be prepared to offer parent company guarantee support. There will be almost no case where this type of credit support will not be required. Indeed, if your offer of parent company credit support is accepted without additional collateral, then you will have obtained relatively low cost Japanese Yen financing in the most efficient way, which can be repaid against future Yen revenues (thereby hedging currency exchange risks).

JAPANESE GOVERNMENT PROGRAMS OFFERING LOW COST FINANCE

Since 1992–93 the topic of Foreign Direct Investment in Japan (FDI) has been a major focus of global attention in the context of continuing international trade negotiations with Japan. Figures produced by the Foreign Investment in Japan Development Corporation (FIND) published in 1994 showed that from 1950–51 through to the end of 1993, Japanese foreign direct investment into other countries amounted to $422.6 billion, while direct investment into Japan from all other countries amounted to only $29.9 billion. This severe imbalance has widely been identified as one of the major sources for the immense trade imbalance between Japan and the rest of the world.

As a result of this continuing international criticism of Japan for its immense trade surpluses, the Japanese government has been working over the past five years to improve the environment for FDI in Japan. Many of these steps involve creation of some tax incentives for increased import of foreign manufactured products, lengthening the period during which start-up operating loss carryforwards could be carried forward for Japanese tax purposes (already increased from five to eight years and likely to be increased to 10 years in the near future) and other informational and advisory programs. The government of Japan has also increased the scope and availability to foreign companies of various subsidised loan programs through the Japan Development Bank and other similar institutions.

These various government programs can be of significant help to foreign companies seeking to begin or expand their operations in Japan. Indeed in September 1995 the Japan Development Bank announced a major low interest loan of about $150 million to General Motors Corporation to finance the building of a new GM research and support facility in Japan. The Japan Export-Import Bank has also similarly announced major loans to the Ford Motor Company with similar objectives in mind. The majority of these loans average a size more in the range of $10 million however.

One word of caution. Foreign companies should not expect from these Japanese government programs any significant free funding, training subsidies or tax holidays. Japan simply does not at this time offer foreign investment incentive programs of that nature. Both Japanese and foreign companies have grown to expect tax holidays and incentive subsidies for new manufacturing and other direct investments in most countries around the world, whether they be OECD or other developed countries or developing or third world economies. Most international business people will be familiar with "pioneer status" industries in Singapore and the Philippines and the lengthy tax holidays and other significant benefits which come with those investment incentives. Even in the United States and the European Union, the nature of the competition for attracting new investment is such that companies can command subsidy packages in the range of $100–150 million for major new factories. Those incentives usually encompass tax holidays, forgiveness of up front sales taxes or VAT on machinery imports, labour employment training and other support incentives, infrastructure development and low interest financing alternatives through industrial revenue bonds or other similar instruments or government loan guarantees. These types of incentive programs do not exist in Japan at present.

In the course of discussing FDI initiatives with the government of Japan, United States government negotiators and foreign private business representatives in Japan have attempted to press home the point that Japan must adopt aggressive incentive programs of this type, from which Japanese companies have been reaping benefits throughout the world for the past 20 years! Unfortunately in the current adverse Japanese economic and fiscal environment anything which involves obtaining the consent of the Ministry of Finance for increased budgetary requirements is guaranteed to be a lost cause. Whether this attitude will change over the coming five years should be watched carefully. There may well be room for tax holidays, improved incentives for tax reductions related to higher imports and increased research and development and other similar types of approaches which may represent foregone tax revenues but at least do not require actual fund outflows from the Japanese government.

Returning to the positive side of this discussion, what is available? One might characterise the possibilities as three: plenty of free advice, cheap loan programs and regional infrastructure opportunities.

A plethora of free advice can be found from a large number of sources. First and foremost in terms of history and scope of offerings is the Japan External Trade Organization (JETRO). As its name suggests, JETRO was originally established in the 1950s under the auspices of the Ministry of International Trade and Industry (MITI) for the purpose of fostering greater and more effective Japanese exports. From about 1985 that mission was modified to include some efforts toward the promotion of imports. With the highly developed capability of Japanese industry to foster exports on their own, JETRO's role in the past five years has become increasingly focused on promoting imports into Japan. Through its substantial network of overseas offices in most major trading countries of the world, JETRO is able to provide access to industry specific information which can be of great assistance to foreign companies engaging in the initial stages of research into the possibility of sales to and/or investing in Japan. JETRO also has a program whereby it offers free of cost for a limited period of time (generally two to three months) shared office facilities for new entrants to the Japanese market. These facilities provide a small dedicated private office space for one to three personnel, together with shared secretarial and conference facilities and full office support (telephone, facsimile, etc.). Some of our clients have used these facilities to excellent effect as a free platform from which to finalise market entry plans and to locate commercial office space without being under severe pressure to take the first thing offered.

JETRO also provides substantial introductions to and information on regional free trade zones and industrial park developments throughout Japan, which can save the foreign investor a lot of leg work, time and expense.

The Foreign Investment in Japan Development Corporation (FIND), founded only in 1993, has quietly become an additional source of information coordination for the foreign companies looking to establish themselves in the Japanese market. Although in some ways the offerings by FIND are confusingly similar to those presented by JETRO, the friendly competition between them can be both amusing and helpful. FIND offers information as to the available Japanese government incentive and loan programs, as well as its own program of free initial office space arrangements similar to those offered by JETRO. Unlike JETRO, however, all of whose services are free, FIND does charge for some of its advisory services or receives "introduction fees" from outside advisors to whom it recommends foreign investors. As a result of that structure, the foreign business community in Japan had been very skeptical of what contribution FIND would be able to make when it was first introduced in late 1992 and incorporated in early 1993. On the whole, however, FIND has been making its own small contribution to the FDI process. Foreign companies would be well advised to visit FIND in the early stages of their investigations into commencing operations in Japan.

Individual ministries within the Japanese government each offer substantial information and assistance in their specific regulatory competencies. Also under MITI you will find the Japan Small Business Corporation, which can be very helpful to foreign companies of smaller size. This agency offers the program for issuing support guarantees for small businesses, including foreign owned businesses, as mentioned above.

Turning to the second major offering of assistance for foreign companies in commencing business operations in Japan, low interest loan programs are available from both the Japan Development Bank (JDB) and the Export-Import Bank of Japan (JEXIM), as well as from a few other specialised regional development agencies. Of these two institutions JEXIM has historically dealt more predominantly with export finance, catering to the financing needs of foreign governments in developing countries and the major Japanese companies seeking to sell equipment to them. JEXIM tends to be very set in its ways and bureaucratic. Even the largest of foreign companies seeking to deal with JEXIM will likely find the experience daunting. Small companies need not apply.

JDB has historically been focussed solely on Japan's domestic development needs, and probably has greater flexibility and better developed programs and practices for dealing with foreign companies seeking to set up new operations in Japan or to expand existing operations by building manufacturing, research or other major facilities in Japan. The interest rates are very low by international standards, reflecting the very low interest rates prevalent for major borrowers in the Japanese market. Certainly if you are able to obtain loan funding from either JEXIM or JDB you will be obtaining some of the lowest cost funding in the world. In the current severe economic environment in Japan resulting from the recession and the adverse effects of the appreciation of the Japanese Yen and the Great Kobe earthquake of January 17, 1995, the Japanese government has been expanding the availability of these JDB and other additional low interest loan programs to small- and medium-sized businesses. These loans will certainly require parent company guarantees and take substantial time to put in place, but can provide very significant benefits to foreign companies. One of the indirect benefits will be the credibility gained vis a vis Japanese commercial banks through JEXIM or JDB financing.

Generally JEXIM and JDB will not finance more than 50% of any project's cost. Thus you will need to include additional equity capital from the foreign company directly or other commercial loans to fully finance such facilities. The interest rates on the most favourable programs currently run in the range of 3.50–3.70% as of September 1995. Interest rates are reset periodically and the programs are subject to expiration, renewal and all other forms of political influences. However, with the building international pressure on Japan to reduce its external trade surplus, any complete elimination or even any substantial reduction of these low interest development and import loan programs in the period 1995–2000 would appear highly unlikely from the political perspective. JETRO and FIND will both have up to date information on all such loan programs currently available. In addition you can always contact both JEXIM and JDB directly.

One criticism or suspicion which has been voiced of these Japanese government or semi-governmental programs in the past has been the fear that disclosing too much of a foreign company's business strategy to the Japanese government could result in that information being used by the government against the foreign company later or result in a leak to Japanese competitors. These concerns perhaps represent an overly suspicious tradition of distrusting the government in Western countries. While occasionally infected by that same suspicion virus myself (the natural state for lawyers is after all one of suspicion), in my experience I have not in recent times directly seen any cases of such abuse of confidential information in Japan by the Japanese government. The sector where such abuses occurred to the largest extent in the past was perhaps the financial sector, where new insurance or finance products were held up in regulatory procedures for months at the bureaus of the Ministry of Finance and when finally approved by the MOF somehow magically a competing Japanese bank or insurer's product was licensed and in the market on virtually a simultaneous basis. Separate issues in respect of intellectual property infringement concerns have been largely addressed in separate negotiations between the American and Japanese governments in 1990–95, as well as multilaterally through the Uruguay Round negotiations and implementation process. In summary, although one needs always to contain sensitive information to the greatest extent possible, it may be said that it will be extremely unlikely that the Japanese government would utilise any of the programs for promotion of foreign direct investment as discussed in this section for that purpose.

Finally in this category one should not overlook the contributions which are available from Japanese local and regional government entities. The programs at this level will involve primarily industrial park facilities and possibly infrastructure enhancement. The 47 prefectures throughout Japan have been working hard in the past 10 years to attract new investment into the outer areas of the Japanese archipelago in order to relieve the congestion and pollution in the main centres of Tokyo, Nagoya and Osaka and bring greater development and jobs to the Japanese countryside. Some additional incentives are available from the central government for this purpose, but usually one will have to deal directly with the prefectural authorities in relation to the purchase or lease price for real estate in the many industrial parks which have been constructed. The program by the prefectures in Kyushu to turn that southernmost of the four main Japanese islands into "silicon island" has met with a large degree of success in attracting high technology silicon wafer, semiconductor and computer facilities, as well as automobile plants and other heavy manufacturing industry base. At the other end of the country, Novo Industri A/S of Denmark constructed a pharmaceutical plant in Hokkaido in the mid-1980s to take advantage of development incentives of this type and the very pure water available in that northernmost of the four main Japanese islands.

Much like in the United States, the fact that these opportunities are spread throughout Japan and require separate contact and negotiation with the individual local and prefectural governments will place large demands on the foreign investor as far as time and effort required to obtain information, analyse opportunities and negotiate a deal. The people at JETRO, FIND, the Japan Small Business Corporation, the Industrial Location Office and other Japanese central government agencies can be a valuable source of information and assistance in managing this process.

OTHER INFORMATION SOURCES

Although they do not provide any financial support or loan programs of their own, we should mention the potential benefit to foreign companies of several additional independent information sources in Japan.

First, the U.S. & Foreign Commercial Service (USFCS) through the American Embassy in Tokyo and American consulates in Osaka, Nagoya, Fukuoka and Sapporo offers a wide range of information and assistance to American companies who want to enter the Japanese market. The USFCS personnel in Japan represent the largest and most active outpost for this Department of Commerce agency in the world outside the U.S. These services are offered free of charge and include substantial information on specific business sectors as well as tips and case studies on entering the Japanese market effectively.

Second, also for American companies primarily but open to other nationalities as well, the American Chamber of Commerce in Japan (ACCJ) provides a wealth of practical information on the process of starting a business in Japan and can put the foreign business person in touch with other foreign business people in Japan in similar or non-competitive business sectors to facilitate sharing of information and experience. ACCJ has a very active volunteer committee structure. Its members have worked with the Japanese and American governments and with Japanese business organisations (*Keidanren, Nikkeiren*, etc.) to improve the environment for foreign investment in Japan, including deregulation, internationalisation of standards and other efforts to make sales of foreign products in Japan more effective and open. The ACCJ is strictly a privately funded volunteer business organisation, affiliated with the US Chamber of Commerce but independent from it.

Third, for European companies the EU delegation has a large and effective staff similar to that offered by the USFCS. In addition, the separate and independent European Business Council represents a broad range of European businesses in Japan on a basis similar to that offered by the ACCJ. Most major countries trading with Japan also have their own national Chambers of Commerce, including the English, French, German, Italian, Canadian and Korean Chambers of Commerce. Some of these groups (particularly the German Chamber) receive direct funding and other support from their national governments to support the efforts of their national companies to export to Japan. For countries with no chambers of commerce in Japan, their embassies and consulates will usually have commercial officers who perform these same functions at least to some degree.

There are other types of government offices in Japan which provide considerable assistance in exporting products to Japan and investing into Japan. These include state and public entity offices (port authorities and other similar government agencies) whose primary function in the 1980s was to promote investment by Japanese companies into the home states, to promote home state employment and increase the home state tax base. During that period these offices were mainly concerned with identifying prospective Japanese companies planning new overseas investments and luring such companies to their home states through investment incentives and other such inducements as described previously. With the severe reduction in Japanese outward investment starting from 1990-91, especially toward the United States and Europe, these many offices have turned a large part of their attention to assisting their home constituents to export to and invest in Japan. Some of these offices are able to offer assistance in identifying potential joint venture partners (a service JETRO and FIND can also assist with), negotiating with Japanese government agencies and introductions to other service providers (accountants, lawyers, consultants, etc.) in the Japanese market who can provide the assistance required in any situation.

HOME COUNTRY FINANCIAL INSTITUTIONS

As the reader has undoubtedly already gleaned from the above discussion, financing options are narrow and difficult to come by in Japan. One additional option which should not be ignored is to seek financing through your home country financial institutions which have branch offices in Japan. These home country banks will know you better and probably have a greater capacity to finance against home country assets as collateral or trade receivables generally. By knowing the company better they will be more likely to get comfortable with financing based solely on the company's parent guaranty. Finally, even where these home country banks may not have their own independent bank branch in Japan through which they could lend directly, they can issue bank letters of credit or letters of guarantee to Japanese financial institutions which can then lend to the foreign company in Japan based on such foreign bank's credit.

The primary drawback in being forced to rely upon the home country banks in Japan is that, as at September 1995, none of the foreign banks participate in the Japanese bank computer clearing system except Citibank of the United States. This means that all foreign banks in Japan other than Citibank must clear their fund transfers through an account of their own at a Japanese bank. This requirement makes utilisation of the home country bank for the purposes as a "main bank" in Japan extremely disadvantageous, if not commercially unacceptable, for the broad range of monetary transfers in the mundane daily operation of a business in Japan. In this case it becomes necessary to hold operating accounts at one or more Japanese banks as well in order that your customers and employees can receive their bank fund transfers efficiently through Japan's instantaneous and country-wide bank computer network. Although the Japanese banking system is far behind its American and European counterparts in many aspects, the nationwide inter-bank computer transfer and settlement system which has already been in use in Japan for over 10 years is probably the most advanced in the world. A Japanese bank customer can access their accounts and funds through any bank ATM anywhere in Japan. The Japanese have become accustomed to this level of convenience and will not take lightly to the inconvenience of having to deal with a foreign company's Japanese branch or subsidiary which does not have its bank accounts directly plugged into this inter-bank computer clearance system.

JOINT VENTURE AND SYNDICATED ENTRY STRATEGIES

The most traditional approach to entering the Japanese market and reducing the burden of financing that entry has been to look for a Japanese joint venture partner. Other such strategies involve a decision for the foreign company to enter the Japanese market initially through only a licensing or distributorship arrangement. These latter two strategies do not involve any direct investment by the foreign company into any Japanese operation of its own, and therefore will not be discussed in this chapter. This section will focus solely on the traditional joint venture strategy for financing of new operations in Japan, and then go on to discuss some recent variations on that joint venture strategy which I refer to as the syndicated entry strategy.

USE OF JOINT VENTURE PARTNERS FOR FINANCING ENTRY

Many thousands of joint ventures have been entered into by foreign companies in an effort to break into the Japanese market. Most typically these joint ventures involved technology or brand edge. The foreign company did not wish to undertake the full risk and investment required to make the product successful in the Japanese market, in most cases due to the financial exposure and capital cost of such effort or possibly because of the opportunity cost of sending senior managers to Japan to direct and build this effort over many years. It has been widely reported that the period of time taken to earn substantial returns on capital investments by foreign companies (indeed even by Japanese companies) in Japan is at least two to three times longer than in other major countries.

Until very recently, the financial issues were seriously complicated by the long-standing tendency and preference of Japanese to work for a Japanese employer. This sentiment probably exists in most countries and is understandable in the sense that a foreign company undoubtedly has less commitment to the Japanese market than a Japanese company does. However, since 1991 and the bursting of the "bubble" economy, with the attendant doubt being created in the minds of Japanese employees as to the durability and stability of even the largest Japanese companies, it has become easier than ever for foreign companies to attract high quality Japanese employees, even recruiting them directly away from major Japanese companies in some cases. In 1995 the "executive search" business has become a very active and vibrant service sector, whereas it could be said to have not even existed in 1985 in Japan.

Moreover the joint venture has been subject to severe academic and business criticism over the past 10 years, both generally and more specifically in relation to foreign company operations in Japan. There have been a number of widely publicised articles and books on this subject, particularly as the joint venture has been used in Japan. The Harvard Business Journal and Clyde Prestowicz have offered very serious criticism based on the perceived result that many of the American joint ventures created in Japan in the 1950s through 1980s had no other tangible effect than to create major international business rivals in exchange for a relatively low cash payout.

Perhaps as a result of those criticisms, or perhaps influenced by the reduction in real estate prices and availability of high level Japanese employees for the first time, the number of new joint ventures since 1990 has decreased significantly. Certainly one hears more of dissolutions of joint ventures (usually through the foreign partner buying out the interest of the Japanese partner) rather than announcements of new joint ventures. The only recent exceptions to this phenomenon may be in the cable television and multi-media sectors.

Notwithstanding this conventional wisdom, the simple fact of the continuing high cost of investment in Japan forces anyone facing this decision to consider the benefits and drawbacks of a joint venture strategy.

The typical joint venture will utilise the financial clout and personnel, as well as the real estate, of a major Japanese trading company or other corporate group to finance the incorporation of a Japanese company. Virtually all joint ventures in Japan take the form of a joint stock company (*kabushiki kaisha*). Please notice here again the plain vanilla approach to the structuring of joint ventures as compared with the greater variations and strategies which can be used for this purpose in other countries for both commercial and tax purposes. In some special situations it has been possible to convince a Japanese joint venture partner to create a more elaborate and tax-effective joint venture structure in Japan, but those successes have been few and far between. Assuming then for the purposes of discussion that the "typical" joint venture pattern is being followed, what will the Japanese partner bring to that venture?

The first contribution of the Japanese party will be cash capital. Frequently the foreign party will put in an equal or other pro rata portion of cash capital up front, but will immediately receive that cash back in exchange for the contribution of (or a fully paid up license for) its technology which is to form the basis for the joint venture business operation. Thus we see the typical pattern, cash being contributed by the Japanese partner and technology being contributed by the foreign partner. The technology can also take the form of licenses, distribution rights and other know-how considered of value in the Japanese market.

The second contribution by the Japanese side of financial significance will generally be real property. The Japanese party will often provide or lease office space to the joint venture (only rarely these days would the joint venture buy the property from the Japanese partner), at a reasonable market rate of course but without requiring the very substantial security deposits or other heavy financial burdens that have come with an arm's length commercial lease in the Japanese market in the past. We have already discussed these costs above, so please refer back to the size of those obligations as to the importance of this element of the Japanese party's contribution to the joint venture.

The third element contributed generally by the Japanese partner will be personnel. One must always be extremely careful that the joint venture is not used as a dumping ground by the Japanese partner to rid itself of personnel whom it no longer desires. This result has occurred on numerous occasions in the past and must be fought resolutely by the foreign partner. However, despite the greater willingness of Japanese generally to switch companies in mid-career as compared to even the recent past in Japan, that mobility is still very restricted as compared with other advanced countries. Especially where the successful market penetration for a foreign product will require the creation of a significant technical support and sales staff throughout Japan in a relatively short time frame, there will be no substitute for a good Japanese joint venture partner. These large Japanese companies currently have significant numbers of underutilised employees which can be refocussed and trained effectively to support a broad-based national sales effort for a newly introduced foreign product. The Japanese trading companies can be particularly adept in this regard for industrial equipment, but less so for commercial and consumer products. All of these employees will come to the joint venture without suffering the expense and time cost of having to advertise, interview and entertain them, and without having to pay any executive search fees.

The fourth and also financially significant contribution of the Japanese joint venture partner is a solid relationship with a bank. By being part of the Japanese partner's *keiretsu* group of companies, the joint venture company will magically and automatically have access to the Japanese partner's main bank. Thus the problems of creating and fostering positive banking relationships in Japan can be avoided from the outset. Although the Japanese partner's main bank may require parent company guarantees from the two joint venture partners depending upon the level of borrowing, that bank will accept these guarantees from the two joint venture partners generally without question or complaint (assuming that the Japanese partner is a substantial company). Thus not only will the joint venture strategy settle the problem of how to capitalise the joint venture company for the initial start-up phase, but it will also have provided for the operational financing needs on a continuing basis.

As stated earlier, the majority of recent news clippings relates to the dissolution of joint ventures rather than the formation of new ones. This fact should not necessarily be taken as an indictment of the wisdom of the joint venture strategy. Indeed, in many cases the opposite could be claimed. Namely, when a foreign company is faced with a decision of how to enter the Japanese market de novo, it is faced with very significant capital requirements and business risks. The natural tendency will be to share those risks with someone else, and especially to reduce the burdens of the capital requirements.

Finding an appropriate joint venture partner is always a difficult proposition. Assuring that the commercial interests of the joint venture partners will remain sufficiently similar so that the joint venture business can be operated smoothly for a lengthy period of time is even more difficult. However, if one looks at this proposition solely from the shorter term perspective of the initial start-up market entry risk allocation decision, then the choice becomes more manageable. In other words, if we approach this decision from the perspective of looking for a partner whose interests and aims would be predictable and reliable for five to 10 years and during that period could share the substantial risk of this new market venture, then buying out that partner's interests after five to 10 years could be taken to represent the successful conclusion of this risk avoidance strategy. Having obtained the assistance in financing the venture start-up, having attracted the necessary personnel for the future and having established the product in the market such that the high risk phase of market introduction has been successfully passed, the foreign partner can then decide that it does not need or desire to "share" the downside risk and upside potential with its Japanese partner any longer. The Japanese partner can have decided for a variety of reasons that it doesn't like this particular product sector as much as it had anticipated and wishes to redeploy its capital resources elsewhere. If these factors come together, the foreign party can purchase the interests of its joint venture partner and then have a wholly-owned Japanese operation fully integrated into its world strategy.

Of course these joint venture dissolutions are most frequently not quite so simple and amicable. Foreseeing such possibilities, the foreign company would be well advised always to consider very carefully the exit strategy and buyout rights when the joint venture agreement is originally being negotiated. Even though many Japanese will tell you that they do not rely on lengthy contracts to dictate the rights of the parties in a business relationship, or that Japan is not litigious or other popular myths about Japan, you can be assured that in case of a dissolution, the first place the Japanese parties will check is the specific terms of the original Joint Venture Agreement. There is no good substitute for having fully covered this exit strategy at the outset.

SYNDICATED JOINT VENTURES

A variation on the traditional joint venture approach which has become quite popular in the high technology field since about 1988 has been the practice of "syndicating" a joint venture subsidiary in Japan. This phenomenon typically involves an American high technology company which has already developed some favourable market reputation for its technology and/or products.

Japanese companies wishing to access such new products and technology rights for use in the Japanese and world markets had since the mid-1980s made frequent small strategic investments into the parent company in the United States in exchange for receiving the target product distribution and/or license rights in Japan and possibly other countries in Asia (only in rare cases would the territory cover additional other countries outside the United States).

The Japanese experience of such investments has been disappointing at best. Whether out of Japanese or American disaffection for that prior approach is not clear, but from the early 1990's two different directions have emerged. One is the general bipolar or multi-polar strategic alliance with only nominal cross-share ownership. This phenomenon has been commented upon broadly and need not be considered further here, since those types of strategic alliances do not commonly involve finance requirements.

The second phenomenon however appears to be a new approach to funding de novo operations in Japan by foreign companies by creating "syndicated" subsidiaries in Japan. By this term I refer to the phenomenon where a high technology company announces to a select few interested companies its intention to enter the Japanese market through its own newly formed marketing subsidiary and invites a select number of Japanese companies to participate in this marketing company through capital contributions. These investors are typically operating companies (not venture capital funds or passive investors) who are most likely seeking to become sub-distributors of the product in Japan or manufacturers who use this product as a component in their own products. Typically each of these investors will subscribe for 2–10% of the new Japanese subsidiary company's shares, with the foreign company retaining in all cases majority control of the shares of the company and complete operating control over the company. In these cases some of the investors may also second employees to the company, but that is not a necessary element of the strategy.

Having in this fashion raised nearly 50% of the required seed capital for the new operation, the new subsidiary company can then of course also rely on this network of investor shareholders for introductions to Japanese banking institutions and other needed business connections in Japan. By taking this route the foreign company has probably been able to avoid any serious limits on its operational control over the Japanese subsidiary. At the same time, however, the mere fact that outside investors have been introduced into the subsidiary company will mean that it cannot operate in the same manner as a wholly-owned subsidiary. Great care will need to be exercised to assure that this Japanese subsidiary is treated for all purposes as essentially a third party entity in order to avoid any claims that the investors have been unfairly treated. For instance, potential transfer pricing issues will arise at all stages of the operations of this type of "syndicated" joint venture in a way which is potentially much more difficult to solve than in the traditional 50–50 joint venture context where the prices are all negotiated at arm's length with the single joint venture partner directly.

These syndicated joint ventures are effected on the basis of a private placement of securities. They therefore do not entail the cost of completing a full public offering of shares, which in most of the cases under consideration here would not be possible in the Japanese market in any event. Identifying and dealing with 3–5 or more such passive investors for this type of strategy can of course be a very daunting process. Joint ventures of this type have not been wildly successful in Japan, with the most successful ones being companies dealing in high technology computer components, software and semiconductor manufacturing equipment. The success of such companies would not be as widely noted as the success of companies producing a finished consumer product. Moreover, since this new strategy has only been tested for several years and only in a relatively small number of cases, it may be as yet too early to judge its comparative success.

Depending upon the product sector of the foreign company, its technology level and the degree of its contacts and recognition in the Japanese market, this "syndicated" joint venture is a strategy which might nevertheless be valuably considered.

FINANCING OF ACQUISITIONS

It would be welcome to many business people and their lawyers around the world if this section could offer some exciting advice about varied and useful structures for financing and leveraging acquisitions in the Japanese market. Unfortunately, as will be discussed elsewhere in this book the number of acquisitions in Japan by foreign companies as a market entry strategy remains one of the lowest among any of the OECD countries. Although in recent years the number of purely domestic Japanese mergers has increased rather substantially, there are no available statistics on those mergers and it is thus impossible to use those examples as a spur for greater cross-border acquisitions.

In keeping with the small number of cases where this market entry strategy will apply, the discussion in this section will be kept short. Unfortunately one of the reasons it must be kept short is once again the nature of this plain vanilla market severely restricting the potential alternatives which may be utilised in Japan for this purpose. Despite the fact that Japanese financial institutions have been major lenders in acquisition financings in the United States for at least 10 years, the same phenomenon has not taken hold in Japan to any degree at all. This result may be related to the absence of more effective security structures in Japan or the general dearth of open bid acquisition transactions in the Japanese market. To date there still are no significant cases where a hostile takeover bid on the open securities market has succeeded in Japan. Japanese securities laws allow for such bids, but none has ever been successful. Japanese domestic acquisitions are virtually all "friendly" transactions arranged by Japanese banks.

There have only been two major examples of attempted international hostile acquisitions. The first was the attempted acquisition by a Hong Kong group of the Katakura Textile company in the early 1980s. This bid was issued shortly after Japan had liberalised its foreign exchange law in 1980 and eliminated the Foreign Investment Law which had constrained such attempts since the 1950s. Strangely, however, the Japanese government deemed the Katakura textile spinning business to fall within the protected category of national strategic interests and effectively blocked the acquisition. The Hong Kong investor finally gave up after a number of years.

The second major such attempt was the well publicised run by T. Boone Pickens at Koito Manufacturing Co., Ltd. Mr. Pickens chose his allies very poorly in this case and the attempt to build it into an international trade dispute failed largely as a result of his inability to generate any sympathy for his position. The entire episode created a very significant black-eye for cross-border acquisition strategies. At the end of the two to three year effort Mr. Pickens sold his block of shares back to the Japanese speculator from whom he had bought them and retreated in total defeat.

In recent years there have been a number of well publicised friendly acquisitions of companies, but not of any real international significance. The largest number of these cases continue to involve a foreign company buying out the equity interest of its Japanese partner in a long-standing joint venture, or purchasing their Japanese distributor or licensee who has either fallen on hard times due to competition from Japanese products or a management succession problem.

Foreign companies which are lucky enough to be able to purchase their joint venture partner's equity interest or their existing distributor's sales force will want to consider how they can best finance and possibly leverage the acquisition cost in Japan. Financing in Japan will be the best alternative because it will allow borrowing of Yen to fund a Yen asset acquisition to be repaid out of future Yen cash flows from the Japanese operations. This financing approach therefore eliminates the extreme vagaries of currency fluctuations and differential interest rates adversely affecting the financing structure chosen. Moreover, as indicated previously, since Japanese interest rates have been among the lowest in the world over the past 10 years, borrowing acquisition funds in Japan would seem to provide the best opportunity for the lowest financing costs.

Leveraging can be introduced into these structures in some limited ways. By leveraging here we are referring both to financial leverage and tax leverage. Being able to take interest deductions against the Japanese target company's cash flow and taxable income needs little additional explanation. One should at the same time remember that Japan's corporate tax remains among the highest in the developed countries, generally being calculated at about a 52% effective tax rate. Obviously, if all the acquisition financing cost could be written off against taxable income in Japan to reduce Japanese corporate taxes, the financing burden of the acquisition could be reduced dramatically.

Financing any such acquisition without support from foreign parent company guarantees will be almost impossible. However, if the target company has sufficient cash flow then you may experiment with strategies to utilise a separate subsidiary company in Japan to borrow the funds needed for acquiring the target shares and then merge the acquisition vehicle into the target company. This approach obliges the target company to repay the borrowed funds and interest expense can thus be taken against the operating profits of the target company to produce the Japanese tax leverage suggested earlier. This strategy faces some complications from the fact that the Japanese Antimonopoly Law continues to prohibit the operation of holding companies in Japan. Thus if a foreign company is considering acquisition strategies for the near term future in Japan there may be a large benefit to be had from establishing a small subsidiary company in Japan for miscellaneous service and market development activities which would not constitute a Japanese holding company during the preparatory period and could then be used as such an acquisition vehicle. This strategy has been used successfully in at least one acquisition, which may still represent the only true example of a leveraged buyout in the Japanese market. Elimination or liberalisation of this ban on holding companies is being actively debated in 1996, which may expand the possibilities of this acquisition leverage strategy.

Even in an optimum case, it may be impossible to find sufficient funding of this type in Japan among the plain vanilla market to finance the entire acquisition on shore in Japan. In these cases it may be possible to borrow some portion of the acquisition price off-shore at the parent level. In these types of circumstances the benefit of considering borrowing from foreign financial institutions in Japan should be explored. As indicated above, those institutions will likely have a greater willingness and capability to analyse the target company on the basis of cash flow and intangible assets to allow for a higher debt level than might be feasible for any Japanese lender institution. Particularly as many foreign banks had drastically trimmed their loan portfolios in Japan in the mid and late 1980s, many are now seeking to engage in renewed lending activities through their Japan branches to produce interest income for covering corporate overheads of their Japanese operations. Utilising such a lender would also have the beneficial possibility of combining additional security for the acquisition outside Japan in order to permit a higher debt leveraging level in Japan where the interest expense deductions would almost certainly provide the highest tax benefit to the acquiring group.

In terms of post-acquisition financing for example by completing an initial public offering in the Japanese securities markets, bear in mind the stringency of the Japanese listing rules. Under recent political pressures the Ministry of Finance has been working with the Tokyo Stock Exchange to loosen listing standards and create a new additional "third" section in the Tokyo Stock Exchange to facilitate public share offerings by smaller "venture" companies. By comparison to other countries, however, these listing requirements in Japan remain archaic and extremely rigid. Adding a new additional tier to the market rather than overhauling the market and relaxing listing standards as a whole, while also continuing to fail to improve the dreadful Japanese disclosure standards, represents a fundamental mistake in emphasis as to how Japan should be reinvigorating its securities markets. No significant hope should be held out that the Ministry of Finance will change its philosophy in respect of share listings in the near future, so expecting to utilise a listing in the Japanese securities markets for take-out financing of an acquisition will remain a distant dream in virtually all cases.

A possible new strategy is to list the Japanese company's shares in the United States or another non-Japanese securities market. Amway Japan Corporation very successfully listed its shares as American Depository Receipts in New York in 1994. Here again, however, this road will be a very difficult and time consuming one. It would be extremely unwise to predicate any decision to acquire a Japanese company on the sole likelihood of being able to complete such a foreign listing as the sole post-acquisition financing strategy. Japanese legal constraints or tax problems would not be the impediment to such a strategy so much as the simple unpredictability of market demand and acceptance over the long time period which would be required to achieve the listing after the acquisition had been completed. In the meantime of course, you would already have purchased the company and could be left with no exit strategy. Thus this financing alternative should be considered only in the context of possible financing or sale strategies for mature businesses in the Japanese market (see next section) and not in the acquisition category.

In summary, if you are lucky enough to identify and successfully negotiate an acquisition in the Japanese market you should not forsake completely the possibility of engaging in some creative financing structures for implementing the acquisition. However, the possibilities will be limited.

FINANCING STRATEGIES FOR MATURE OPERATIONS

These alternatives will be discussed in greater detail in the chapter on the Japanese securities markets, so we shall only mention them briefly here.

Since about 1985 there have been a small number of cases of Japanese subsidiaries of foreign companies becoming listed in the Japanese over-the-counter securities markets. Shaklee, Amway and a few other companies have achieved very high Japanese sale multiples for their foreign owners, usually both bringing in new money for financing company expansion in Japan as well as allowing for some secondary offering of the parent's original shares to cash out capital gains.

Another alternative which has only been done to date by Amway Japan Corporation, is for the Japanese subsidiary to also list its shares on a securities market outside Japan.

Either of these two listing alternatives need to be considered very carefully from the corporate perspective of the future relationship between the parent company and the Japanese "subsidiary". After completing such public offerings the Japanese subsidiary company will in all cases remain controlled by the foreign parent company, but continuing to treat the Japanese company as a wholly-owned subsidiary will be fraught with risk. The subsidiary's directors will have fiduciary duties to the public shareholders as well as the major shareholder which the foreign "parent" company will continue to be. Transfer pricing issues and other corporate profit and liability issues can become extremely complicated in this setting. With the liberalisation of the Japanese rules regarding shareholder derivative suits in October of 1993, any perceived abuses favouring the foreign parent company over the Japanese public shareholders could easily attract litigation against the Japanese company's directors.

Since 1993 it has become possible to securitise lease and other receivables in the Japanese securities markets on a much broader scale than previously. However to date these structures have not developed very well and the market remains rather moribund. It may be more interesting to use these available securitisation structures to back issuances of securities outside Japan, or as collateral for the issuance of commercial paper financing programs in the United States. This latter financing structure has been used quietly in some large cases since about 1985 through financing vehicles and commercial paper programs in the United States.

Domestic issuances of bonds or commercial paper in the Japanese markets remain rather high cost and uncompetitive alternatives to the other financing alternatives available in the international markets.

One final alternative which can be considered in some cases will be to conduct a financing of trademark or other intangibles in Japan. Walt Disney Company performed the best known such financing in the Japanese market when in 1988 it successfully completed a forward financing of the trademark royalties payable to it from the owner of Tokyo Disneyland. However, if the transaction to be financed is not sufficiently large, then the registration fees for securing the lender's rights against the trademarks or other intellectual property rights may be prohibitive. This problem has been experienced in some movie copyright financings.

In summary, the plain vanilla nature of the Japanese finance market severely limits the choices of international corporate groups looking to finance their Japan operations. The best advice is simply to be patient and consult with effective leaders in the securities and banking markets, as well as creative legal and tax advisors who can provide the latest information on alternative structures.

CHAPTER 7
SECURITIES LAW AND THE REGULATION
OF FINANCIAL MARKETS

by Norifumi Tateishi and Jeffrey P. Clemente

INTRODUCTION

In Japan, as in most countries with highly developed economies, "securities regulation" is a substantial and highly technical area of the law. It encompasses all of the statutory, government regulatory and "self-regulatory" material pertaining to (i) the means by which corporate and government entities may obtain direct financing, i.e., raise capital through the issuance of shares, debentures and bonds ("securities"), (ii) the manner in which securities may be distributed initially to the investing public, (iii) the institutions, entities and devices available to facilitate the initial distribution and subsequent trading of securities by investors in the so-called "secondary markets," and (iv) the civil and criminal means by which compliance with the legal and regulatory requirements is ensured.

The issuance of securities to investors, as a means of direct financing, stands in contrast to the more customary means of indirect financing, borrowing from banking entities. When a corporate or governmental entity, or an individual, for that matter, seeks financing from a commercial bank, the skill and sophistication of the bank's personnel, presumably expert in the evaluation of investment risk and creditworthiness, stand between the ultimate investors and the entity seeking access to the investors' money. In the event of an error in the evaluation process, the resources and credit of the bank and the banking system are theoretically available to shield the indirect investors (e.g., depositors and other creditors of the bank) from the losses that may result from the bank's mistaken judgment. However, when direct financing is sought, through the issuance of securities, there is no bank present to assist and mediate in the evaluation of risks or to absorb the consequences of wrong investment decisions. In the absence of sophisticated and financially well-muscled intermediaries, such as banks, it falls to the law, devices and institutions of "securities regulation" to ensure that direct financings take place in an orderly environment, characterised by adequate and accurate disclosure, and that the securities investment environment is rendered at least "fair," if not safe.

Because of the vastness of the subject matter and the amounts of money typically involved, any attempt to summarise securities regulation in the space of a few pages is fraught with danger. It is axiomatic that no serious corporate financial planning, involving the use of securities, should even be contemplated, without invoking the assistance of highly specialised legal and financial advisers at an early stage in the process.

LEGAL, REGULATORY AND SELF-REGULATORY STRUCTURES

PRIMARY STATUTES

The legal matrix governing the issuance, distribution and secondary trading of securities in Japan consists of two primary statutes, the Securities Exchange Law (SEL) and Foreign Securities Firms Law (FSFL), several other statutes relating to specific aspects of the securities business, such as the Securities Investment Trust Law and the Investment Advisory Business Law, as well as a number of other statutes of more general applicability, e.g., the Commercial Code, the Civil Code and the Foreign Exchange and Foreign Trade Control Law (FEL), any or all of which may have relevance in the context of a particular transaction or problem. The SEL deals exclusively with the public offering and trading of securities, the regulation of firms engaged in securities-related businesses and the organisation and operation of securities exchanges and markets, while the FSFL regulates foreign firms engaged in securities-related businesses in Japan.

The Ministry of Finance (MOF), acting principally through its Securities Bureau, is the governmental agency primarily responsible for the oversight and regulation of securities, securities markets and all firms engaged in the securities business. The MOF also exercises, through other of its bureaus and under authority derived from a number of other statutes not ordinarily regarded as securities laws, per se, a very significant degree of control over the largest players in the securities markets — the institutional investors — primarily insurance companies, trust banks and mutual funds.

Securities and Exchange Law — The cornerstone of Japanese securities regulation is the SEL (Law No. 25 of 1948, as amended). The SEL is a product of the post-war occupation and is modelled, not surprisingly, after the basic securities laws of the United States. It resembles a composite of the U.S. Securities Act of 1933 and the Securities Exchange Act of 1934. The stated purpose of the SEL is to foster and facilitate proper operation of the Japanese economy and to protect investors by assuring the fairness of securities issuance and trading and the smoothness and efficiency of securities distribution. The SEL attempts to achieve these purposes by (i) defining "securities" and "securities business" falling within its scope, (ii) imposing registration and disclosure requirements upon companies and others wishing to issue and distribute securities to the public, (iii) regulating and establishing procedures for public tender offers, (iv) regulating the business, capital structure and operations of Japanese firms engaged in the securities business, (v) regulating the formation and functions of securities dealers associations, (vi) enabling the organisation of securities exchanges, over-the-counter markets and securities finance companies, (vii) implementing a system for the mediation of securities-related disputes between securities firms and between securities firms and investors, (viii) providing for the establishment of an advisory Securities and Exchange Council, to study, investigate and make recommendations to the MOF concerning the issuance, distribution and trading of securities and derivative investment products and (ix) criminalising or providing for the civil punishment of non-compliance with SEL's requirements or the requirements of subordinate regulations.

Foreign Securities Firm Law — The FSFL (Law No. 5 of 1971, as amended) provides a basis for the establishment by foreign securities companies of branch offices in Japan, for the licensing of such branch offices and for the regulation of their business activities. As a general proposition, the FSFL, usually by direct reference, subjects foreign securities firms to all of the requirements and limitations that are imposed by the SEL upon domestic Japanese securities firms. In principle, foreign securities firms are eligible to engage in all types of securities business. As a practical matter, however, because foreign securities firm branch offices tend to be less heavily capitalised than most Japanese securities firms, the business licenses granted to them under the FSFL are generally somewhat narrower than the business licenses of domestic securities firms.

Securities Investment Trust Law — The Securities Investment Trust Law (Law No. 198 of 1951, as amended) is the statute pursuant to which Investment Trust Management companies are licensed and regulated by the MOF, for the protection of investors in so-called "investment trusts," analogous to what are known in other jurisdictions as unit trusts or mutual funds.

Investment Advisory Business Law — The Investment Advisory Business Law (Law No. 74 of 1986, as amended) is the basic statute pursuant to which the MOF regulates the business of rendering investment advisory services with respect to securities. It is the statute which governs the registration of both resident and non-resident professional securities investment advisors and pursuant to which resident investment managers may be licensed to engage, on behalf and for the account of their clients, in discretionary trading of securities.

Commercial Code of Japan — In Japan, the Commercial Code (Law No. 48 of 1899, as amended) serves, among other things, as the analog of what in other jurisdictions might be referred to as a companies act or business corporations act. As such, it is the defining statute for corporate shares and debentures, two of the largest and most important types of "securities," as that term is defined by the SEL. It is the Commercial Code which imparts substantive content, i.e, ownership and basic creditors' rights, to the primary trading units that are the subject and focus of securities regulation. Furthermore, the principles embodied in the Commercial Code and in the commentary and cases relating thereto have been influential, even if not legally determinative, in defining the rights and obligations associated with and the contractual form of securities issued by governmental and other entities not actually organised under the Commercial Code.

Civil Code of Japan — The Civil Code (Law No. 89 of 1896, as amended) is the basic source of contract, tort and remedial principles in Japan and, consequently, figures prominently in the definition of all legal relationships to which a more specialised statute does not apply.

Foreign Exchange and Foreign Trade Control Law — Despite successive waves of so-called liberalisation, the Japanese Yen remains a controlled currency. The FEL (Law No. 228 of 1949, as amended) and the foreign exchange regulations subordinate thereto constitute the basic means by which the Japanese government, acting primarily through the MOF and The Bank of Japan (BOJ), exercises control in this regard. Although often invisible to a portfolio investor, these days, any cross-border securities transaction involving more than

¥100,000,000 continues to have FEL aspects that must be regarded as part of the overall system of securities regulation. The FEL influences, among other things, the manner in which cross-border securities transactions are executed and settled, as well as the manner in which foreign securities are "held" by or on behalf of, Japanese investors.

GOVERNMENT AGENCIES

Ministry of Finance — This ministry was established pursuant to the Law concerning the Ministry of Finance (Law No. 144 of 1949 as amended). Preeminent among the various ministries constituting the government of Japan, the MOF is responsible for, among many other things, (i) the fiscal and budgetary affairs of the nation, (ii) general oversight of the national economy, (iii) the printing of currency and the minting of coins (iv) regulation of the financial industry, (v) control and regulation of foreign exchange and (vi) government printing. Primarily through its Securities Bureau, the MOF exercises direct control of or supervisory responsibility over all aspects of, and those institutions associated with, the securities industry in Japan.

Securities and Exchange Surveillance Commission — The Securities and Exchange Surveillance Commission, a "watchdog" body to oversee, investigate and make recommendations to the MOF concerning the securities industry, securities markets and exchanges, was established in 1992. Governed by the Law concerning the Ministry of Finance, this semi-autonomous commission is attached to the MOF and is charged with responsibility for the inspection and surveillance of securities and derivatives markets. The Commission has the authority to conduct unannounced inspections of securities companies and other financial institutions, to search, seize and attach, to recommend to the MOF the initiation of administrative proceedings, and to law enforcement authorities the initiation of criminal proceedings.

SELF-REGULATORY BODIES

Organised Exchanges — The eight stock exchanges organised pursuant to the SEL, of which more will be said below, are among the most important non-governmental, self-regulating institutions involved in the securities industry. The principal purpose of the exchanges is to operate highly organised and easily identifiable markets for the trading of stocks and other securities, including certain derivative products. The exchanges seek to achieve this objective through the promulgation, administration and enforcement of internal rules governing membership, listing and trading which go beyond the legal minimums imposed by the SEL, FSFL and regulations subordinate thereto. The rules relating to membership require participating securities firms to satisfy standards for financial soundness and to conduct their businesses in conformity with established practices; those relating to listing impose disclosure requirements upon issuers of listed securities as well as liquidity requirements upon the listed securities themselves; while those relating to trading regulate the manner in which member firms may execute and settle purchase and sale transactions involving listed securities.

Japan Securities Dealers Association — The other principal self-regulatory organisation involved in the Japanese securities industry is the Japan Securities Dealers Association (JSDA). As with the stock exchanges, the SEL is the relevant enabling statute and, as with the stock exchanges, the JSDA promulgates, administers and enforces, under government supervision, rules relating to a number of residual aspects of the securities business. In particular, JSDA rules serve as the primary regulatory basis (i) for over-the-counter (OTC) trading of publicly tradable securities not listed on one of the stock exchanges and (ii) for the licensing of securities industry professionals, such as brokers, dealers and customer account representatives. Recent amendments to the SEL have imposed a higher degree of accountability upon and have added weight to the internal rules of self-regulatory associations such as the JSDA.

Others — There are several other self-regulatory bodies, the Securities Investment Trust Association and the Securities Investment Advisers' Association, which have similar rule making and enforcement responsibility within their respective spheres of competence. As in the case of the JSDA, these self-regulatory bodies are now under the scrutiny, if not the active superintendence, of the Securities and Exchange Surveillance Commission, the securities industry watch-dog, and their internal rules have been given a legal recognition and force which renders them functionally equivalent to direct MOF regulations.

KEY DEFINITIONS AND CONCEPTS

Securities — A clear concept of what constitutes a security is a predicate to any system of securities regulation and to any discussion of capital markets. In Japan, the definition is drawn from the SEL, which identifies the following as "securities":

(1) national government bonds;

(2) local government bonds;

(3) bonds issued by "corporations" organised under special statutes (i.e., *Shoko Chukin* or *Norin Chukin*, Electric Power Company Bond, etc.);

(4) corporate bonds and debentures (secured or unsecured);

(5) certificates of contribution issued by "corporations" organised under special statutes (same as (2) above);

(6) share certificates and warrants for new shares;

(7) beneficiary certificates issued by securities investment trusts or loan trusts (i.e., mutual fund shares);

(8) certain promissory notes (as determined by MOF ordinance) issued by corporations (i.e., commercial paper);

(9) securities or certificates issued by foreign governments or foreign corporations which are similar in nature to any of the items specified above;

(10) certain securities and trust certificates, as determined by MOF ordinance, issued by foreign corporations and representing interests in trusts consisting of claimable rights arising from mortgage, home equity or credit card loans (i.e. "securitised" consumer debt);

(11) such other securities or certificates as may be designated by cabinet order.

Although the foregoing definition appears to be quite comprehensive and, by virtue of item (11), to have an elastic quality capable of reaching any potentially abusive investment vehicle not expressly identified in the statutory definition, there has been virtually no administrative and even less judicial expansion of the definition of "securities". In consequence of the relatively static character of the foregoing definition, certain widely-offered instruments, such as domestic golf club membership and foreign limited partnership interests, have remained largely beyond the reach of the SEL's anti-fraud and other remedial provisions. On occasion, in

Japan, public offerings and distributions of such peripheral, security-like instruments, which in other jurisdictions might well be regarded as securities and regulated accordingly, have resulted in swindles of spectacular scale and public notoriety. In such cases, law enforcement authorities generally have had to make do with the criminal provisions and penal devices available to them under the Criminal Code and, in some cases, under the tax statutes.

Securities Business — The definition of "securities business" is another key concept and serves multiple purposes. It delimits the field of business in which licensed securities firms and foreign securities firms may engage, serves as a basis for prohibiting unlicensed persons from conducting business activities in respect of securities and, together with the statutes governing the organisation and business of financial institutions such as banks, trust banks and insurance companies, provides a basis for segregating and, to some extent, insulating the principal sectors of the Japanese financial industry from one another.

The SEL definition of "securities business" includes the following:

(i) the purchase and sale of securities (including derivatives, etc.);

(ii) acting as an intermediary, agent or broker in connection with the purchase and sale securities;

(iii) acting as an intermediary agent or broker, on behalf of third parties, in connection with:

(a) the purchase and sale of securities on a securities market or exchange; and

(b) the execution and settlement of similar purchase and sale transactions on comparable markets or exchanges located in foreign countries;

(iv) the underwriting of securities;

(v) the public offering for sale of securities;

(vi) handling the flotation, public offering or private placement of newly issued or outstanding securities.

While most Japanese securities firms hold plenary licenses to engage in all of the foregoing lines of business, because of the capitalisation and reserve requirements associated with each, the branch operations of many foreign securities firms are licensed to engage in some, but not all lines of business.

Securities Firms and Foreign Securities Firms — A "securities firm" is a *kabushiki kaisha* (stock corporation) licensed by the MOF under the SEL and regulations subordinate thereto, to engage in "securities business" and related commercial activities incidental thereto. With the exception of branch offices of "foreign securities firms" (see below), no other form of enterprise may be licensed to engage in "securities business" and, except to the extent that banks, trust banks and insurance companies are permitted, by the respective special statutes applicable to each of them, to engage in one or another aspect of "securities business," no unlicensed entity may engage in "securities business." MOF regulations establish capitalisation and reserve requirements for corporations wishing to become securities firms which are intended to and do constitute significant barriers to entry.

While it is technically possible for a foreign securities firm to organise and operate through a subsidiary corporation, to date all foreign securities firms that have sought to engage in securities business in Japan, under the FSFL, have done so by establishing and securing a license for an operating branch office of either the foreign securities firm itself or a specially-formed foreign (non-Japanese) subsidiary corporation. Pursuant to the SEL, by virtue of the FSFL, a foreign securities firm may qualify for licenses to engage in all or any of four types of securities business. While the various licenses are separate and relate to different lines of securities business, a foreign securities firm seeking a higher level license ordinarily would seek all lower order licenses as well. In ascending order (in term of the costs associated with bonding, capitalisation and reserve requirements), the types of licenses which a foreign securities firm may hold are:

(i)   dealing (purchase and sale of securities);

(ii) broking (acting as an intermediary, agent or broker with respect to securities transactions on or off a securities exchange);

(iii) limited underwriting (underwriting and arranging public offerings of securities);

(iv) general underwriting (arranging the public offering and/or flotation of new or outstanding securities).

At the present time, virtually all foreign securities firms hold dealing and broking licenses. Only the largest foreign firms, in terms of the paid-in-capital, hold limited or general underwriting licenses as well.

STOCK EXCHANGES, THE OTC MARKET AND THE ROLE OF SECURITIES FIRMS IN ROUTINE TRADING ACTIVITIES

EXCHANGES, MARKETS AND TRADING ACTIVITIES

Japanese stocks are traded on eight domestic stock exchanges in Tokyo, Osaka, Nagoya, Sapporo, Niigata, Kyoto, Hiroshima and Fukuoka, as well as on an over-the counter (OTC) market organised by the JSDA. The listing of a stock on a stock exchange requires the approvals of the MOF and the listing stock exchange. Similarly, the trading of a stock on the OTC market requires prior registration of the stock with the JSDA.

The exchanges operate trading markets that are characterised by the following attributes: (i) trading prices are determined through competitive bidding in transactions that are concluded consecutively during fixed trading sessions, (ii) trading activity is restricted to members who satisfy established criteria pertaining to financial soundness and personnel management, (iii) trading is limited to "listed" securities, with listing being contingent upon the satisfaction of certain basic criteria by both the issuer and the securities themselves, and (iv) trades are settled by means of an expedited system involving the periodic clearing of member accounts. In contrast, in the OTC market: (i) purchase and sale transactions are executed, literally, "over the counters" at various securities firms; (ii) no fixed marketplace exists; (iii) individual trades are concluded by "negotiation" between individual buyers and sellers, acting in relative isolation; in consequence of which (iv) prices in simultaneous or nearly simultaneous transactions in the same securities may vary widely from one securities firm to another.

Among the eight stock exchanges, the Tokyo Stock Exchange (TSE) is by far the largest. The Osaka Securities Exchange (OSE) and Nagoya Stock Exchange (NSE) are the second and third largest. The other exchanges are insignificant, both in terms of the number of stocks listed and trading volume, when compared with the three larger exchanges. Stocks listed on the TSE are traded on either its First or Second divisions. The First Division is for the stock of large corporations, while the Second Division is mainly for smaller corporations. Similarly, the OSE has three divisions and the NSE two divisions. Trading volume on the OTC market has increased rapidly in recent years, and its trading volume is now routinely as large as that of the Second Division of the TSE.

In principle, listed securities may be sold on a stock exchange only in "ordinary trading." This requires the selling securities company (acting as a broker or dealer) to deliver the securities to the buying securities company for settlement by 3 p.m. on the third business day after the trading day. In most instances, the delivery of traded securities is accomplished through the posting of debit and credit entries in the selling and purchasing securities companies' securities accounts with a clearing organisation designated by the stock exchange (e.g., Japan Securities Clearing Corporation in the case of trading on the TSE). A customer in physical possession of securities who has requested a broker to effect a sale must deliver the securities to his/her broker by 9 a.m. of the above-mentioned settlement day. The same requirements apply to the settlement of sales of OTC stocks.

Investors who purchase securities normally leave the securities in a custodial account with the securities company which acted as the broker for the purchase. It is also common for institutional investors to direct that their securities be delivered to a bank or specialised custodian company. In either case, the securities company, bank or specialised company acting as the custodian for the purchasing investor is ordinarily granted no authority to lend or otherwise deal in the deposited securities. The custodian's function is strictly limited to safekeeping.

The SEL and stock exchange regulations do not prohibit an investor from selling securities, on a stock exchange, which are not in his/her possession at the time of trading (i.e., engaging in a short sale). However, an investor and his/her broker are required to indicate, for each sale, whether it is short or long. When a short sale is made on a stock exchange, other than from a margin account, the seller may not quote a sales price below the market price immediately prior to such quotation. In effect, this restriction on price quotation precludes short sales on a stock exchange, other than by margin traders.

Accordingly, as a practical matter, a customer's order for the sale of securities on a stock exchange must be from a long position, unless the customer is selling from a margin account. In order for a customer's order to be considered a long sale, certificates must be in the customer's custodial account with the broker, otherwise the customer must prove to the broker that he/she has actual possession of such securities elsewhere, either by virtue of ownership or a securities borrowing arrangement. Without such proof, the broker will not accept the sale order.

Although the short sale of listed securities is restricted, the SEL recognises that excessive stock price fluctuation might result from limiting investors to those who actually possess securities or funds at the time of a desired trade. The need to encourage more investment in the stock market by making credit facilities (i.e., margin trading) available is also recognised. Accordingly, the SEL permits a securities firm, acting as a broker, to lend money to buying investors and stocks to selling investors, subject to MOF and stock exchange regulations. Presently, margin trading is limited to those stocks listed on the First Divisions of the TSE, OSE and NSE and certain stocks listed on the Second Division of the TSE. Margin trading is not permitted for other stocks (e.g., most of the TSE Second Division stocks and OTC stocks).

ROLE OF SECURITIES FIRMS

Only a licensed securities firm, including a Japanese branch of a foreign securities firm, may act as a broker (i.e., to buy and sell stocks for customers' accounts and to charge commissions for such services) or a dealer (i.e., to buy and sell stocks as a principal for its own account) in the stock market. Certain specialised securities firms, Nihon Tento Shoken K.K. and Nakadachi Securities Co., Ltd. act as brokers' brokers in the OTC market.

In principle, the SEL and FSFL limit the activities that may be undertaken by securities firms to (i) those activities that fall within the definition of "securities business," contained in the SEL and the FSFL and (ii) certain activities ancillary or related to "securities business" or "securities" (discussed in II.A. above) that securities firms have been specifically authorised, by the MOF, to engage in ("related business"). Securities firms are prohibited from engaging in any other business.

Despite the narrow scope of business activities permitted securities firms, the MOF has, in the past, allowed them to undertake "related businesses" without MOF approval. The MOF will permit such activities when securities firms appear naturally better suited to undertake the given business than companies in other industries. Securities lending is one such business. Securities firms are implicitly authorised to engage in all aspects of securities lending business, as a borrower, lender, broker, agent or arranger, for all types of "securities," as defined in the SEL, including both stocks and Japanese government bonds.

PUBLIC OFFERINGS AND EXEMPTIONS FROM REGISTRATION

The SEL imposes a general prohibition against the "public offering" of new or outstanding securities, the aggregate issue or selling price of which equals or exceed ¥500,000,000, without the prior filing, with the MOF, of a registration statement (for most smaller public offerings, the filing of a pre-cleared notification is required). Furthermore, no underwriter, securities firm or foreign securities firm may publicly offer or sell to any person, new or outstanding securities to which the above-described registration requirement applies, unless and until the registration statement relating to the public offering of such securities has become effective. The SEL also imposes a requirement that any issuer, underwriter or securities firm engaged in a public offering of securities deliver to the offeree, unless the offeree is another securities firm, a prospectus prepared in connection with and describing the public offering.

The preparation of a registration statement and prospectus, for filing and use in connection with an initial or secondary-market public offering, is a highly technical exercise, involving the disclosure of detailed information concerning both the securities to be offered and the business and financial condition of the issuer. Inadequate or inaccurate disclosure can result in disruption and delay of the offering and can have subsequent legal consequences. Because the preparation of these documents would never be attempted without the comprehensive assistance of legal, accounting and securities business professionals, a detailed discussion of their contents and the procedures involved in seeking their preliminary clearance by the MOF, is beyond the scope of this chapter. It would be worthwhile, however, to examine briefly the concept of a "public offering," the making of which will necessitate prior compliance with the registration requirements of the SEL.

As used in the context of Japanese securities regulation, a "public offering" of new or outstanding securities involves the solicitation of offers to acquire newly issued securities or to purchase existing securities from "many and unspecified persons." In the case of outstanding securities, a solicitation would have to seek offers on "uniform terms and conditions" in order to constitute a "public offering." The concept of "many and unspecified persons" is given content in an internal MOF circular which indicates that a solicitation or offer will be regarded as having been made to "many and unspecified persons" if it has been made to "50 or more persons," in Japan. Thus, as many as 49 persons may be solicited without causing the particular offer to be deemed a "public offering," thereby triggering the registration, notification and other requirements applicable thereto. It bears emphasis, that the foregoing test relates not to the number of persons who ultimately purchase or subscribe, but rather to the number initially solicited. Acquisitions or purchases of securities, the aggregate subscription or purchase price of which exceeds the ¥500 million threshold, under circumstances not involving a public offering (i.e., less than 50 solicitees) constitute private placements. The regulatory assumption is that such securities are being acquired for long-term investment purposes and not for resale. Thus, resale restrictions apply.

There is another type of "private" placement that may involve an offering to 50 or more persons, but may nevertheless be exempt from registration requirements. Under recent amendments to the relevant MOF regulation, a distinction has been drawn between qualified institutional investors (QII's), generally banks, trust banks, insurance companies, securities firms, etc., and certain other investors. If a solicitation of offers to acquire newly issued securities is restricted to QII's, the solicitation of more than 50 persons will not result in the solicitation being deemed a "public offering." In such cases, as in the case of conventional private placements, resale restrictions will apply.

In order to avoid circumvention of the SEL's registration requirements by the holders of unregistered securities, initially offered in private placements, either to less than 50 investors or exclusively to QII's, the resale of such securities, without registration, is permitted only under the following circumstances:

i.   the securities are non-equity securities originally offered to QII's and resalable only to other QII's;

ii. the securities are equity securities of a non-public nature (i.e., no securities of the same class have ever been listed, registered for OTC trading, publicly offered and the securities are not subject to continuous disclosure requirements under the SEL);

iii. the securities are part of an issue (small in number; less than 50 securities and indivisible into smaller units) of bonds in registered form with or without an equity feature (i.e., convertible bonds, or bonds with warrants).

ACQUISITIONS AND TAKEOVER BIDS

Acquisitions of publicly traded companies (those whose shares are listed on an exchange or registered for trading on the OTC market) are very rare occurrences in Japan. Nevertheless, in order to protect investors and markets from the price volatility that may attend large block transactions, reporting requirements are imposed on large shareholders of publicly traded companies and there are specific rules applicable to public tender offers. Under the SEL and subordinate regulations, any person who acquires 5% or more of the shares (including rights, warrants or securities convertible into shares) of a publicly traded company must file a report with the MOF concerning his/her shareholding. This reporting requirement applies regardless of the manner in which the acquisition occurred (i.e. in an on or off market transaction). Once the reporting threshold has been crossed and for so long as the percentage shareholding remains at or above 5%, further reports are required with respect to any acquisition or disposition of the shares in question by the reporting person.

In addition to the general reporting requirement imposed on large shareholders, any purchaser of listed shares (or securities likely to result in the acquisition of listed shares) outside of a stock exchange or the OTC market is required to comply with MOF prescribed Takeover Bid (TOB) Rules, unless the acquisition transaction is expressly exempted. Both the exemptions and the TOB Rules are highly technical.

Generally, the TOB rules require (i) the filing of a registration statement with the MOF, (ii) the publication of notice of the terms of the TOB, (iii) the holding of the TOB open for a stated period of between 20 and 60 days, which period may be extended, in certain circumstances, and (iv) the appointment of a bank or securities company to manage the safekeeping of shares tendered and disbursements of the bid price.

A failure to comply with the TOB Rules, when required to do so, or the making of any intentional misstatements in the required filings will subject a violator to criminal penalties of up to one year imprisonment or a fine of ¥1,000,000.

INSIDER TRADING

Article 166 of the SEL contains a broad prohibition against trading in the securities of a publicly traded company by "insiders" or "persons related to the company," on the basis of material information not generally available to the public. The statute defines "insiders" to include, among others: (i) officers, agents, employees and other personnel who become aware of material information in the course of the discharge of their respective duties; (ii) significant shareholder, if they have become aware of the information through the exercise of shareholder rights not generally enjoyed by other shareholders (i.e., through the inspection of corporate books and records); (iii) persons having authority over the company, who have become aware of the information through the exercise of their authority; and (iv) persons who have become aware of such information through the conclusion or performance of a contract with the company.

Although the statutory provisions delineating those facts and items of corporate information that will be deemed material are quite detailed, the operative test boils down to the question of whether, given the circumstances of the company, a particular fact or item of information concerning its performance, operations or finances would have a material effect on the investment decisions of investors. If so, insiders or persons related to the company, with knowledge of such fact or item of information are prohibited from trading in the company's securities until such material fact or item of corporate information has been publicly announced.

Violations of the prohibitions against insider trading may be punished criminally, by imprisonment or fine. In theory, a violation of the statutory prohibitions will also support a private right of action, by allegedly injured investors against the wrongdoer. However, such an action would be predicated upon the general tort provisions of the Civil Code, and not directly upon the SEL. For this reason and because of the general procedural difficulties which confront private, civil litigants in Japan, to date, very few private actions have been pursued to a successful conclusion.

PORTFOLIO MANAGEMENT

With the growth of capital markets in Japan and with Japanese investors increasingly seeking investment opportunities outside of Japan, there has been an increase in the demand for the services of professional investment advisors and managers as well as an increase in the number of domestic and foreign entities interested in providing such services to Japanese investors. The relevant statute is the Investment Advisory Business Law (Law No. 74 of 1986, as amended) (IABL).

Any person who intends to engage in the business of rendering to investors in Japan advice relating to investments in securities is required, unless authorised by a separate statute to engage in such business, to register with the MOF as an investment advisor. This registration requirement applies not only to investment advisors resident in Japan, but also to non-residents who wish to furnish securities investment advice to investors in Japan.

A registered investment advisor may not render discretionary investment management services, with respect to securities, to investors in Japan unless the advisor has been specifically licensed by the MOF, under the IABL, as an "investment manager." Obtaining a license to engage in the business of discretionary investment management is a much more involved and rigorous process than seeking registration as an investment advisor. Most significantly, a foreign registered investment advisor may not be granted a discretionary investment management license, unless it establishes a branch office in Japan.

In response to certain abusive practices, involving the management of discretionary investment accounts, which has come to light in the early 1990s, MOF regulations now prohibit licensed investment managers from engaging in securities transactions, on behalf of discretionary accounts, with an affiliated entity, i.e. a securities firm or bank, unless the client in question has given written consent, in advance, to each proposed securities transaction with the affiliated entity.

In situations where such prior approvals, on a transactional basis would be difficult or impractical to obtain, as in cases involving the operation of automated trading programs for institutional investors, the investment manager must prepare a written explanation and then, on the basis of that written explanation, seek its client's blanket prior approval to place the trade with its affiliate.

Whenever an investment manager seeks to avail itself of one of the exceptions to the prohibition against trading for discretionary accounts with an affiliate, it must disclose certain statistical information, concerning the percentage of its trades placed with affiliates, to its client and, in certain circumstances to competent regulatory authorities (i.e., the local finance bureau having jurisdiction over the investment manager).

As indicated at the beginning of this chapter, securities regulation, in Japan as elsewhere, is a vast and complex area of the law. Those planning their corporate finances, and contemplating the use of securities would be well advised to seek specialised legal and financial advise.

PART III
DOING BUSINESS IN JAPAN

CHAPTER 8

EMPLOYMENT AND LABOUR LAW
by Gerald Paul McAlinn

INTRODUCTION

While all law is ultimately rooted in local customs and values, few areas of substantive law reflect as deeply the fundamental mores of society than do employment and labour law. Employment law as used in this chapter addresses the general principles which apply to the employer/employee relationship. Labour law, on the other hand, refers to the specific rules and regulations arising in the context of concerted and collective (usually by a union) action by workers. Both bodies of law regulate the core human relationships found in the work place.

Because work is a central and self-defining experience which contributes greatly to an employee's sense of self-esteem and human dignity, a society which fails to protect the basic rights of its workers inevitably falls prey to social instability or worse. Japanese law and practice have not neglected this lesson of history and, indeed as is suggested throughout this chapter, have embraced it to a degree far beyond the logical extension of positive law. This chapter maps the broad parameters of employment and labour law, paying particular attention to their specific application in the context of the foreign employer.

Before exploring some of the more prominent features of these areas of law and practice, there are four caveats which must be stated at the outset. First, precisely because this area of law reflects deeply held social values, it is subject to the same process of change as society at large. In Japan an outer face of social harmony is often used to mask from outsiders an internal collective process of dissent and change. It is not easy for a foreigner to access, let alone to understand, the inner workings of the Japanese mind at the collective or the individual level. For those adept at doing so, there is much to suggest that Japanese society is evolving at a rapid pace and that this evolution will soon begin to impact on all areas of Japanese law. A Japanese reader of this chapter might, however, provide an entirely different explanation for various of the practices described while acknowledging their existence. One is not necessarily right and the other wrong. It is entirely possible and not at all inconsistent for both perceptions of reality to be correct. Foreign managers will quickly come to appreciate this cross-cultural conundrum.

Second, it is almost impossible to discuss such a basic and far-reaching topic within the confines of a single chapter without resorting to gross generalisations. For every general statement made, there are many individual instances where different variables combine to produce a result at variance with the general rule. Japan is a situation sensitive environment where the role of law in providing predictability and certainty is largely subordinated to other more highly valued social objectives, mainly the desire to avoid conflict and the need to maintain group harmony.[1] Put another way, when a dispute arises much more attention is likely to be paid by workers and employers, and judges for that matter, to the "equities"[2] of the particular situation and the "reasonableness" of the behaviour of the parties than it is to a hard analysis of the legal rights of the respective parties.

Third, the practices of large traditional Japanese companies (large being a relative term, but for our purposes those employing 500 or more people) are often quite different from those of medium sized companies, which are, in turn, unlike those of smaller sized Japanese companies in many material respects. Employment and labour practices also vary from industry to industry. Thus, generalisations which apply to workers in large companies will not always precisely fit workers who are employed in the multitude of small and medium sized companies. There is, nevertheless, much common ground in the legal and practical relationship of all Japanese workers and employers and that common ground will make up the substance of this chapter.

Finally, the realities faced by foreign companies in Japan, irrespective of size, are subtly (and some times not so subtly) different from those faced by Japanese companies. This chapter highlights the major attributes of the Japanese employment and labour environment, at the same time contrasting where appropriate how and when the general rules and practices are likely to differ in the context of a foreign company doing business in Japan.

There is one final point of general application which merits noting before embarking on our journey into the realm of Japanese employment and labour law. Japan does not have a regime of detailed anti-discrimination laws enforceable by sanction such as can be found in the U.S. or Europe. To the extent that such laws do exist, they are generally not triggered until after the basic employment relationship has been created. There is, for example, no legal problem with help wanted ads expressly stating, as they almost always do, that the company is looking for either male or female applicants and that applicants must not be over an express age limit, typically between 30 to 35 years of age. Another good example of this point is the Equal Employment Opportunity Act (Law No. 113 of 1985; *Danjo Koyo Kikai Kinto Ho*), enacted by the Japanese Diet to rectify a long history of discrimination against women in the work place. This law expressly prohibits employers from discriminating against women in a variety of contexts within the employment relationship (e.g., termination and retirement age) but obligates the company only to make good faith efforts to eliminate discrimination in the recruiting and hiring of female employees. The law, unfortunately, does not carry any sanctions for violation whether the same occur before or after the start of the employment relationship.

THE CONSTITUTIONAL AND LEGAL FRAMEWORK OF EMPLOYMENT AND LABOUR LAW

THE CONSTITUTION OF JAPAN

The Constitution of Japan contains four major provisions relevant to employment and labour law. Article 22 guarantees to every person the right to choose an occupation freely, provided the chosen occupation does not interfere with public welfare or order. Involuntary servitude is prohibited by Article 23. Of more direct significance in the contemporary environment are Articles 27 and 28 of the Constitution.

Article 27 provides, in relevant part, that: "All people shall have the right and the obligation to work. Standards for wages, hours, rest and other working conditions shall be fixed by law." The first sentence of this Article is understood to be an expression of a social, rather than a legal, obligation on the part of all Japanese citizens. It establishes a principle to which all citizens are to aspire without creating a concomitant legal obligation. The second sentence is, in contrast, legally significant insofar as it provides constitutional support for implementing legislation enacted by the Diet regulating virtually all aspects of the work place. The main body of legislation promulgated pursuant to the mandate of Article 27 is the Labour Standards Law (Law No. 49 of 1947, as amended; *Rodo Kijun Ho*).

An equally important provision of the Constitution is Article 28. This Article guarantees "the right of workers to organise and to bargain and act collectively." As with Article 27, this Article provides a constitutional basis for legislation governing collective bargaining relationships between organised labour and management, as well as other traditional areas of union activity and governance. The main statutory expression of the principles contained in Article 28 is the Labour Union Law (Law No. 174 of 1979; *Rodo Kumiai Ho*).

In simple terms, the Labour Standards Law governs the general conditions pertaining in the work place, and sets ground rules for the individual employer and employee relationship. The Labour Union Law, for its part, deals with the management and labour relationship in the context of unions and collective action by workers.

Both the Labour Standards Law and the Labour Union Law come under the administrative jurisdiction of the Ministry of Labour (MOL). The MOL was established in 1947 for the purpose of "promoting workers' welfare and contributing to the stability of national life." It is responsible for regulating and overseeing the Japanese work place. This is done through a bureaucratic labyrinth of specialised bureaus and divisions. The most important of these for most purposes are the regional and local Labour Standards Offices and Labour Relations Commissions.

The constitutional protection of Articles 27 and 28, as implemented by the Labour Standards Law, the Labour Union Law and a myriad of other laws, ordinances, rules and regulations, and administrative guidance (formal and informal) promulgated by the MOL provide workers in Japan with rights and working conditions equal to or exceeding those found in the most highly developed industrial nations. There can be little doubt that these conditions, coupled with an enviably low, nation-wide unemployment rate, have contributed substantially to the social harmony, well being and prosperity of Japanese society.[4]

LABOUR STANDARDS LAW

General The Labour Standards Law is a comprehensive body of legislation establishing minimum standards for working conditions applicable in all places of employment. The minimum standards are intended to provide all workers with a means to achieve a socially acceptable standard of living. The Labour Standards Law sets forth detailed rules concerning employment contracts, wages, working hours (including breaks, rest days, the annual paid vacation), occupational safety and health, the treatment of minors and women, rules of employment and other related matters. Violating specified provisions of the Labour Standards Law, such as by forcing an individual to work under threat of violence, intimidation or unfair mental or physical restraint, can result in criminal prosecution.

In addition to prohibiting employers from setting working conditions below the minimum standard, the Labour Standards Law also articulates a number of other general principles which set the tone for the employment relationship. The first and most fundamental principle is that working conditions are to be determined by workers and employers on an equal basis. This does not mean that an employer cannot, in practice, effectively determine the terms and conditions of employment. It does, however, mean that once an employer has established working conditions in excess of the minimum standard required by the Labour Standards Law (as virtually all employers do in Japan) the employer may encounter difficulties unilaterally altering the conditions of employment to the detriment of the employees. The employer may be effectively required to obtain the consent of a majority of the workers before the desired changes can be implemented. Other generally applicable principles of the Labour Standards Law prohibit employers from discriminating in the treatment of men and women with respect to wages (still honoured more in the breach), forcing a person to work against his/her will, or refusing to allow an employee, upon request, to take the necessary time off from work to exercise the right to vote or other civil rights or to perform public duties.

The Labour Standards Law applies to virtually every business or enterprise operating in Japan regardless of its nature or form (i.e. incorporated entities, partnerships, branch and representative offices, etc.), and irrespective of the number of persons employed. The term employer is very broadly defined to include the owner and manager of any enterprise, as well as any person acting on behalf of the owner or the manager. A worker, on the other hand, is equally broadly defined to encompass any person who is employed at an enterprise and receives wages therefrom. As will be discussed later, even the president and directors of the company may be considered to be employees for purposes of the Labour Standards Law.

Wages Wages, as used in the Law, include salary, allowance, bonus and all other forms of payment as remuneration for labour regardless of how the payment may be characterised. Wages must, absent a collective agreement or as provided for by specific laws or ordinances, be paid directly to the employee in full (subject to certain permitted deductions such as for taxes, national health and pension, and other voluntary savings plans) and in cash when due. The standard method of payment of wages is by direct deposit into the employee's designated bank account.

The payment of wages must be at least on a monthly basis and must be paid on a fixed date. Most Japanese companies pay their employees on a monthly basis usually on a fixed day between the 20th and 25th of the month. In addition to a monthly salary, a large part of each employee's gross annual compensation is paid in the form of semi-annual bonuses. These bonuses are paid in the winter and summer, usually around December and July, respectively.

There is a fair amount of variety from company to company with respect to the calculation and payment of bonuses. The most common model provides for the company to calculate the bonus component of compensation in terms of months of salary. A major portion of the bonus is determined by the company work rules (see the discussion of work rules below) and a smaller discretionary portion is fixed by the company based on recent business results. It is rare for a company to base any portion of the bonus on individual performance, although some foreign companies pay bonuses based on individual performance as a means of differentiating themselves from traditional "lock step" Japanese employers. Some foreign companies have gone a step further and eliminated the bonus system altogether, electing instead to pay their local employees a gross annual salary.

The exact number of months of salary to be paid to each employee (beyond the non-discretionary amount) as a bonus is decided by the company a few months before the date of payment. For example, if the work rules require the company to pay two months of salary as a winter bonus and two months as a summer bonus, the company may decide, based on overall company performance, to pay a winter bonus to each employee equal to 2.5 months of salary and a summer bonus equal to three months of salary. These figures are fairly typical for Japanese companies and, to the extent that a portion of each semi-annual bonus is non-discretionary on the part of the company, it can be said that employees have a legal entitlement, and certainly a firmly entrenched expectation as to its receipt.

Even where bonuses are not required by the work rules, companies find themselves (including most foreign companies) compelled to pay bonuses if they want to remain competitive and to keep a happy and productive work force. The bonuses are usually determined in such cases by reference to the relevant industry standard if there is one, or the nation-wide average, information about both of which is widely reported in the major Japanese dailies and in the industry papers.

Thus, even though denominated as a "bonus", these payments should more properly be thought of as being fully vested, forced savings (without interest) programs for employees. The bonus system at the same time provides an obvious cash flow benefit to employers. Indeed, so institutionalised and widespread is the bonus system that manufacturers and retailers of big ticket consumer products run major sales compaigns coinciding with the summer and winter bonus seasons aimed at inducing employees to purchase these expensive consumer goods. Similarly, banks offer mortgage repayment schedules with a low monthly payment and two large balloon payments payable from the seasonal bonuses.

Japanese wages have continued to increase, notwithstanding the general recessionary trend of the Japanese economy. While the rate of salary growth has slowed as a result of the financial hardships faced by Japanese industry, personnel costs are and will continue to remain a major component of the cost of doing business in Japan. This dictum regarding personnel costs is truer still for foreign companies which can expect to pay wages to their Japanese employees ranging from 10 to 15% over that paid by Japanese companies for comparable workers. There are a number of reasons for this. First, Japanese employees working for foreign companies must be able to speak at least one foreign language, usually English. The number of Japanese who are competent and comfortable working in a foreign language work environment is small and those who are willing and able to do so can command a premium in the foreign job market.

Second, Japanese companies provide their employees with a complete and integrated package of non-cash compensation benefits, such as housing (either in company dormitories or in the form of subsidised rent or housing loans), meals, medical benefits, professional and social activities, recreational facilities and, most importantly, prestige. Few foreign companies can duplicate this in Japan. Money is often the only lure available to the foreign employer and is the main motivating factor for the Japanese worker to leave his/her Japanese employer. Other factors such as the chance to advance based on merit and the decreased competition for top spots in foreign companies also play a role to a greater or lesser extent depending on the individual involved.

Third, foreign employers have traditionally been viewed by Japanese workers as being inherently unreliable. Many Japanese feel it is quite risky to leave the security of the fabled lifetime employment system and the stability of working in a culturally homogenous work force. The foreign company may make demands that a Japanese employer would not, or it may decide to close its Japan operations in order to protect jobs in the more politically sensitive home market. Similarly, absentee management may change its business priorities, seemingly on a whim, opportunistically entering and withdrawing from the market in response to global trends. This can leave local employees in the embarrassing position of trying to explain to highly dissatisfied customers the company's apparent lack of commitment to the Japanese market.

Finally, many foreign companies simply lack the know-how and resources to recruit and to train less expensive new entrants to the work force. They must, as a result, staff their operations with experienced, and more expensive, senior workers who have been lured away from their former employers with the promise of higher wages. There are other, less benign, reasons for why foreign companies have historically had to pay a premium to attract good local employees. Many foreign executives sent to Japan simply do not have enough background or information to make informed decisions about what the going rates are for various categories of workers and end up relying on their local staff for guidance. More than one hapless foreign executive has fallen prey to the myths spun by local employees about what is "traditional and standard practice" in the Japanese work place. At the risk of putting too fine a point on this topic, suffice it to say that all such information should be verified by independent legal and business advisors before being accepted.

Foreign companies with knowledgeable expatriate staffs that have worked in Japan for a long time have, as might be expected, tended to do much better in this area than companies entering for the first time. They usually still pay a premium, but it is not as great. The one bright spot for foreign personnel managers is that the depth and duration of the post — Bubble economic recession plaguing Japan has made local employees more willing than ever to consider leaving their companies for a foreign firm, making it an excellent time to recruit qualified Japanese staff.

Employment Contracts Except in the case of temporary workers and more senior executives in foreign affiliated companies, employment contracts do not usually exist. Where a contract is used, any provision not meeting the minimum standard set by the Labour Standards Law will be invalid. In a similar vein, a provision in an employment contract which is less favourable than that provided to all workers in the company's work rules is invalid.

An employment contract with a fixed term in excess of one year (indefinite terms and contracts for specific projects likely to last more than one year are excluded) is not enforceable beyond a one year term by the employer, but can be enforced by the employee. A one year or longer fixed term contract for full-time employment with a renewal provision will be treated by the courts as creating a permanent employment relationship if the contract is, in fact, renewed after the expiration of its initial term. This means that the employer may not be able to end the relationship after the first renewal merely by refusing to renew the contract in accordance with its terms at the expiry of the then current term.

The employment contract must provide a clear statement of the applicable working conditions. It cannot obligate the employee to pay liquidated damages in the event of breach or authorise the employer to offset wages against advances. Non-competition clauses are sometimes found in the contracts of senior Japanese executives working for foreign companies. They are generally enforceable to the extent that they are reasonable in geographic and functional scope. Reasonableness depends on the level of the employee, the degree to which the employee has had access to confidential information and all other relevant facts and circumstances.

Other than the above restrictions and subject to the minimum standards in the Labour Standards Law, the parties to an individual employment contract are essentially free to set the terms and conditions of their employment relationship through the bargaining process. In the case of senior executives working for foreign companies, experience has amply demonstrated the merit of including clear and unambiguous termination provisions. The topic of terminating employees is dealt with in greater detail below, but it is worthwhile to note at this point that companies desiring to discharge an employee, even for cause under an otherwise valid employment contract, could face a high hurdle in order to justify their action. Japanese courts have long recognised the imbalance of economic power between the company and the individual employee and are sympathetic to the financial and social dislocation the employee and his/her family will experience if the company is permitted to exercise its power unreasonably, i.e. without good and substantial cause.

Work Rules Every employer employing 10 or more workers is required to prepare work rules (often called rules of employment, or in Japanese; *Shugyo Kisoku*) and to submit them to the local Labour Standards Office. The work rules must address, among other things, the following major items:

(a) Starting and ending time of work, rest periods, rest days, leave and shift work, if any.

(b) Methods of calculating wages, and payment thereof, dates of closing of the account and payment of wages, and increases in wages.

(c) Retirement provisions and, if there is a retirement allowance plan, the qualifications therefor, the workers covered and the methods of calculation and payment.

If the work rules provide for extraordinary or minimum wages, the provision of supplies or equipment necessary for work, safety and health, vocational training, accidents, commendations and sanctions, or any other provisions generally applicable to workers, then the details of the same must also be specified.

Prior to submission of work rules to the appropriate Labour Standards Office, the employer is required to solicit the opinion of any trade union organised by a majority of the workers, or, if no union exists, of a person representing a majority of the workers. The employer is obligated to submit along with the work rules a statement of the opinion of the union or the representative of the majority of the workers. Changes to work rules must also be submitted to the Labour Standards Office and must follow the same employee solicitation procedure.

The relevant Labour Standards Office is authorised to order the revision of any rule or condition in the work rules which violates the law or any applicable collective agreements. It is not entirely clear under the law what happens when the company is not able to obtain the approval of its workers for a proposed amendment to the work rules but the changes do not rise to the level of a violation of the law or a collective agreement. The reality is, however, that the Labour Standards Office would probably pressure the company directly or indirectly to reach a compromise with the employees so as to remove any points of contention (thereby restoring harmony) before the work rules as amended are "accepted" for filing.[5]

Employers are free in the work rules to provide for any other aspect of the employment relationship they may desire, in addition to those required to be addressed. A standard additional provision found in the work rules of almost every company is a probationary period of employment lasting from 30 to 90 days. Many companies go much farther and have work rules dealing with virtually every aspect of the employment relationship. There are two theories on this. The first holds that the work rules, which in the broadest of senses form a kind of implied contract with the employees, should be kept to the minimum so that the company can retain maximum flexibility to change the non-mandatory terms and conditions of employment. The other school of thought contends that, unless the work rules clearly cover all aspects of the employment relationship, the company may find itself being "second guessed" by a disgruntled employee or, worse, a court if a major dispute arises. A second rationale in support of detailed work rules is that the company might find it hard to attract the best employees if the work rules do not contain competitive policies and benefits consistent with a secure and desirable work place.

Regardless of the school of thought ascribed to, the work rules should have strong and unambiguous provisions spelling out how and when the company can discipline (including discharge) an employee. All other topics in the work rules must be prepared with equal care in order to avoid confusion and unnecessary argument. It is easy to find standard form work rules, but a company would be wise to obtain outside professional help in the preparation, adoption and implementation of work rules tailored to its needs and policies.

Work rules are another area where expatriate management can find itself suffering under the burden of disadvantageous provisions which were adopted without a full appreciation on the part of the company of their impact. A good example all too frequently found is a provision providing for automatic annual wage increases. In the early years this item may go unnoticed. However, as the work force matures, or if the business turns down quickly, management can be surprised to learn that the employees must continue to receive pay raises. This kind of provision can result in a company where secretaries and other support staff over time end up with salaries of eight or nine million yen a year (approximately, $80,000 to $90,000) with no "top out" cap.

The Retirement Allowance System It is customary for companies to pay employees in Japan a non-contributory, lump sum retirement allowance (*Taishokukin*) payment upon leaving the company. The calculation method of the retirement allowance is typically determined by multiplying the number of months of employment by the monthly salary of the employee at the time of retirement. Retirement allowance payments are taxed under an extremely favourable scheme which exempts a large portion of the lump sum allowance. The method of calculating retirement allowance payments and the preferential tax treatment accorded to them provide a strong incentive for workers to remain with one employer until the age of mandatory retirement. This is another factor making it difficult for foreign firms to recruit Japanese employees from Japanese companies.

The retirement allowance "vests" as soon as the employee finishes the probationary period of employment, and it is paid out regardless of the age of the employee at retirement from the company, the years of service or the reason for leaving. There are no portability provisions allowing an employee to carry-over a retirement benefit from one company to another. For an employee with only a few years of service with the company, the amount received at retirement from the company will be small. Employees who spend their entire careers with one company can ordinarily expect to receive an amount somewhere between ¥30 million to ¥50 million at retirement. Most companies do not fund their retirement allowance obligations and there are no provident fund type arrangements as are found in many other countries of Asia.

While a lump sum payment of ¥50 million may sound like a lot of money, it must be remembered that the Japanese enjoy the highest longevity rate in the world. In order to supplement the private company retirement allowance plans, the government manages a mandatory, employee and employer contributory, pension scheme which pays retirees a relatively small monthly pension for life.

Finally, a word about the related topic of mandatory retirement is in order. All Japanese companies set a mandatory retirement age in their work rules. There is no age discrimination legislation applicable to mandatory retirement such as exists in the U.S. The standard retirement age varies from industry to industry, but as recently as 10 years ago the average age for mandatory retirement was somewhere around 55 years of age. It has crept up over the intervening years and is now set at 60 years of age by most companies. Foreign companies by establishing a mandatory retirement age of 65 can use this fact as a substantial competitive advantage in recruiting Japanese employees.

Company Directors The role and function of directors in a Japanese corporation, as separate from employees, are dealt with more fully in Chapter 5. It is sufficient to note for our purposes that there is a major distinction between the treatment of directors under the Commercial Code and that of employees under the Labour Standards Law.

In simple terms, directors have the responsibility of overseeing the operations of the company, and are accountable directly to the shareholders. They are elected by, and serve at the will of, the shareholders. Under the Commercial Code, a director can be removed from office by the shareholders at any time, with or without cause. A director removed without cause before the end of the director's then current term is entitled to claim damages against the company. The measure of damages for removal without cause is the payment of an amount equal to the unpaid compensation due to the director for the remaining portion of the director's term. Employees, on the other hand, are employed directly by the company and are ultimately accountable through the chain of command to the directors.

For purposes of the Labour Standards Law, a director may nevertheless continue to be deemed to be an employee. The test ultimately comes down to one of substance, i.e., whether or not the director had substantial independence in the performance of his/her duties. Since Japanese companies rarely have outside directors and usually have a strong president who is responsible for directing the business and operations of the company, directors frequently retain their employee status. The practical effect of this is that the shareholders may easily terminate an individual as a director under the Commercial Code, but the individual may still have a right to continued employment with the company under the Labour Standards Law. This is very often the case in foreign companies where director titles are handed out freely, but decision making authority remains closely held by the home office.

Many companies try to sharpen the distinction between directors and employees by having the individual formally resign as an employee of the company before being elected as a director. The former employee receives his/her retirement allowance under the work rules for employees and then joins the board of directors, where a separate set of rules and regulations applicable only to directors will apply. These special rules for directors often include a multiplier that increases the retirement allowance payment received upon retirement as a director of the company and other benefits and perquisites such as a car and a driver, club memberships and special bonuses. A representative director who has served as the president of the company for many years can receive as much as three times the ordinary amount of ordinary retirement allowance calculated under the employee work rules.

Foreign companies who elect local employees to directorships may face complaints if the company does not adopt a separate set of rules and regulations for directors giving them some of the perks enjoyed by directors in Japanese companies. Of even greater importance is to provide the directors with a sense of autonomy so that they feel as if they have a meaningful voice in the direction and the formulation of policies of the company. One obvious example would be for the company to hold regular and substantive board meetings at which the directors can actively participate in the management of the company.

Many foreign companies elect local employees to the board and then treat them no differently than before they were elected. This often leads to a deep sense of alienation which can spread to the whole work force, resulting in a variation of what is known in the U.S. as the "Glass Ceiling Syndrome." The obvious cure is to promote directors only on merit (i.e., to avoid promoting local employees just because they have the right "face") and then to give the directors the trust and authority commensurate with their positions. An even bolder move is to honour the local president and representative director with a position on the board of the parent company. Not only will the company have the benefit of the counsel and experience of the senior Japanese executive, the rest of the employees and the marketplace at large will immediately perceive the foreign company as one which values Japanese perspectives and is committed to Japan. This advice must, of course, be tempered by the realities of the situation and it assumes that the company has been able to attract and train local employees of director level quality.

LABOUR UNION LAW

General The stated purposes of the Labour Union Law are as follows:

(a) To elevate the status of workers to an equal footing with their employer.
(b) To protect the right of workers to form autonomous labour organisations and to affiliate with other unions for the purpose of undertaking collective action.
(c) To encourage collective bargaining resulting in labour agreements governing the employer/employee relationship.

Article 1 of the Labour Union Law expressly exempts collective bargaining and other acts of a labour union, not involving violence, from the provisions of the Criminal Law of Japan. In practice, this means that it is virtually impossible to obtain legal relief in the courts against employees engaging in traditional, non-violent collective activity such as occupying company facilities, picketing, distributing pro-union or anti-management literature, or striking. This is true even when the action takes place on company facilities during working hours and results in the disruption of production. For example, a disorderly crowd of boisterous employees could not be required to move from company facilities unless their actions involve direct violence to other individuals or the destruction of company property. On the other hand, action by workers taken against safety equipment or facilities could be stopped since safety is given a higher value than labour rights.

Definition of a Labour Union A labour union is any organisation, or federation thereof, formed autonomously and substantially by workers for the main purpose of maintaining and improving the conditions of work and for raising the economic status of workers. Labour organisations which admit supervisory workers (defined as those having direct authority to hire, discharge, promote or transfer other workers) having access to confidential company information relating to labour relations as well as other persons representing the interests of the company are disqualified from being treated as labour unions under the Law.

The precise level of members with supervisory responsibility sufficient to disqualify a labour union is unclear and can only be determined on a case by case basis. A union which admits workers from the lowest levels of management (i.e., section heads; *Kacho*) will probably not be disqualified if the authority of the individuals in this position is limited in scope and subject, especially if approval by a superior is routinely required before action can be taken. Likewise, groups receiving financial support from the company (other than indirectly by way of pension contributions, provisions of office space, time off to conduct union activities, etc.), or whose object is confined to mutual aid work, or whose principal goal is political or social, are not deemed to be labour unions.

Establishment and Registration of Unions At least in theory if a single employee desires to form a union or to join an industry-wide union, the company is powerless to prevent it. The right "to organise and to bargain and act collectively is guaranteed" by Article 28 of the Constitution. There are no certification or election procedures required by the Labour Union Law to verify the representational status of the union. A labour union is not required to take any particular form, to represent a majority of the employees or to have a written constitution. A company can have more than one labour union representing different workers in the same work place or unit.

The Labour Union Law does provide, however, that if a labour union desires to participate in the formal process established under the Labour Union Law it must submit written evidence that it meets the definition of a labour union. In other words, it must show that it is not disqualified by virtue of admitting supervisory personnel, receiving financial support from the company, or having as its main objective matters outside of the scope of the labour management relationship. The written evidence must be submitted to the Labour Relations Commission.

A union recognised by the Labour Relations Commission, and thereby afforded the full protection of the Labour Union Law, must have a written constitution showing, among other things, the name and address of the union, and stipulating that all members are entitled to participate equally and without discrimination in the affairs of the union. Membership must be open to all qualified workers without regard to race, religion, sex, social status or family origin, and officials must be elected by secret ballot. Finally, the financial particulars of the union have to be made available to the members and no strike action can be taken without a secret ballot showing majority approval.

Powers A labour union has the power and the right, on behalf of its members, to negotiate a collective bargaining agreement or any other matter with the employer. Labour agreements are not permitted to have terms of longer than three years. The company cannot refuse to recognise the union or to negotiate with it without a compelling reason. There is no legal requirement that one or more representatives from the union be given seats on the board of directors of the company as in certain other countries and this would be highly unusual in practice.

Unfair Labour Practices by the Employer The following actions constitute unfair labour practices if committed by the employer:

(a) Discriminating in employment (hiring, firing, disciplining, refusing promotions, transferring etc. a worker) based on union membership or participation in union activities.

(b) Making it a condition of employment that an individual will not join a union, or requiring the individual to resign from a union.

(c) Refusing to bargain collectively without a good reason. This includes refusing to bargain in good faith.

(d) Dominating a union, including interfering in the formation or administration of a union.

(e) Providing financial support to a union.

(f) Disciplining, or discriminating against, an employee who has lodged a complaint with the Labour Relations Commission or who has given evidence in any relevant forum.

The standard remedy against employers who commit unfair labour practices is a cease and desist order issued by the Labour Relations Commission. An employer can be fined for refusing to follow a valid order of the Commission which has been approved by the courts.

Significantly, the Labour Union Law does *not* contain a comparable list of unfair labour practices on the part of labour unions. This fact strongly suggests a bias in favour of organised labour in the Labour Union Law. It is generally understood that the MOL and the Labour Relations Commissions also hold a deeply embedded bias towards labour.

Company Unions and Employee Associations The formal prohibition against company unions notwithstanding, many Japanese companies have them. This is accomplished through the careful cultivation of "safe and reliable" individuals who are encouraged to take leadership positions in the union. This is supported by the fact that employees tend to remain with one company for life and must look to the company for promotions, job security and a wide range of other financial and social supports. There is little to be gained and much to be lost from engaging in "slash and burn" labour tactics under these circumstances. Although there is little direct evidence, it also seems apparent that indirect financial support of company unions is substantial.

Another favourite tactic employed by companies desiring to control labour relations, is the formation of an employee association which in many ways looks and acts like, but is definitely not, a union. The typical employee association serves as a semi-formal channel for the exchange of labour and management information. A successful employee association removes much of the incentive for individual workers to form a union by giving the workers a collective forum for airing concerns about working conditions, grievances and other matters of common interest in the work environment. It also allows the company to diffuse and correct potentially harmful rumours and to disseminate its views on important matters directly to the work force. For this reason an employee association will almost always have as one of its main purposes the promotion of communications between the company and all of the workers. It will, at the same time, be responsible for coordinating a whole variety of social activities and programs instituted and funded by the company for the benefit of employees.

One of the main objectives of companies in fostering company unions and employee associations is to insure that the labour management relationship does not become "contaminated" by the influence of outside forces. As indicated above, unions can be formed solely within a single company or they can be part of a larger federation of unions operating on an industry and a nation-wide basis. Many of the federated unions have, at least historically, been dominated by strident socialists and communists. Their labour relations tactics have been characterised by confrontation and the desire to achieve "political" agendas rather than to advance the more traditional interests of workers.

In general, organised labour has been very quiet with a few notable exceptions over the past 25 years. The younger generation of workers outside of selected industries does not seem interested in joining or supporting unions. This is due in large part to the widespread prosperity enjoyed by the Japanese in recent years. It should be noted, however, that this was not always the case and during the 1970s Japan experienced some of its worst violence and labour turmoil in the modern era. There is little to suggest that the labour movement is poised for a resurgence, although the downsizing going on in much of Japanese industry is the kind of spark which could rekindle this fire. Be that as it may management needs to be continually vigilant and responsive to the legitimate needs of all workers so that the seeds of labour dissension are not given soil in which to take root.

Unions and the Foreign Company While the labour movement has been relatively quiet in Japan, foreign companies with substantial work forces continue to be targets for unionisation. Professional union organisers and sympathisers have little difficulty gaining access to foreign employers and many foreign companies actually end up hiring such individuals as employees without knowing it. This happens because many foreign companies lack the basic know-how for screening applicants for positions with the company.

Once inside the company, these new employees often find fertile ground for dissension in the "We/Them" environment too often existing between foreign management and the local workers. Additionally, many foreign company operations in Japan are inherently unstable, leading employees to join a union out of a real or perceived fear for job security. This perception is exacerbated by reports of the accordion-like labour practices of many foreign companies during economic boom and bust cycles. A foreign enterprise planning to do business in Japan on a long-term basis would be well advised to hire a highly competent employment relations manager and to institute company wide programs before labour problems arise. It is too late once a rift appears and a union has been formed.

THE EMPLOYMENT ENVIRONMENT IN JAPAN

Lifetime Employment It is often said that Japanese workers enjoy the benefits of a system of lifetime employment (*Shushin Koyo Seido*). This may be largely true in practice for workers in major Japanese companies, but it becomes progressively less so for those (blue and white collar alike) in the many small shops, companies and factories located across Japan. Lifetime employment to the extent that it exists at all is based more on custom and practice than it is on law. The foundation for this concept is an unwritten social contract between employers and their employees the essence of which is that the company will supply each employee with a safe and secure work place and with a decent wage capable of supporting the employee and his/her family in return for a lifetime of loyal and dedicated service (rewarded at the end with a large retirement allowance payment) to the company.

Professor Wiltshire has summarised the gist of the lifetime employment system in his book entitled *Relocating the Japanese Worker*, as follows:

> "Under this system, core workers are hired directly from universities, colleges and schools, and are granted conditional tenure of employment, generally through custom and collective bargaining in the private sector, but through law in the public sector, until the age fixed for retirement. In return for a moral or contractual guarantee of secure employment, the employee concedes to the employer the right, with or without consultation, to determine not only the tasks that he/she will be expected to perform, but also the locations where the work must be undertaken."

While Professor Wiltshire was writing in the specific context of the employer's right to determine the nature and place of work, it is true that Japanese workers have an expectation of permanent employment. This expectation has been fostered by an unusually high degree of employment stability across the board, coupled with very low unemployment, since the end of the Second World War and a reluctance on the part of the government and the courts to permit companies to terminate or lay-off employees at will. At any rate, Japanese employees have come to expect that once hired they will spend their entire careers with the same company or an affiliated company within the same group.

This attitude on the part of Japanese workers produces three very positive effects. First, workers do indeed develop a strong identification with and loyalty to their employers. Status and prestige in Japanese society are very much associated with one's position and company affiliation. Every self-introduction by a Japanese person invariably begins with a statement of the individual's company name and position thereby allowing the listener to place the person in the proper identifying group. In formal business settings this is also accomplished by the universal practice of exchanging business cards. Second, because the employees are likely to be with the company for life, employers can afford to hire predominantly from the ranks of recent graduates and then to spend the necessary time and money to train each new employee in the policies, objectives and management style of the company. This training is accomplished primarily by having the new employees rotate through a variety of jobs and locations in the company over the early years of their careers. Third, a stable work force, starting with the most senior executives of the company and extending down to the lowest levels of workers, produces an enviable consistency in corporate direction, philosophy and objective. Because promotion is always from within, succession is orderly (although internal power struggles and competition for the top posts do occur) and instances where a change in senior management produces a radical change in corporate direction are extremely rare.

Seniority Closely related to the system of lifetime employment is the practice of promoting and paying employees exclusively on the basis of age and seniority. As for salary, many companies have detailed personnel charts to determine the exact salary of each employee based on job title and age. No individual variation is permitted.

Promotion is based on a highly subjective assessment of the individual's character, ability to work in a group and commitment to the company, rather than on any objective review of individual business results or performance. Differentiation does begin to appear when promotions are made at the section chief (*Kacho*) or department manager (*Bucho*) level. There is a cultural bias in Japan against singling out an employee from the group for individual merit promotion. Successes are thought of as being the result of group effort. Calling attention to one individual is as likely to produce a profound sense of embarrassment as it is to have the intended effect of encouraging positive behaviour. It is very difficult for all of the parties involved to leapfrog one employee over more senior "next in line" employees when it comes time for promotion.

This system has the effect of reducing competition among workers, fostering a cooperative sense of team spirit, and advancing the interests of the group over those of the individual. People who make it to the management levels in Japanese companies must be as strong in the area of human relationships (*Ningen Kankei*) as they are in the conventional areas of business performance, which, of course, is also a major part of the equation for advancement.

The Social Contract of Employment Another very important aspect for understanding the dynamics of the work environment is an appreciation of the role played by the company in Japanese society. At the risk of wearing out the cliche, Japan is a group oriented society. Life in Japanese society, from kindergarten to retirement, involves identifying with one primary group or another. In the case of full-time employees, the primary identifying group is the company. A young Japanese male fresh out of school becomes a "salary man" when he joins the company. Women, who are fairly new to the white collar, non-secretarial work force, have not yet become the female equivalent of a salary man because they are still expected to marry and leave the company within a few years. Upon joining the company, the individual and the company assume a full range of mutual duties and responsibilities which form the basis of the "social contract" of employment.

There are two other major elements to this "social contract". First, Japan has, at least in the modern era, looked to the company, rather than to government, to provide much of the social support and service system required by society. Companies provide employees with housing and access to recreational facilities for company sponsored sports and social club activities. Employees and their families are covered by company subsidised medical insurance through the National Health System and rely on the retirement allowance paid by the company (which strongly rewards long service) instead of the government pension scheme.

Second, and closely tied to the first point, is the strong emphasis placed on human relationships in Japanese society, including those of the work place. The company for its part is expected to provide a stable and secure work place replete with amenities and to treat its employees as part of an extended family. To push the analogy of a family one step further, the company assumes the role of parent, and the workers of children. Dutiful children move through the company smoothly while disobedient ones are disciplined but rarely expelled from the family. To wantonly terminate the social contract of employment will not only do violence to the human relationships of the work place, it will also cause hardship for society which will then have to provide for the needs of the terminated worker and his/her family. In this sense, the social contract of employment extends to society as well as to the employee and the employer.

In return for the comprehensive social network provided by the company, employees are expected to devote themselves body and soul to the company. This means more than just doing the job assigned. It also means subordinating individual desire and convenience, such as taking time off from work for family or leisure, to the needs of the company. The typical salary man works five days a week (until recently it was six days a week, a policy which still continues in certain industries) from 09:00 to 20:00 or later. At the end of the workday employees are expected to go out to eat and drink with their colleagues from the office at a local drinking establishment. This system is essential for creating and maintaining the close social harmony and strong human relationships required in the Japanese work place.

So legendary is the devotion of the Japanese "salary man" to work that the MOL and the courts have been actively trying for years to reduce working hours and to increase vacation time. The MOL and the courts have also been pressed recently to recognise a new form of worker compensation claim, namely, a claim for *karoshi* (literally, death from overwork). A claim for *karoshi* arises when a worker (not infreqeuntly a white collar one) dies, usually of cerebral hemorrhage or heart failure, after having worked over an extended period of time without adequate time off for rest. Such cases have been reported sensationally in the newspapers, but have met with only limited legal success.

Recruiting and Hiring Japan has one of the highest literacy rates in the world and the Japanese work force, as a whole, is remarkably skilled and disciplined. Japanese factories, by way of example, approach a level of safety, order and cleanliness more usually associated with a head office in many other countries. As noted above, Japanese companies hire virtually all of their employees directly upon graduation from school and train them internally. There is almost no lateral hiring except in the unskilled fields.

The Japanese academic year runs from April to March and the job hunting season begins, at least for university students, at the start of their last year of school. The recruiting and hiring process begins with students sending postcards to selected companies requesting general recruiting and company information.[9] Employers hold a series of information seminars (some attended by thousands of interested students) through the spring followed by a battery of standardised tests designed to screen candidates. Students passing the company test are invited back for official interviews and unofficial meetings with company employees who graduated from the same university.

Successful candidates receive an informal promise of employment

(*Naitei*) in July or August. Students who are not fortunate enough to receive a *Naitei* in the first round repeat the process through the fall until they either find a job or drop out of the market. The average male student can expect to receive two or three *Naitei* whereas female students consider themselves lucky to get one for a good career track position. Astute foreign employers have exploited this bias on the part of Japanese company recruiters and have begun to tap into this large, under utilised pool of qualified candidates as a prime source for recruiting new employees.

A second narrower method of recruiting new employees is through direct recommendations from professors and teachers. Companies carefully cultivate these key educators, especially those in the sciences, in the hope that they will channel their top students to the favoured companies. This system works well for companies that need specialised skills but it does have the drawback of obligating the company to take (as a matter of *Ningen Kankei* and not as a matter of legal obligation) at least one student a year on the recommendation of the professor or teacher. Failing to take a student without good cause can result in the cutting off of the pipeline.

Many Japanese companies routinely conduct background searches on new employees. These searches are usually performed by independent private investigators and can run the gamut from a simple check of each candidate's family registration (at a cost of about $50.00 per candidate) to a more extensive background check including verifying school records and checking the candidate's references and activities at school. Special attention is paid to students who may have been caught up in the more radical political groups found, albeit in small numbers, on many university campuses.

Because employees are hired with the expectation of lifetime employment, there is almost no employee initiated job hopping among mid-career employees. In fact, a willingness to change companies (i.e., to switch corporate or group allegiance) is perceived by the Japanese as a sign of instability and evidences an underlying lack of trustworthiness. This is in marked contrast to the West where job hopping is seen as one of the principal methods of résumé building and skills acquisition.

There is one major exception to the general rule against changing companies in mid-career. It occurs when a company shifts some of its less productive or redundant employees off to subsidiary companies, suppliers and other affiliated entities. This is done to make way for newly hired employees or to reduce personnel costs. The usual methods are to dispatch the employee on a long or short term basis

(*Shukko*) or to permanently transfer (*Tensoku*) the employee. In both cases, the parent company may agree to continue to pay all or a portion of the employee's salary for a period of time in order to lessen the burden of the company taking the employee. Affiliated companies and suppliers are obviously not always pleased to accept these employees and frequently a considerable amount of arm twisting and negotiating precedes the move. The employee often is required to take a reduction in pay or in benefits. This is not seen as violating the social contract between the employee and the parent company if reasonably necessitated by business circumstances. The employee continues to have a job and the company has fulfilled its duty by making adequate provisions for the employee. By any objective standard, this is far more preferable to all concerned including society at large, than laying off the employee.

Joint venture companies are a favourite repository for excess employees. Every foreign corporation negotiating a joint venture in Japan should be aware of this hidden secondary agenda on the part of the potential Japanese partner. It does not happen in all cases, but it does occur with sufficient frequency to bear a general caution.

Recruiting by Foreign Companies Since very few foreign companies possess the size or resources to duplicate the system described above, it is necessary for them to recruit management level personnel almost exclusively from the ranks of mid-level employees in Japanese companies, or from other foreign enterprises. The standard lures used to attract these employees are money and promotion. The result is a work force that tends to be older, top heavy and more expensive than what one would expect to find in Japanese competitors.

There are two major problems with this form of recruiting. A person motivated solely by money may lack the desired loyalty. Similarly, an employee who is not able to advance in the rigorous environment of a Japanese company and therefore looks to the foreign job market as an easy avenue to promotion may lack the necessary business skills to succeed once employed at the foreign company.

Japanese working at the management level in foreign companies can be separated into two broad categories. The first is the person who feels stifled by the hierarchical nature of the Japanese system and is confident of success in a performance based environment. This individual has the basic skills and abilities to succeed in business in Japan, but is not willing to suffer a system where seniority outweighs ability. A foreign company capable of identifying and recruiting this type of individual will be very successful in building a strong local work force.

The second type of person is one who lacks the basic business skills or personality to prosper in the wholly Japanese environment. This employee is working at a relatively low level when recruited and sees the foreign employer as an avenue for rapid advancement. Although this person would never be hired for a equally responsible position in the home office, the fact that he/she is Japanese, speaks good English and is willing to move to the new employer, makes the candidate seem like an ideal choice. In the environment faced by foreign companies in Japan where needs are immediate and choices few, this type of person makes up the bread and butter of recruiting firms working on a commission and relying on rapid and frequent placements of middle and upper level executives.

It does not take long for a company which has hired this second type of person to realise its mistake. Since the individual lacks the necessary skills to function effectively in the Japanese business arena, the company must either invest substantially in the employee's training or induce the employee to resign from the company. If jobs in the foreign marketplace are plentiful (the employee will never be able to return to a Japanese company), the employee may accept a cash payout in return for retirement.

Many of the senior employees in foreign companies have been with more than one foreign employer and indeed are continuously getting on and off the employment conveyor belt as it passes through the foreign company community. Sad but amusing anecdotal stories are told by lawyers who have been asked by one client to prepare a separation contract for such an employee only to be asked a few months later by a different client to prepare an employment agreement for the same individual!

It would be wrong to leave the reader with the impression that all, or even most, of the many thousands of Japanese workers diligently and gainfully employed by foreign companies in Japan are incompetents who have failed in the purely Japanese environment. Nevertheless, just as one would naturally ask why a candidate for a lateral job at the home office is interested in leaving his/her present position, so too should the same question be asked in Japan. If there is any question, it is prudent to have a trusted Japanese adviser, such as outside counsel, meet with the individual to make an independent assessment. It may also be worthwhile to engage an investigation firm in order to get a fuller picture of the candidate's character, current responsibilities, and true reasons for leaving the present employer.

Managing, Disciplining and Terminating Japanese Employees.
There is little science, and much art, in the area of managing
Japanese employees. If ample attention is given to building a strong
human relationship with the employees many mistakes (even major
ones) can be overlooked or forgiven. Japanese workers are generous.
They do not expect a foreigner to understand fully all of the intricacies
of Japanese social conventions and mores. Making an effort to do so,
however, will be greatly appreciated and rewarded. It should also be
remembered that the sensitivities of Japanese workers may not be the
same as in one's home country. The actions of a foreign manager can
be forceful, but they must always be seen as being fair and reasonable
under the circumstances. A warm heart, an honest demeanour and
the willingness to express a sincere apology when an error has been
made can go a long way towards resolving many difficult situations.

As mentioned above, company work rules usually provide for a
series of punishments for violation of the company's rules and orders.
The range of punishment for misbehaviour runs from an oral or
written warning to a reprimand, reduction in wages, suspension,
demotion or, finally, discharge. With respect to disciplining employees,
even where the work rules specify violations and punishments, a
company whose actions are perceived by the other employees as being
too harsh under the circumstances will find itself with an alienated
and disgruntled work force. The attitude of the company must be firm,
but it should also be merciful when the employee acknowledges his/
her improper behaviour.

The company should be more concerned with rehabilitation than with
punishment. When rehabilitation is not possible, either because of the
character of the individual or the nature of the offense, the company
must act decisively and then be certain to let the other employees know,
either directly or indirectly, the reasons for its actions. Japanese
employees will readily accept the reasonable exercise of authority by the
company, especially where the actions of the employee are perceived as
having left the company with little choice.

The legal concern for preserving the human relationship and
protecting the worker from overly harsh action by the employer is
strongly manifested in the area of termination. The written law is
simple and straightforward. Under Article 20 of the Labour Standards
Law, an employer is permitted to terminate an employee, with or
without cause, by either giving 30 days notice in advance of the date
of termination or by paying 30 days pay in lieu of notice. Japanese
courts have routinely rejected following this provision literally in
favour of a judicially created doctrine holding that a termination
without "just cause" amounts to an abuse of right prohibited by

Article 1 of the Civil Code. Thus, the termination of an employee will be considered void by the courts (i.e., without just cause) when it is deemed to be unreasonable in light of all of the facts and circumstances and it violates prevailing social norms. Courts are particularly critical of terminations which are for the economic convenience of the employer.

The "just cause" hurdle is a high one indeed. For example, mere incompetence would probably not satisfy the standard unless the company had made every effort to train the employee or to find a job within the company which the employee could handle. Employers are expected to carry unproductive employees on the payroll until retirement out of social duty and sympathy. They are not given responsibilities or duties commensurate with their age or position, but they receive their full pay. This enables the employees to support themselves and their families and prevents them from becoming unemployable burdens on society. This condition is so widespread that a special term exists in the language for such people. They are called the *madogiwazoku* (literally, members of the family who sit by the window) because their seats are located near the window, which in a Japanese organisation is the least influential position being the furthest from the centre of the group.

On the other hand, an employee who violates the criminal law or who repeatedly refuses to obey the lawful orders of superiors can probably be terminated. It is impossible to say in general terms and with any degree of certainty what would qualify as just cause. Employers have a greater degree of discretion to terminate employees in the senior management ranks where employees may be reasonably expected to be able to perform competently the assignments given to them and where their lack of skill could ultimately endanger the company including the jobs of ordinary workers in the company.

As a practical matter, most employment disputes are resolved without recourse to third party dispute resolution since the Japanese abhor social conflict and are extremely reluctant to expose internal matters to the public. When a company decides to terminate an employee, it could however find itself in a lawsuit.[10] Judges in employment and labour cases (there is no jury system) are notorious for making herculean efforts to persuade the parties to the dispute to reach an amicable settlement in the course of extensive pre-trial conferences. One favourite tactic for encouraging settlement is to simply refuse to render a decision. A Japanese court will, of course, eventually render a decision if both parties absolutely refuse to reach a settlement. The court does not have the legal power to compel the parties to settle. The reality is that it is almost always better for the company to settle out of court in order to avoid the negative impact of a prolonged lawsuit, the lost time and diverted energies of key members of the management team and the legal fees likely to be incurred. Figures showing average settlement amounts are not available, but payments from around six months to one year of salary would not be uncommon.

Assuming a decision is finally rendered, it is relatively rare for courts to order reinstatement of middle and senior level employees once the basic trust inherent in the employment relationship has been broken. Most of these cases result in monetary awards sufficient to insure that the employee will have an adequate means of support for a reasonable period until new employment can be located. A court is more likely to order reinstatement with back pay when a union is involved or the employee holds a lower position in the company.

The terminated employee has one other very powerful weapon in his/her arsenal. The employee can petition the court for a provisional disposition (*Kari Shobun*) order requiring the company to continue to pay salary and benefits so that the employee can maintain a reasonable standard of living while the suit is pending. Yoichiro Hamabe, a Japanese attorney, has succintly described the practical impact of provisional disposition proceedings as follows:

> "Provisional, or temporary, disposition originated as an optional special proceeding for the purpose of securing temporary relief, in addition to and separate from a regular lawsuit. Although this proceeding was designed for use in an emergency situation during or prior to a lawsuit, it can provide relatively quick relief for the discharged employee. And that relief frequently leads to a fast, final resolution because often the parties resolve the dispute by settlement during the provisional disposition proceedings. In practice, provisional disposition is so important in termination disputes that it has become as critical as the principal lawsuit. Accordingly, Japanese employees may assert procedural as well as substantive protection against involuntary discharge."[11]

Judges are inclined to grant such provisional orders expeditiously if the parties cannot reach a settlement. The company is usually not ordered to pay the full salary of the employee, but only the amount required for the employee to maintain an acceptable standard of living. This money is paid monthly until the dispute can be resolved in court (a process taking many years) and is effectively non-recoverable even if the company prevails on the merits.

Downsizing and Voluntary Retirement Plans. Mass lay-offs and other collective involuntary personnel reductions are highly disfavoured in Japan. In the early 1990s a number of Japanese companies began to talk publicly about the need to reduce bloated work forces in order to maintain global competitiveness in the era of the high yen. Newspapers promptly reported that a number of these executives were summoned by the government and strongly advised to stop making such statements. This is now one of the silent problems facing Japanese society.

The need to reduce personnel from time to time is a reality of Japanese business and most companies accomplish it by a mixture of attrition and the transfer of redundant employees to affiliated companies as mentioned above. Many large Japanese companies couple plant closings with offers of job transfers to other distant company facilities, rather than laying off redundant employees. The companies obviously expect and hope that many of the employees will not accept transfers to far away locations and will quit instead. Some major Japanese companies have instituted retirement incentive programs for management employees whereby the amount of the incentive is scaled to the age of the employee at retirement. For example, if the employee retires at 50 years of age, he/she receives the ordinary retirement allowance amount under the company work rules plus the maximum early retirement incentive amount. At 51 the incentive amount is reduced and so on until it reaches zero at the mandatory retirement age of 60.

Foreign companies lack the leverage and the affiliated company network required to take the "soft landing" approach practiced by large Japanese companies. This has left foreign companies with few choices. Companies which have tried the "American" way of bluntly laying off redundant employees have quickly found themselves in a bitter fight with employees, who usually end up forming a union.

The preferred method of reducing personnel at foreign companies has been the voluntary retirement plan. Under such plans, the company identifies the number of employees it wants to reduce and then offers an economic incentive to each employee to take an early retirement package. The amount of incentive is calculated to reflect length of service. It is difficult to obtain solid information on the average amount of incentive a company must pay to get a sufficient number of employees to resign. Three to six months of extra salary would probably be considered the minimum, whereas an additional one year of salary would be generous. These plans were popular and quite successful during the late 1980s when employees were almost guaranteed of finding a new position immediately upon leaving the company. In the current economic environment, finding a new position is much more difficult and the number of willing volunteers for early retirement has decreased.

EXPATRIATE EMPLOYEES

A separate chapter could be written on the topic of expatriate management in foreign-affliliated subsidiaries in Japan. There are many aspects from which this issue can be examined. First and foremost is the fact that it is a very expensive proposition to send an employee with his/her family to Japan for an extended period of time. Rents in the "Golden Ghetto" area of Hiroo and Moto Azabu, where many foreign executives live, range from the yen equivalent of $10,000 to $20,000 per month and usually require as a deposit an amount equal to two months' rent. To this is added the cost of school for children (around $15,000 per year per child at one of the international schools), a cost of living allowance (COLA payments for employees in the $100,000 to $150,000 salary range can be anywhere from $50,000 to $150,000 per year after tax depending on the rate of exchange), home leave and tax equalization. This is, of course, all in addition to the regular salary of the employee.

The largest single cost is the tax equalization burden which is treated in detail in chapter 12. For our purposes it is enough to note that the Japanese tax authorities tax resident aliens on world-wide income after five years and treat all of the benefits received by the expatriate employee as taxable income, including tax equalization payments. Few companies can afford to keep an expatriate employee in Japan for longer than five years because of this "tax on tax" spiral.

Unfortunately, this happens to be just about the period of time it takes for the employee to develop a sound base of knowledge and the network of contacts and personal relationships necessary for doing business in Japan. Repatriating the employee at this critical point can be devastating to the company in a country like Japan where so much attention is paid to human relationship and the bonds of trust that facilitate the smooth functioning of business. It could well be argued that it is the height of folly for companies to think, as some seem to do, that these relationships can be easily and automatically passed on to the next person sent out to replace the repatriated employee. Few companies could flourish in their home markets operating in this fashion and it is unclear why so many think it is possible to penetrate the Japanese market with such tactics.

There is a negative effect to all of this as well within the company. Japanese employees catch on quickly to the fact that foreign managers are not around long enough to be a permanent force in the local business and affairs of the company. The short-term expatriate manager cannot, due to the language barrier, fully understand the complete inner workings of the company, nor control its destiny. Efforts to do so may be perceived as meddling with and disturbing the harmony of the group. This can lead to an unhealthy stratification of the company and, in particularly bad cases, a polarization of forces that is only relieved when the foreign manager is repatriated. Japanese employees are quite skillful at "waiting out" unpopular foreign managers.

At the same time, it is important to realise that having employees from the headquarters stationed in Japan is critical to developing a unified corporate culture. The inability of many Japanese to express themselves fluently and comfortably in English (and the inability of foreign managers to do the same in Japanese) can result in a major communication gap. The gap increases if employees from both the local company and the head office do not have the opportunity to work together on a daily basis. The Japanese way of doing things, business and otherwise, is very different from that in the West. It takes many hours of patient listening and observing to understand what is really being said by employees and customers. This understanding cannot be obtained by phone, fax or periodic trips out to the region. There is no substitute for being on the scene full-time.

Dispatching a senior, and well respected, executive from the head office is particularly critical at the start-up stage of any new venture. This is the time when new Japanese employees must be hired and trained in the company's culture and way of doing business. New employees need to observe first hand the course set by the head office management, if not the company is likely to drift in unintended and undesirable directions.

Many companies make the mistake of trying to start out from scratch with a local Japanese president. The president is the most important person in a Japanese organisation and commands great respect and loyalty. The president is literally the human face of the company both to the employees and to the outside world. Picking the wrong person will set the company back many years and will cost a great deal of time and money to correct. Equally disastrous is picking a Japanese out of the misguided belief that the company needs a Japanese president and then emasculating the president by not giving him the authority and discretion traditionally attached to the position. The time for appointing a local president will come after the operations of the company have been stabilised and then only assuming a highly qualified and trustworthy person can be found. The best situation of all is to have the first local president emerge naturally from the ranks of the senior managers recruited and trained by the company. In this way the senior management in the home office knows and is comfortable with the new president and the new president is in the same position with respect to the practices, policies and products of the company.

The time is ripe for companies to reconsider the basic philosophy of expatriation. A good starting point would be to examine the underlying operative tenet of most expatriate policies, i.e., the company should provide a complete package of salary and benefits so as to enable the employee and his/her family to duplicate in Japan the lifestyle in their home country, irrespective of cost. This is fallacious. Tokyo is not Peoria and to turn a foreign assignment, which many would consider sufficient incentive by itself, into a lavish life divorced from the lifestyle of the ordinary Japanese employees in the company, sends the wrong message to the expatriates and to the local employees. Moreover, local employees cannot fail to miss the irony of cost-cutting programs instituted during hard times by foreign managers living in $15,000 a month apartments.

Japan is an exciting and challenging place to live and work with rewards that cannot be calculated in terms of the comparative cost of a market basket of goods and services. Companies need to identify people from inside and outside of the company who are willing to make a long-term commitment to Japan. This market demands no less.

CONCLUSION

The most critical resources of any company are its employees. This is doubly so in the case of a foreign enterprise where home office management must rely so deeply on the local staff to be its eyes and ears, and interpreter. There are few functions within a company which require more time and care at the outset as the selection of competent personnel, both local and expatriate. The time and effort exerted at the beginning of operations must continue for the duration of the company's presence in Japan. Vigilance is rewarded with success, and neglect with disaster.

In closing, it is well to reflect on the words of advice offered by Miyamoto Musashi, a legendary swordsman and master strategist of 16th century Japan. Musashi likened strategy in battle to the work of a master carpenter when he wrote in his famous *Book of Five Rings* as follows:

"The foreman carpenter must know the architecture theory of towers and temples, and the plans of palaces, and must employ men to raise up houses. The Way of the foreman carpenter is the same as the Way of the commander of a warrior house.

"In the construction of houses, choice of woods is made. Straight un-knotted timber of good appearance is used for the revealed pillars, straight timber with small defects is used for the inner pillars.

"Timber of the finest appearance, even if a little weak, is used for the thresholds, lintels, doors, and sliding doors, and so on. Good strong timber, though it be gnarled and knotted, can always be used discreetly in construction. Timber which is weak or knotted throughout should be used as scaffolding, and later for firewood.

"The foreman carpenter allots his men according to their ability. Floor layers, makers of sliding doors, thresholds and lintels, ceilings and so on. Those of poor ability lay the floor joists, and those of lesser ability carve wedges and do such miscellaneous work. If the foreman knows and deploys his men well the finished work will be good.

"The foreman should take into account the abilities and limitations of his men, circulating among them and asking nothing unreasonable. He should know their morale and spirit, and encourage them when necessary. This is the same principle of strategy."[12]

To the timeless words of Miyamoto Musashi could be added the final sentence: "This is the same principle of human resource management."

---

[1] John O. Haley, *Authority without Power Law and the Japanese Paradox* (Oxford University Press, 1991).

[2] Japanese law does not possess the doctrine of equity in the same manner as Anglo-American law. Nevertheless, the deep concern on the part of Japanese legislators, bureaucrats and courts for fairness and reasonableness often produces the same *de facto* result.

[3] *Labour Administration Seeking a More Comfortable Life for Workers* (Ministry of Labour Japan, 1993) at p. 1.

[4] The first page of the evening edition of the *Nihon Keizai Shimbun* on December 26, 1995 reported that unemployment in Japan reached its highest point at 3.4% in the month of December. The rate had held steady at 3.2% for the months of October and November.

[5] It is a common attribute of bureaucratic practice in Japan to refuse to accept a filing with which the relevant ministry or administrative office does not agree. This makes even the routine notification provisions of Japanese law *de facto* approval standards.

[6] The work rules of many companies provide that the retirement allowance may be withheld if the employee is discharged for cause. It is unclear whether a courts would honor this type of provision even if a company sought to utilize it which would be highly unusual in any event.

[7] Richard Wiltshire, Relocating the Japanese Worker (Japan Library; 1995) at p. 2.

[8] Professor Wilshire has surely overstated the case since a company can only unilaterally require an employee to move if such a move would be within the reasonable expectation of the employee. Likewise, the company does not have the unilateral right, at least as a matter of law, to unreasonably change a worker's job assignment.

[9] The Japan Times

[10] As a result of the harsh economic climate in Japan, formal Labour disputes rose to record levels in 1995. Yoichiro Hamabe, 12 UCLA Pacific Basin Law Journal (Spring 1994) 306, 312.

[12] Miyamoto Musashi, *A Book of Five Rings* (The Overlook Press; 1974; transl. by Victor Harris) at pp. 41–42.

As noted previously, the retirement allowance is payable regardless of the reason for separation of the employee from the company. Many companies provide in their work rules for forfeiture of all or a portion of the retirement allowance in the case of dismissal for cause and/or for actions resulting in material damage to the company. This type of provision in the work rules is rarely invoked and it is highly doubtful that any court would permit a forfeiture absent the most egregious of circumstances.

A recent article in *The Japan Times,* an English language daily, reported that a survey of 1,396 graduating university students conducted by a magazine specialising in recruiting, found that students sent cards to approximately 199 companies this year and ended up visiting nearly 25 companies in pursuit of a job.

CHAPTER 9

PRODUCT DISTRIBUTION, THE ANTIMONOPOLY LAW AND PRODUCT LIABILITY
by Yoshikazu Takaishi

OVERVIEW

Japan has one of the most complex distribution systems in the world. This distribution system alone has been perceived by many foreign analysts and manufacturers to be the most significant barrier to penetrating the Japanese market. Distribution is responsible for providing roughly one out of six jobs in Japan, and provides nearly 15% of domestic production[1]. The system is often criticised for being inefficient and costly, in many cases adding nearly 50% to the price of the identical product sold outside of Japan.

Distribution channels contain many layers, and are tightly controlled. The product moves from the factory to the trading company, and then on to the large wholesaler, who will deliver the product to the chain of smaller wholesalers that might be one to four wholesalers deep, or directly to one of the hundreds of thousands retail outlets. The larger wholesalers seem to be the most efficient channel, as they usually sell to larger retailers such as supermarket chains, who in turn can offer the product to consumers at a lower price.

The relationship between manufacturers and distributors is extremely close, exceeding those of any other country in the world. Distribution *keiretsu* (affiliated companies) dominate the system. Basically, the distribution *keiretsu* consists of a manufacturer, which often owns all or some portion of the stock of the related distributors, a bank and various suppliers. In this sense, the distributor is often simply an extension of the manufacturer itself. For this reason, the distributor has traditionally carried only the manufacturer's goods and excluded other competitors' products, resulting in a network that is closed to new or unrelated companies, foreign or local. Building a distribution network from scratch is extremely difficult and takes years, making joint ventures look very attractive to foreign companies, who can only enter the market by utilising the existing distribution networks of their Japanese counterparts.

Such a grouping allows the manufacturer to create a uniform image through coordinated publicity, marketing research, etc. Manufacturers can also gain useful feedback from these distributors, as distributors may loan salespeople to large retailers, who can see firsthand how products perform, what improvements can be made, as well as what products are missing or in demand. Furthermore, this control of the distribution network encourages resale price maintenance. Japanese manufacturers often have a network of 50 to 500 primary wholesalers who exclusively carry that manufacturer's products. The wholesalers cater to the retail stores many of which are also effectively controlled by the manufacturer. By controlling most of the wholesale and retail outlets in the marketplace, a manufacturer can impose fixed prices for its goods and increase its profits.

While distribution *keiretsu* are not present in every sector of the market, they dominate the ones in which they appear, and outlets exclusively deal with one brand or name. The household appliance and consumer electronics sector provides a useful illustration: In 1991, Matsushita had approximately 27,000 stores, Toshiba 14,000, Hitachi 12,000, Sanyo 6,000, Sharp 5,800, and Mitsubishi 5,500.[2] Very few of these stores carried other brands, and fewer still carried foreign brands. Automobiles, motorcycles, cosmetics, watches, and eyeglasses all are dominated by similar retail outlets, and the market share is reflected in the number of retail outlets owned by the manufacturer.

Westerners think this system is very strange; you can walk into any J.C. Penney's in the U.S. or Curry's in England and find every major brand of consumer electronics on sale, and usually there are salespeople who can explain any product they carry. The same is not true in Japan, where you must visit different shops to see different brands. Department stores in Japan do carry different brands, but the selection is not as extensive as in the West and these department stores cannot compete with the smaller retail outlets where manufacturers have exclusive distributorships. It is rare for these Japanese department stores to have trained salespeople, since manufacturers often refuse to cooperate with non-exclusive distributors.

WHOLESALERS

The gateways to the Japanese market are wholesalers and trading companies. They are frequently multilayered, and products reach the retailer only after passing through at least two and as many as five wholesalers, depending on the type of product and manufacturer. Wholesalers generally fall into one of three types: functional, geographic, or product. Functional wholesalers usually specialise in foreign or domestic goods, or occupy a specific position in the distribution chain as primary, secondary or tertiary wholesalers. Geographic wholesalers concentrate on either a specific region or the entire nation. Product-specific wholesalers tend to focus on a specific regional comparative advantage, such as pearls or kimonos or fish; namely whatever the region produces in abundance and at a competitive cost. Of course, there are combinations of these types.

While manufacturers often operate wholesale distributorships, it is not uncommon for the wholesaler to own small manufacturing companies or to loan storage facilities, managerial or marketing know-how or other assistance to manufacturers. Wholesalers often provide invaluable financial assistance to manufacturers in procuring raw materials and perform break bulk functions to allow the many smaller retailers to purchase smaller quantities of merchandise that otherwise would be unavailable to them. Again, the storage facilities of the wholesaler are vital to the distribution network, this time on the retail side, as real estate prices prevent the smaller retail stores from maintaining larger inventories. Similarly, the demand for smaller purchases has created the need for secondary and tertiary wholesalers, who serve these small retailers.

The wholesale distribution network in Japan is built on very close ties at the business and social levels, with personal relationships maintained through frequent visits and elaborate courtesies. These relationships far outweigh short term profits or sales targets. There is generally not such strong pressure on retailers to sell products. Wholesalers, on the other hand, are expected by retailers to assist in developing new retail business, and are pressured by manufacturers to remain competitive in price and product lines.

Introducing a new product illustrates the importance of these relationships. Often an entirely new distribution system must be created to support a new product, and even when existing channels are used, it is still a costly process. Meetings between major wholesalers and the manufacturer are held across the country to receive input from wholesalers as to effective marketing of the product. To this end, the distribution network serves as a market research tool. A more important function of these meetings, however, is to strengthen and develop existing and new relationships with wholesalers.

Regardless of the manufacturer's willingness to bear introductory costs of new products, it is customary for wholesalers to insist on improvements to the product. If improvements are not made, competitors will enter the market and the efforts of the wholesaler will be wasted. This is of particular importance in the case of imports where feedback and improvements may not be practical. It will be extremely difficult for wholesalers to resist carrying a Japanese competitor's product when offered through their long-standing supplier. The Japanese market strategy of incremental product development is in direct conflict with the giant leap forward approach toward innovation.

Wholesalers are also expected to supply support staff to retailers to promote new products, as they are thoroughly trained to promote and explain the product to customers. Although these staff wear the uniform of the retail store, their salary is paid by the wholesaler. The wholesaler is also expected to offer a generous return policy to retailers, covering damaged goods as well as goods that don't sell. This is mainly to help small stores that can't sacrifice valuable floor space to low turnover inventory. Because of the lack of storage space and its associated cost, the responsiveness of suppliers is of paramount importance, particularly for foreign suppliers. A reliable, quick response often is more desirable than a lower price.

Wholesalers play a significant role in financing the distribution network. Extended payment terms are common, with promissory notes that range from 90 to 120 days being the norm. Wholesalers also maintain a complex system of rebates to manufacturers and downstream wholesalers. Wholesalers receive rebates from manufacturers of 2–5% for invoicing and collecting from downstream wholesalers and retailers. Similar to the U.S., cash discounts of 3% are generally offered for payment within 30 days. Quantity discounts of 1–2% are common for certain minimum orders, and although the wholesaler can easily accumulate high discounts in this manner due to their storage capacity, such rebates often must be passed on to retailers, for cooperation in promotion, keeping the number of returns low, etc. Some wholesalers are completely disconnected from actual distribution activities, but serve only to finance other wholesalers and act as a clearinghouse for manufacturers.

The wholesale sector is undergoing significant changes. During the 70s and much of the 80s, the wholesale sector grew rapidly, with the increase in wholesale businesses outpacing the increase in personnel. This means that most of the growth was in small wholesalers, resulting in longer distribution chains and higher markups.

In recent years, however, growth in this area of the wholesale sector has nearly stalled. The annual growth rate of small wholesalers has slowed to only 0.35%, and the growth rate for employees is down to 1% annually.[3] The result is that the size of wholesalers is now increasing for the first time in nearly 30 years.

Wholesalers are responding to this trend by engaging in horizontal and vertical integration, and it is common for wholesalers to merge with manufacturers. Typically, such a firm will manufacture some items, but subcontract the vast majority of its product line. This is often seen in the apparel industry, where manufacturers absorb wholesalers, but the opposite also occurs, i.e. a wholesaler will acquire the manufacturer and lean toward the retail side of the distribution chain.

Such integration may threaten imports in the future, unless foreign manufacturers are bought up, as horizontal and vertical integration, in typical *keiretsu* style, to encourage group members to purchase from within the family of companies. Even if imports are purchased, these purchases may be short-term and opportunistic until the manufacturing arm of the group begins producing a competing product.

Apart from structural changes, wholesaling is also experiencing new patterns. Population shifts to cities are congesting urban areas, causing increased problems for storage and transportation. Increases in the standard of living and greater varieties of products are placing greater demands on wholesalers. Due to the increasing responsibilities to finance downstream wholesalers and retailers, wholesalers are experiencing diminishing returns on their investment.

The Japanese government has responded by sponsoring joint ventures between small firms, large warehouse companies and distribution terminals in order to create improved storage facilities. These new centres include distribution warehouses, display space, office buildings and ample parking space. Tall warehouse buildings with direct truck access have been constructed to utilise space more efficiently, and are fully climatised and automated to a great extent. Administration of such centres also provides maintenance, security and other services. As a result, tenants need only be concerned with their specific rented space, and have less responsibilities than in the past. This government involvement has helped streamline the industry. Wholesalers now need less storage space within crowded urban areas, and require far fewer employees than in the past.

Manufacturers themselves are forming their own retail groups in order to offer a variety of products, and in many cases have eliminated the wholesale chain and now deliver directly to the retailer.

The recent trend towards order consolidation, particularly in warehousing zones, is solving wholesalers' increasing inability to provide delivery service in urban areas. New transportation companies are being formed specifically to handle consolidated orders.

Consolidation orders cut transportation costs by 30%–60%. By delegating transportation responsibilities to outside firms, wholesalers can focus on providing financing, break bulk, and provide assortment services to their downstream wholesalers.[4]

Regional wholesalers are decreasing in number, particularly in the consumer product areas, as many smaller manufacturers cannot compete with larger firms, and larger manufacturers generally do not need financing provided by regional wholesalers. The existing regional wholesalers, instead of bringing products from their region to consumption centres, now more often are bringing products from those areas to distribute in their respective regions. In the high technology product area both the nation-wide and regional distributors are more frequently used.

Traditional business relations in the wholesale sector are changing with everything else. The time-honoured tradition of close business ties is giving way to more temporary arrangements, with switches being made when financially necessary. Cash-and-carry wholesalers are growing in number. By eliminating their financing functions and catering only to retailers who can make payment at the time of delivery, such wholesalers have cut their cost and can now sell and deliver products at lower prices. These wholesalers buy from small manufacturers, select suppliers based strictly on price, and refuse to accept returns, offering to discount slow-moving items instead. Generally, these wholesalers do not carry national brands as many large manufacturers refuse to sell to them. No personal relationships are developed and no bonuses or rebates are generated. Frequent customers for these wholesalers are small retailers who purchase small quantities on a daily basis. Despite their fast and loose business style, these distributors often turn over inventory 30 times annually, compared to an annual turnover of seven for conventional wholesalers of equal size. As these wholesalers usually handle their own importing and exporting, they can be excellent gateways to the Japanese market for foreign manufacturers.

RETAILERS

Retailing in Japan is an extremely difficult and competitive business, as Japanese consumers are among the most demanding customers in the world. Products must be of high quality, food items must be fresh, clothing must fit exactly, and there is no tolerance for defective merchandise. Service is vital to the survival of any retailer, large or small.

Retailers are categorised as to the type of store and/or products carried. Stores usually fall under the classification of department stores (*depato*), superstores or supermarkets (*supa*), general merchandise stores, specialty stores or convenience stores. Each of these types of stores may specialise in the types of products offered, i.e. food, clothing, consumer electronics and household appliances, etc.

Department stores generally offer products at higher prices and carry luxury goods. Specialty items are also usually marketed in department stores, with outside vendors frequently occupying space within the department store and paying sales commissions to the store and possibly rent for their floorspace.

Superstores or supermarkets and general merchandise stores are quite similar in nature but differ in size. Both offer products at lower prices. A few leading supermarket chains in Japan are Daiei, Itoh-Yokado and Seiyu. These stores have incorporated general merchandise stores into their operations. Generally these stores sell food items on the bottom floors and household products on the top floors.

Specialty stores can be found selling virtually any type of product, from household goods or consumer electronics to luxury items such as jewellery. Others specialise in selling bulk quantities to keep prices low.

Convenience stores occupy the vast majority of all retail stores in Japan. These are neighbourhood stores, often "mom and pop" operations that cater to a very small geographical area. They are able to compete with the larger stores for a variety of reasons. The prices at these convenience stores are competitive because of low overheads, and these stores offer services to customers that larger stores do not. Because most Japanese consumers shop by train, bicycle or on foot, they do not want to travel far and cannot carry large amounts of goods over significant distances, so the neighbourhood convenience store is the preferred choice. Also, because the neighbourhood store serves a social function and Japanese homes generally do not have much storage space, the average Japanese consumer prefers to shop at the neighborhood convenience store twice per week. The sheer number of convenience stores in Japan undercuts the number of large retailers, so that the largest Japanese retailers are very small when compared to their counterparts in other countries.

Service is very important to the success of a Japanese retailer, and retailers demand the same high level of service from wholesalers and manufacturers that they must in turn supply to their customers. Retailers require wholesalers to provide financing in the same manner that wholesalers require extended payment terms from manufacturers. Retailers make the same efforts to build relationships with customers as wholesalers seek to establish ties with retailers.

Despite all the support that retailers receive from wholesalers and manufacturers, the retail business in Japan is not easy, and retailers are highly competitive in the service they provide to consumers. Great attention is paid to packaging and wrapping, particularly during the gift-giving seasons during July and December. Store personnel carefully check every part of the product for defects, and defective or damaged products will not be sold, even if the consumer wants it, because it is believed that such a sale would threaten the long-term satisfaction of the consumer and therefore damage the store's reputation.

Retailers organise purchasing clubs for their customers, whereby a customer registers with the store and his/her purchases are tracked. When a customer reaches a certain level of purchases, a bonus is awarded. This also provides the retailer with valuable feedback as to a particular customer's taste or preference.

Competition makes service and customer satisfaction more important to Japanese retailers than in other countries in the area of food sales. The Tsukiji fish market in Tokyo, for example, supplies more than one fourth of the Japanese population with fresh fish and seafood on a daily basis! Grocers demand equally tight delivery schedules of their farm producers to guarantee freshness, often within several hours of harvest.

Imported products are sold primarily through department stores and superstores or supermarkets, because of their significantly shorter wholesale distribution chain and increased buying power. Imports until recently have cost more than domestic products, so as a result most smaller stores have marketed primarily domestic items to consumers who rely on the small store's competitive prices.

Imports constitute between 10% and 20% of sales of department stores and supermarkets or superstores. Large retailers may import directly from the foreign manufacturer or indirectly through a trading house or agent. In the case of direct import, the cost of importing generally costs about 30% to 40% of the price of the imported product, and includes import duties, freight, insurance, ground transportation costs and customs fees. Given a retail markup of 100%, this increases the shelf price to 260%–280% of the manufacturer's price. In the case of indirect imports, the cost is even higher, with trading houses and agents increasing the price to well over 300% of the manufacturer's price.[5] This generally forces retailers to cut their sales margin to remain competitive, so direct importing is far more popular among large retailers, who often form importing groups with each other.

Just as the wholesale sector is undergoing change, the retail sector is experiencing numerous changes and restructuring.

Convenience stores and specialty stores have traditionally provided employment for workers who have reached retirement age but do not have sufficient resources to stop working. These people often take their lump sum retirement payments and open convenience stores or small specialty stores. Many specialty shops that carry only one brand name product are family operations. These types of stores are usually in small buildings, with the proprietor living in an apartment above or behind the storefront. However, in the area of technology, the small family operations have not been able to provide the high level of customer support demanded by the Japanese consumer. While able to explain and demonstrate the next generation rice steamer or portable radio, it is very difficult to keep up with advances in personal computers and CD ROM viewers. As a result, elderly storekeepers who retire are not replaced. Instead, manufacturers rely more on larger retailers and superstores.

LARGE-SCALE RETAIL STORES ACT

Small retailers have traditionally relied on the government to protect their markets from larger, better capitalised retailers. This protection has been implemented largely through the Large-Scale Retail Stores Act (LSRSL) and its predecessors, dating back to the 1930s. MITI cited industry rationalisation and consumer protection as goals for the LSRSL when it was passed in 1974. The law guarantees small retailers an enterprising opportunity, and also requires due consideration to consumer interests and the well-being of the retail industry as a whole.

The law, which was a sticking point in the Japan-U.S. Structural Impediments Initiative (SII) talks, requires retailers who wish to open large stores to seek approval from local retailers. Strong opposition from these retailers can in some cases prolong the process indefinitely. Local retailers, of course, cite among their reasons for opposition the loss of customers, and their fear of being forced to close their stores. Community local assemblies dominated by local retailers have routinely passed resolutions opposing revision or abolition of the LSRSL.

The procedural requirements of the LSRSL are fairly simple and straightforward. Persons wishing to construct a building with more than 1500 square metres (454.5 *tsubo*) of retail space and prospective retailers have to notify MITI under the LSRSL of their plans. If MITI determines that opening the new store would have a significant impact on local small and medium retailers, it has four months to issue a recommendation that the prospective retailer delay the proposed opening date, decrease the floor space, or otherwise modify its plans.

During these four months, MITI has to solicit the opinion of the Large-Scale Retail Stores Deliberative Council at the regional level and the Commercial Activities Adjustment Board (CAAB) established within the local chamber of commerce, both groups consisting of retailers, consumers, and other representatives of the public interest. The board investigates local conditions, negotiates with the prospective large retailer regarding possible changes to its plans, and reports to the regional council, which in turn gives its opinion to MITI. Acceptance of a recommendation by the prospective large retailer is voluntary, but Article 8 of the LSRSL gives MITI the power to order compliance if necessary to protect the interests of local retailers. Legislators intended for the entire process to take no more than eight months.

From the outset, however, the law was implemented with little adherence its formal structure. The shift from the permit system of the prior Department Store Law to the notification system of the LSRSL was supposed to mean that government intervention would be the exception rather than the norm, and free market principles played a role in convincing large retailers to support the law. At the same time that MITI was espousing free market principles to the large retailers, it was also ensuring small and medium sized retailers that the notifications system would operate in the same fashion as the previous permit system. This latter promise proved to be the rule, and the LSRSL created a system that placed significant barriers to entry by large retailers into retail markets that far surpassed any imposed under the previous Department Store Law.

Local governments responded by passing ordinances and issuing administrative guidance that restricted stores even if floorspace was less than 1500 square metres, and small retailers pushed hard for tighter restrictions on retailers entering the industry. In 1977, the Diet passed a resolution urging action to protect small retailers, and the following year amended the LSRSL to apply to stores with as little as 500 square metres of floorspace. Two classifications were created for retail stores under this amendment; class one stores were those with more than 1500 square metres and class two included stores with floorspace between 500 and 1500 square metres. MITI followed in 1979 by issuing administrative guidance that required Article 3 notification be given to MITI 13 months prior to the proposed opening date rather than the statutory seven months.

Regardless of such tough measures, there was an increasing number of store openings in 1979 and 1980, so small retailers pressured government to return to the permit approach of the Department Store Law and regulation of stores according to the type of retail activity as well as floorspace. This new requirement was in response to the new chain convenience stores that threatened local family run neighbourhood convenience stores by operating 24 hours per day. In 1982, MITI again issued administrative guidance that required builders of class one retail stores to explain their plans to local merchants before notification to MITI.

MITI increasingly began to refuse to "accept" Article 3 notification unless the builder appended a document setting forth terms to which the local retailers unanimously agreed. With such veto power in the hands of local retailers, it became common for negotiations to take seven to eight years, and sometimes delays continued for more than 10 years. The opening of any store could be made financially unattractive. Often, a new store could only be opened if the local merchants were included as subtenants or large "donations" were made to local merchant groups.

The overall results of this system was that the opening of large stores plunged and foreign firms pressured their respective governments to address this barrier to entry in trade negotiations. The international business community, both inside and outside of Japan, pushed hard for the repeal of this law and an end to related administrative guidance. MITI responded by both denying the inhibitory effect upon foreign firms but also promising to change the law.

Finally, in 1990, in large part due to the SII talks, MITI announced a number of changes to the LSRSL and its administration. The length of the application process was to be limited to a maximum of 18 months, store expansions of 100 square metres or less that were designed for the promotion of imports were exempt from the process altogether, regardless of the total floorspace in the store after expansion, and local governments were to adjust their policies to comply with these new measures.

The measures have been enacted to a large extent, and major retail stores such as Toys "R" Us from the U.S. were able to open in Japan beginning in 1991. Opening the retail sector to any increased participation by new, larger competitors is likely to have an adverse impact on smaller retailers, which as mentioned before, are a major source of post-retirement employment in Japan. The number of retirees will rise sharply over the near term in Japan, and given the combination of changes to the Large Scale Retail Stores Act and manufacturers' increasing preference to deal with larger stores, it is entirely possible that there will be serious pressure again from powerful voting blocks to pass legislation to protect Japan's small retailers.

Japan's political institutions are already rallying against the new measures that help large stores open in Japan. Japanese unions as well as the Ministry of Home Affairs, have been voicing opposition. Conflict within MITI is also visible, when one examines MITI's industrial policy for the 90s. The Ministry calls for restrictions on further congestion of Tokyo by limiting government support for large-scale projects, cutting demand for new land, and transferring authority from national government to local governments.

Existing larger retailers must struggle to maintain their position in the marketplace. Department stores, superstores and supermarkets are focusing on operating more efficiently and improving their business. More of these stores are importing directly, relying less on trading houses and agents. Direct imports account for nearly half of all imports retailed in Japan.

New forms of retailers are emerging as well. Chain stores, discount stores, and non-store retailers are growing in number. While discount stores are successful mainly because of their prices, chain stores and no-store retailers offer the convenience and service of the traditional neighbourhood stores. Chain stores are typically located in residential areas, are open long hours, and carry a limited range of goods needed on a daily basis. Customers for these stores are usually working couples or singles, people who do not have time to shop in larger stores. Stores are usually franchised to individuals, who receive training and support from the chain in the area of store management, service and stocking techniques.

Centralised purchasing is the dominant feature of these chains. Despite the small size of individual stores, the combined stores often are the largest purchasers of a given manufacturer. However, despite the economies of scale reached through such purchasing power, chains still directly import relatively few products, and rely on trading houses and agents for imported items. However, technology may play a role in stimulating direct importing, as detailed inventory tracking systems may indicate customer preferences that outweigh long-standing supplier relationships as these convenience chains move away from fresh foods into products with longer shelf life.

The increase in non-store retailing has been the other significant change to the retail industry, usually through direct marketing. Direct marketing generally takes one of three forms, namely door-to-door sales (*Homon Hanbai*), mail-order sales (*Tsushin Hanbai*) and chain sales (*Rensa Hanbai*). Recently, door-to-door sales and mail-order sales have sharply increased. Door-to-door sales does not necessarily mean only sales recruiting from a door-to-door visit. Sales outside the seller's office, store or other business locations are defined as "door-to-door sales" under the Direct Sales Law. Mail-order sales are those through mail, telephone, fax or electronic mail and the like. Chain sales has been defined as "Sales of goods or services under the conditions that a purchaser shall bear the specific economic burden the amount of which shall be ¥20,000 (roughly US $200) or more with a solicitation of the purchaser".

The term "chain-sales" was perhaps initially adapted from the term "multi-level-marketing", which has a very unique and specific meaning in Japan. It is often expressed as "multi business" and has negative connotations. This is because many Japanese multi-businesses in the past imitated the U.S. "multi-level-marketing", which closely resembled pyramid schemes, without adopting the business philosophy, ethics and practices of the U.S. model. As many Japanese multi-businesses tried to make huge profits over the short term without adequate management capability or experience, they eventually went into bankruptcy.

Many people who paid sums of the yen equivalent of US$1,000 to $10,000 not only did not gain the economic benefits promised, but were also unable to recover their initial investments. This became a serious social issue. A large number of such unethical or even illegal multi-businesses were organised in the 1980s and 1990s and many of them went into bankruptcy. MITI, the ministry in charge, in response defined multi-business as a bad-nature business in its commentary on the Direct Sales Law. Due to negative public opinion and stringent government control and vigilance, it is now almost impossible for a multi-business to succeed in Japan.

Another rapidly emerging form of direct sales is the mail-order business. This type of direct sales is fairly new in Japan and has become popular over the recent years. Direct sales have become more and more popular in Japan, first, due to high store cost and, second, many women now work and no longer have sufficient time to shop. As mail-order sales increase, problems also increase. Therefore, MITI has just started a study to amend the Direct Sales Law mainly in the area of mail-order sales.

In order for a foreign direct sales company to be successful in the Japanese market, it should have (1) products with good quality and service, (2) a good management system, (3) a good educational system for its sales representatives, and (4) good business practices including a warranty. Consultation with experts in the direct sales industry is advised prior to entry to the Japanese market — particularly with respect to the legal and regulatory focus.

Amway is the most successful direct sales company in Japan. Although popular in the early 80s, growth in the area of door-to-door sales has nearly stalled, primarily due to Japanese culture, which is less open to home visits by strangers, and also because more Japanese women are currently employed. Amway has experienced growth rates of 50% and still its annual sales growth has been in double digits in recent years. It is now one of the largest American companies in Japan. Its sales volume is the second largest, next to Coca Cola, among foreign companies. Amway's sales in Japan account for more than 50% of its total world-wide sales.

Another successful foreign direct marketer is Franklin Mint of the U.S. Franklin Mint uses printed advertisements to attract new customers and direct mailings to communicate with its customers. Like Amway, one of Franklin Mint's largest markets is Japan.

The mail order business has grown very rapidly in recent years in Japan, with annual growth rates of around 17%.[6] In a recent survey by MITI, 72% of married women polled indicated that they had purchased merchandise through catalogues, and half of these women answered that they had made purchases within the last year.[7] In 1989, the postal service discounted mailing rates, which led to a sharp increase in catalogue retailers.

Regardless of all this growth, mail order retail is still in its infancy in Japan. There are only 2000 to 3000 companies engaging in mail order sales presently, and mail order sales only account for 1% of retail sales in Japan.[8] Domestic firms dominate this market, with foreign firms accounting for less than 1% of the market.[9]

Mail order items commonly include furniture, clothing, sporting goods, jewellery, cassette tapes and shoes, with most products in the ¥10,000 to ¥40,000 range. Regardless of the relatively small market share of foreign firms, several retail chains have developed mail order service for imported goods, with some stores stocking catalogues for several different foreign retailers. For example, Yunyua, the mail order department of the Seiyu chain, offers catalogue service for Sears, L.L. Bean, Sheplers, Tiffany, Bloomingdales and many other foreign retailers. A customer visits the Seiyu store, browses through the catalogue, and makes a selection. The selection is checked for air mail availability, the purchase is made in yen, and the customer returns in several weeks to pick up the merchandise.

Technology has also been introduced to catalogue sales. Matsuzakaya, a Nagoya based department store, has an arrangement with a German department store where the two stores are connected by direct satellite link. Catalogue purchases are transmitted directly via computer terminals located in the stores, and after checking availability on the on-line system, the merchandise can be shipped with a very early delivery date of less than two weeks.

In the works is the World Shopping Network, another technological marketing wonder. Based on data communication links between Japan and other nations, this network is built on a database of foreign products and suppliers, and provides access to department stores and supermarkets around the world. The network is also linked to major credit card companies and financial institutions around the world to facilitate payment.

Television shopping is also highly advanced in Japan. MITI has supported a two-way interactive cable television service by HI-OVIS, which allows transmission of voice and picture. Customers can dial up and order videotape, and retail functions are offered as well. Companies rent timeslots to explain their products and interact with viewers. A teleshopping program is transmitted during which viewers can examine merchandise and compare prices.

The Fuji Television Network carries a successful teleshopping program that offers foreign products directly to the Japanese audience. Viewers can call a toll-free telephone number to order the product directly from the television network's Fujisankei Living Service, which handles payment, delivery and import.

Despite the technological advances that have fuelled this recently developed branch of the retail sector, significant impediments keep the mail order business from becoming a major marketing tool. Mailing costs remain quite high, and mailing lists are less available than in other countries such as the U.S. where they are bought, sold and rented. Few of the mailing lists in Japan are computerised, and there is no standard format as in other countries as the use of four different alphabets (*hiragana, katakana, kanji and romaji*) make standards nearly impossible. However, given the convenience and growing acceptance of such retail methods, and the size of the market, non-store retailing are expected to blossom in the future.

LAWS RELATED TO MARKETING

OVERVIEW

The Japanese legal system is a civil code system based on the German legal system. After World War II, however, the Japanese legal system has been very much influenced by the U.S. legal system, particularly in the area of the tax and economic regulatory laws such as antitrust, securities exchange transactions, labour laws and so forth.

With respect to marketing contracts, freedom of contract is the basic guiding principle. An oral agreement is valid and binding under the Japanese legal system. There is no requirement of consideration as found in Anglo-American law. The freedom of contract has been one of the driving legal forces together with the negligent liability theory and the absolute protection of private ownership of property to develop and enhance capitalism in Japan. However, as freedom of contract can sometimes lead to social and legal troubles, the government has enacted various laws and regulations to address problem areas, real or perceived. A company which comes under an applicable regulatory scheme must strictly comply with these regulatory laws. Below are brief explanations on each of the major applicable regulatory laws.

ANTIMONOPOLY LAW

One of the safeguards installed after World War II to protect markets in Japan was the Antimonopoly Law of 1947. There were no such laws before the war, and in fact, prewar legislation permitted and in some cases rather encouraged cartels and monopolies. Enacted at the behest of the Occupation Forces, and reflecting largely foreign values, the Antimonopoly Law is often at odds with accepted business practices. This is one of the reasons why cartels are still prevalent in Japan. The free enterprise system became one of the goals of postwar reforms, and accordingly the Antimonopoly Law became a fundamental piece of legislation for industrial development in Japan. However, this law has never been strictly enforced in Japan because of policy conflict.

The Japanese government adopted the so-called industrial policy under which certain industries were identified for rapid development and the products developed and manufactured in such a industry are required to be world class in quality and price competitiveness. To achieve this goal, the government enacted laws for the promotion of such identified industries under which the government was authorised to give a subsidy for R & D of new technologies and provide low-interest and long-term government loans to the designated companies and industries. Such designated or "strategic industries" were protected by the industry promotion law. This law gave the government the power to restrict excessive domestic competition which might be destructive to a young strategic industry. The industry promotion often contained an antitrust exemption clause.

There was another set of laws to completely control foreign companies doing business in Japan. The first was the Foreign Investment Law (FIL), abolished in 1980, and the Foreign Exchange & Foreign Trade Control Law (FEL) which continues in force today. Under the FIL, all investments (minor exceptions were gradually given at the later stage of this law) must be approved by the competent government bodies such as MITI and the Ministry of Finance (MOF). The government can attach various restrictions as conditions to an approval of certain foreign investments. Such conditions include, inter alia, the governmental approval for an expansion of manufacturing facilities, and the manufacture and/or sale of new products. The government willingly approves a new foreign investment into Japan where such a foreign company brings valuable technologies into the Japanese market and, more importantly, where such a foreign company is willing to license its technology to Japanese competitors. The Japanese competitors aggressively reverse engineer the products of the foreign company brought into the Japanese market in order to implement the licensed technology more effectively and efficiently. To identify the strategic industry and the government assistance required — a subsidy, low-interest loans, the legislation of industry promotion law with an antitrust exemption clause, etc. — the government established the so-called Industrial Structure Council (*Sangyo Kozo Shingikai*, its abbreviation is *Sanko Shin*) as a consultative body to MITI. *Sanko Shin* has consisted of industry leaders, influential scholars, opinion leaders, and government bureaucrats. This nation-wide cabal of government and industry utilises skills, knowledge and power to raise strategic Japanese industries to world-class. All of the Japanese industries which have been successful have benefitted from the Japanese government's industrial policy, including, among others, the steel, shipbuilding, textile, automobile, computer, and semiconductor industries.

The Japanese industrial policy which restricts competition in the industry, particularly by foreign companies, completely contradicts the antitrust policy which encourages free competition. Since the Japanese government previously put priority on the industry promotion policy, the Antimonopoly Law was superficial and was never vigorously enforced. The 1947 Antimonopoly Law was one of the most advanced antitrust laws in the world at that time. However, since the strict enforcement of the Antimonopoly Law would have made Japanese industrial policy more difficult, if not illegal, a series of revisions were made to weaken the law.

Japan's economic success on the world market, however, has made it difficult for Japan to continue its protective industry policy. Japan-U.S. SII talks have been effective at focusing attention on Japanese industrial policy. The role of *Sanko Shin* has been greatly changed since the mid 1980s.

The Antimonopoly Law prohibits three types of conduct as anti-competitive: private monopoly, unreasonable restraints on trade which is synonymous to a cartel as interpreted by the Japanese courts, and unfair trade practices.

PRIVATE MONOPOLY

The Antimonopoly Law was originally based on conduct, and not on a dominant market position in and of itself. Therefore, the Law did not address the natural monopoly position enjoyed by a single enterprise or a few big enterprises, as usually referred to in economic theory. The Law was concerned instead with behaviour aimed at attaining, maintaining, or strengthening the monopolistic position by excluding or controlling other entrepreneurs.

"Private monopoly" is defined in the Law in Article 2(5) as follows: "The term 'private monopoly' as used in this Law shall mean such business activities by which any entrepreneur, individually, by combination of conspiracy with other entrepreneurs, or in any other manner, excludes or controls the business activities of other entrepreneurs, thereby causing, contrary to the public interest, a substantial restraint of competition in any particular field of trade." The language "excludes or controls" refers to restraints on the free decisions on business activities of an excluded entrepreneur by unilateral or combined actions of a single entrepreneur or group of entrepreneurs to the extent that the excluded or controlled entrepreneur is forced to comply with the excluding or controlling entrepreneur(s), or leave the market.

According to Article 2(5) of the Law, private monopoly exists if the excluding or controlling conduct of the entrepreneur is the cause of substantial restraint of competition in a particular field of trade. Three concepts must be examined here. The restraint must be "contrary to public interest," it must result in a "substantial restraint of competition," and it must involve "a particular field of trade."

There is no clear definition of what is "contrary to public interest," however, the opinion held by most courts, legal scholars, and most importantly, the Japan Fair Trade Commission (JFTC), is that public interest in connection with the Antimonopoly Law is primarily concerned with the maintenance of competition in the marketplace.

Hence, the public interest is threatened whenever competition is restrained in any market.

"Substantial restraint of competition" occurs when there is a decrease in competition as a result of an entrepreneur or group of entrepreneurs being able to effectively control the market by controlling the price, supply or quality of products as well as other business conditions. There is no objective criteria in determining the existence of such market control, but evaluation must include the prevailing economic conditions surrounding the conduct in question.

"A particular field of trade" means "the relevant market", as that term is commonly used in connection with the U.S. antitrust law. The market can be geographical, or product or service-related. There is no numeric standard by which an entrepreneur is determined to have a dominant power in such a market.

Any situation where the net result of action of an entrepreneur or group of entrepreneurs is to effectively eliminate competition is considered a violation of the Law. Entrepreneurs holding dominant market positions who sell below cost to drive out competition, or maintain predatory pricing policies that discriminate on the basis of geographical distribution or different kinds of customers are possible violations; causing a company to comply with another company's decision through stockholding or interlocking directorates is another possible violation. Restrictive covenants which deny access to distribution channels or sources of raw materials also constitute "exclusion" under the definition of private monopoly if competition is substantially reduced. Finally, if a manufacturer enters agreements with its distributors which restricts these distributors from purchasing and reselling products of competing manufacturers, then the dominant manufacturer may be in violation of the Law by engaging in the exclusion of the business activities of other entrepreneurs.

While private monopoly under the Law traditionally referred to conduct, Section 8-4 of the revised Act of 1977 empowers the JFTC to take action against a monopolistic organisation, even if the firm achieved its market position through ordinary business practices and did not engage in any prohibited conduct. Under this provision, when the JFTC determines that a monopolistic situation exists it may order the enterprise concerned to transfer a part of the business or take other measures necessary to restore competition.

A "monopolistic situation" is defined as a situation where the total amount of sales of goods and services of the same and similar description during the latest one-year period exceeds ¥50 billion; the market share of a single entrepreneur is above 50% or a combined market share of two entrepreneurs is above 75%; it is extremely difficult for other entrepreneurs to enter the market; and the price of particular goods or services has experienced a sharp increase or decrease marginally over a period of time, despite changes in costs and fluctuations of supply and demand, during which time the entrepreneur has experienced a very high profit margin or very high selling and administrative costs.

Enforcement of the Antimonopoly Law, especially ordering the transfer of business, is considered drastic action and only occurs as a last resort, and the JFTC may not order such measures where such a measure is expected to reduce economies of scale, weaken the entrepreneur's financial position or make it difficult for the firm to remain competitive on an international scale, or where other measures may be taken to restore competition.

Further revisions to the Act of 1977 empowers the JFTC to request reports justifying price increases from enterprises in an oligopolistic market – especially if such enterprises raise the prices of their products by a similar amount or rate within three months of each other. The reports may be required only when the total sales of the products supplied in Japan exceed ¥30 billion and the combined market share of the three largest firms exceeds 70% of market share.

Interlocking directorates of companies in Japan are prohibited in the case where they substantially restrain competition in any particular market. Every director of a company who concurrently holds a position as officer in another domestic company engaged in competition with the first company, must, where the total assets of either of the companies exceeds ¥2 billion, file a notification with the JFTC within 30 days of the date of assuming such director position

Mergers or acquisitions are prohibited where their effect may be to substantially restrain competition in any particular market or where unfair trade practices have been employed. Furthermore, any firms proposing a merger or acquisition of a business must file a notification with the JFTC at least 30 days in advance of such action, and the JFTC is required to take action within that 30-day waiting period if it determines that such restructuring violates the related provision. Stock acquisitions by individuals or corporations are prohibited if the acquisition may substantially restrain competition in any particular market or where unfair trade practices have been employed.

The original Antimonopoly Law prohibited stockholding by any company other than a financial company if the competition in a particular market was substantially restrained. This provision was thwarted by the growing trend toward affiliation or grouping of companies, so Section 9-2 of the Act of 1977 was added in order to prevent giant groups of non-financial companies from acquiring massive amounts of stock. Section 9-2 provides that any stock company whose business is other than financial services and whose capital is larger than ¥10 billion or whose net assets exceed ¥30 billion shall not acquire or hold stock of companies if the total acquisition price of the stock of the Japanese companies it has acquired or holds exceeds its capital or assets, whichever is larger. The original Antimonopoly Law also prohibited a financial company, including foreign financial companies, from acquiring or holding stock in a domestic company in excess of 10% of the total outstanding stocks of the issuing company. The revised Act of 1977 reduced this limit to 5%, with an exception for insurance companies, which rarely have close relations with other companies through deposits or exchanges, and supply only occasional long term credit. They are considered in character to be similar to a mutual fund supplier. Insurance companies were allowed to retain the old 10% limit.

UNREASONABLE RESTRAINT OF TRADE (CARTELS)

Article 2-6 of the Law defines "unreasonable restraint of trade" as follows: "The term 'unreasonable restraint of trade' as used in this Law shall mean such business activities by which entrepreneurs by contract, agreement, or any other concerted activities mutually restrict or conduct their business activities in such a manner as to fix, maintain, or enhance prices; or to limit production, technology, products, facilities, or customers or suppliers, thereby causing, contrary to the public interest, a substantial restraint of competition within any particular field of trade." This definition would include collusion by entrepreneurs which results in a substantial restraint of trade in a particular field of trade contrary to the interests of the public. For this reason, "unreasonable restraint of trade" is synonymous with "cartel." The Japanese courts have uniformly interpreted this term in the same way. This prohibition is concerned only with horizontal agreement among competitors. Restriction on business activities of the parties to an agreement, contract, or undertaking must be mutual. Therefore, a vertical agreement or contract made between a buyer and a seller does not fall under the definition of "unreasonable restraint of trade."

Cartels are permitted under the Antimonopoly Law in certain situations. Article 24-3 provides an exception for a depression cartel agreement between manufacturers when the price of their product drops below the cost of production and it would be difficult to rectify the situation through rationalisation. Entrepreneurs wishing to form such a cartel agreement must first limit the quantity of production, and only after demonstrating that such measures fail to overcome the depression can they receive permission to fix prices.

Article 24-4 permits rationalisation cartels. Entrepreneurs wishing to enter agreements to build or operate special facilities may file a request with the JFTC, and proceed once permission has been granted.

Other laws besides the Antimonopoly Law allow certain types of cartels. The Export and Import Transactions Law permits the creation of an export and import cartel under MITI's supervision. The Small and Medium Business Organisation Law allows cartels between small and medium entrepreneurs, and the Marine Transportation Law allows tariff agreements to be executed among shipping companies. The Insurance Business Law allows insurance companies to make agreements which unify and standardise insurance policies. As long as agreements are allowed by specific laws of this type, they are exempt from the Antimonopoly Law.

It is very difficult to prove the existence of a cartel. Cartels are usually formed on verbal agreement, the type of tacit communication that occurs in oligopolistic markets that results in agreements among large-scale manufacturers regarding price, quantity, and other business terms. Material evidence such as written contracts, correspondence, or minutes of board meetings are difficult to secure, if in fact they even exist. There is no effective private cause of action and discovery is severely limited.

The existence of uniformity as the result of unilateral acts by entrepreneurs is not sufficient to establish an unreasonable restraint of trade. There must exist some collaborative intent among the persons involved. However, the JFTC has recently investigated and revealed large scale cartels in the construction industry, electric industry and others. If the JFTC were to seriously investigate a cartel, it would likely be successful in proving its existence even if there is no written documents as evidenced by the recent cases.

Trade associations are carefully watched by the JFTC, as they are composed of entrepreneurs in a particular industry and often function like a cartel. As trade associations are frequently responsible for various restrictive acts toward competition, Section 8(1) specifically prohibits the following acts by trade associations:

(a) Substantially restraining competition in any particular field of trade;

(b) Entering into an international agreement or an international contract which contains provisions as provided for in Section 6(1) (described below);

(c) Limiting the present or future number of entrepreneurs in any particular field of business;

(d) Unjustly restricting the function or activities of the constituent entrepreneurs;

(e) Causing entrepreneurs to employ such acts as will constitute unfair trade.

A "trade association" is defined as "any combination of two or more entrepreneurs or federation of such combinations, having as its principle purpose the furtherance of their common interest as entrepreneurs." There is no requirement that the trade association be a legal entity. However, organisations having equity capital shares for profit such as joint sales companies are subject to the same control as entrepreneurs and are not considered trade associations. Trade associations, except for various cooperative associations, are required to file notice of their formation with the JFTC.

Section 6(1) prohibits entrepreneurs from entering into an international contract or agreement which includes matters that constitute unreasonable restraint of trade or unfair trade practices. Entrepreneurs in Japan who have entered into an international contract or agreement are required to file notice with the JFTC within 30 days from the date of execution of such contract or agreement. Specific types of international contracts or agreements were designated by the JFTC Rules No. 1 issued in 1971 for the notice requirement. The rules specify six different categories of contracts or agreements:

(i) Technological tie-up contract or agreement: A contract or agreement between a domestic entrepreneur and a foreign entrepreneur, involving the transfer of intellectual property rights, such as patent rights, utility model rights, licensing of any of these rights or licensing of know-how, etc. for a period of more than one year.

(ii) Continuous sales contract or agreement: A contract or agreement between a domestic entrepreneur and a foreign entrepreneur related to sales transactions of objects to be resold to a third party to be conducted continuously for a period of more than one year.

(iii) Joint venture contract or agreement: A contract or agreement between a domestic entrepreneur and a foreign entrepreneur related to joint management of a business through holding stocks and shares of a company to be conducted for a period of more than one year.

(iv) Trademark right or copyright contract or agreement: A contract or agreement between a domestic entrepreneur and a foreign entrepreneur related to the transfer of rights of a trademark or copyright (including neighbouring rights) or the licensing of such rights for a period of more than one year.

(v) Continuous sales contract or agreement involving domestic entrepreneurs in a competitive relationship with one another: A contract or agreement between domestic entrepreneurs who are in a competitive relationship with each other and a foreign entrepreneur related to sales transactions to be conducted continuously for a period of over one year.

(vi) Export or import restricting contract or agreement: A contract or agreement between a domestic entrepreneur and a foreign entrepreneur (who are in a competitive relationship) involving continuous restriction on business activities relating to export or import such as restricting prices, quantities, or areas in export or import trading.

UNFAIR TRADE PRACTICES

Unfair trade practices when employed by individual entrepreneurs violate Article 19 of the Antimonopoly Law. Trade associations causing their individual members to employ such practices violate Section 8 of the Antimonopoly Law.

"Unfair trade practices" are those specifically enumerated in the JFTC's "General Designation on Unfair Trade Practices of 1982." The earlier version (Notification No. 11 of 1953) specified 12 practices that were banned by the Antimonopoly Law, and the amendments made in 1982 completely replaced this list with a second version (Notification No. 15 of 1982) with a total of 16 practices. The 1982 version refined and sub-divided the practices into more specific types.

There are six basic types or categories of restrictive trade practices: unjust discriminatory treatment, unjust pricing, unjust inducement or coercion, dealing on unjust restrictive terms, abuse of dominant bargaining position and unjust business interference.

There are also two groups of classifications, one which applies generally to all industries and another containing specific designations that pertain to specific areas or industries, such as to patent and know-how licensing agreements, or industries such as canned food, newspaper publishing, and department stores. The latter group is subject to the Specific Designation on Unfair Trade Practices with respect to Newspapers, Department Stores and so forth.

Designations in the category of unjust discriminatory treatment include activities such as boycott or collective refusal to deal, individual refusal to deal, price discrimination, discriminatory treatment on transaction terms, and discriminatory treatment by a trade association. The existence of any of these actions does not constitute a violation per se, and each designation is qualified with language such as "without proper justification" or "unreasonable." Such activities do not violate the Antimonopoly Law if it can be shown that the discrimination or refusal to deal in question is an act of self defence, or that price fluctuations between geographical locations are the results of higher costs, etc.

Designations in the area of unjust pricing include activities such as selling products or services below cost or purchasing a commodity or service at a high price in order to drive competition out of the market. These designations are also violated only when such action is "unjust."

Unjust inducement or coercion of customers of a competitor includes activities such as deception, offering benefits which are unjust in the light of normal business practices, and unjustly causing a trading party to purchase a commodity or service from oneself by tying the purchase to the supply of another commodity or service.

Designations related to dealing on restrictive terms include unjustly dealing with a trading party on the condition that the trading party does not deal with a competitor, or supplying a commodity or service to a trading party while imposing certain restrictive terms without justification.

Abuse of dominant bargaining position is conduct which unjustly creates disadvantage for the other trading party, preventing that party from freely competing and thereby reducing competition in the particular market in which the parties are involved.

Unjust business interference includes interference with a competitor's transaction or internal operations that hinders or obstructs fair competition by lowering prices or raising quantities, generally by inducing, abetting, or otherwise coercing a stockholder or officer of the competitor.

Certain exemptions have been made in the Antimonopoly Law. Exemptions exist for activities related to railways, electricity, gas and other industries which by their nature constitute public utility monopolies. Where there is special legislation for a specific industry, the Antimonopoly Law does not apply to the legitimate acts of an entrepreneur or trade association that are in accordance with the specific legislation. Any conduct that is in accordance with rights granted by the Patent Act, Utility Model Act, Copyright Act, Design Act or Trademark Act also is exempted from application of the Antimonopoly Law, as long as the conduct does not exceed the legitimate scope of rights granted by the respective law.

OTHER COMPETITION LAWS AND REGULATIONS

In addition to the Antimonopoly Law which forms the main substantive body of Japanese antitrust law, there are other competition laws and regulations. The Antimonopoly Law mainly addresses an abuse of the monopoly power on the supply side as is the case with many other country's antitrust laws. However, Japan enacted a law to prevent a delay of payment to a subcontractor in 1956 which prohibits an abuse of dominant power on the purchaser side. As explained above, large-scale purchasers or distributors who purchase goods and/or services on the large scale from small/medium manufacturers or suppliers have a dominant procurement power over the suppliers. Therefore, this law prohibits an abuse of such power just like a prohibition of an abuse of supplier's dominant power. This law has been separately enacted from the Antimonopoly Law.

Another important competition law is the Undue Prizes and Undue Representation Law (enacted in 1962). This law along with its supporting regulations and notifications restrict the amount of prizes or premiums which can be offered to the public in connection with the sale of goods or services. There are two methods of restricting the amounts of prizes so that an excessive or unhealthy competition can be avoided by an escalation of prize wars with disregard for quality or value of goods or service itself. One method is to restrict the maximum amount of each individual prize. This approach is taken when a prize is given to all purchasers. Another method is to restrict the maximum aggregate amount of the total prizes. This method is applied to the prizes which will be given based on a prize competition.

OTHER LAWS RELATED TO MARKETING

There are many other laws which may regulate or restrict freedom of contract and marketing activities. Following is a very brief description of these laws. Those who are interested in details of such laws and regulations must check the relevant laws and regulations.

UNFAIR COMPETITION LAW

The original law was enacted in 1940 before the Antimonopoly Law, with the purpose of prohibiting unfair competition by creating confusion in the marketplace by using confusing or deceptive trademarks, logos, trade names, containers, wrappings, or indications of other famous merchandise, confusing or misleading representation of the function or quality or shapes similar to other's goods, or misappropriating or infringing other's trade secrets. This law partially has a similar purpose to the Antimonopoly Law. Its competent ministry (MITI) is different from that of the Antimonopoly Law (JFTC). The two laws have not been integrated and co-exist under separate bureaucratic regimes today. The significance of this law is that it protects trade secrets under Articles 2 to 8. The relief against unfair competition under this law are (1) injunctive relief, (2) damages and (3) measures for restoring a business reputation of the damaged.

PRODUCT LIABILITY LAW

This law became effective as of July 1, 1995. The Japanese PL Law was drafted using the EC Product Liability Directive as its model. However, the Japanese PL Law is more lenient to a manufacturer than the EC Directive. The law contains only six articles. The law recognises the strict liability of the manufacturer, importer or other persons who are statutorily regarded as "manufacturers" (Art. 3). The state of arts defense and a defense of the manufacturer's instruction where a part or components contain a defect due to the manufacturer's instruction are recognised (Art. 4). The statute of limitation on the claim of damages is three years from the time when the injured person becomes aware of the damage and the liable party for the damage, or the expiry of a period of 10 years from the time when the manufacturer delivered the product (Art. 5).

Other civil remedies available under the Civil Code can be utilised together to supplement the PL Law (Art. 6).

DIRECT SALES LAW

This law has been explained earlier. Reflecting an excessively high cost of store or office space, direct sales are sharply increasing in Japan. Therefore, this law is expected to become increasingly important in the future, especially for foreign companies desiring to enter the Japanese market.

FOOD HYGIENE LAW AND THE PHARMACEUTICAL LAW

There are stringent laws controlling the quality of foods and drugs. If a violation is found, the government has the power to suspend a sale of such a merchandise, suspend a business, or order a recall of defective merchandise.

ENVIRONMENTAL PROTECTION LAWS

Japan has enacted stringent environment protection laws. Therefore, a product which may pollute air, water or land, or manufacturing plants which may produce such pollution are subject to the Air Pollution Control Law (Law No. 97 of 1968, as amended), the Water Pollution Prevention Law (Law No. 138 of 1970, as amended) and the Noise Control Law (Law No. 98 of 1968, as amended). When a product becomes industrial garbage or waste, the Law concerning the Industrial Wastes may be applied (Law No. 137 of 1970). Particularly, TV, audio equipment and other electric and electronic waste are potentially hazardous waste which may damage the environment and must be disposed in accordance with this law. Normally the responsibility is imposed on the consumer. However, if such a product contains harmful chemical substance such as PCB, or displays radiation, the manufacturer may be ordered to collect such industrial waste.

CONCLUSION

The Japanese law and practice relating to marketing and distribution obviously differ greatly from law and practice in other countries. Traditional practices, and the latest technology, co-exist to create an environment many outsiders will find difficult to deal with. Japanese consumers are among the most demanding in the world, and have traditionally held a deep distrust of foreign companies and products. Western companies wishing to enter Japanese markets would be well advised to learn from companies already operating in the market, and to take the advice of lawyers and consultants experienced in dealing with Japan.

---

[1] Czinkota, Michael R. & Woronoff, Jon *Unlocking Japan's Markets*, Charles E. Tuttle Company, 1991, pp. 75.
Takahide Shiotani, "Outline of Japanese Distribution System," *Business Japan*, August 1988; pp. 89–94.

2   Czinkota, Michael R. & Woronoff, Jon *Unlocking Japan's Markets*, Charles E. Tuttle Company, 1991, pp. 62.
The Economist, September 9, 1989, pp. 28.
3   Czinkota, Michael R. & Woronoff, Jon *Unlocking Japan's Markets*, Charles E. Tuttle Company, 1991, pp. 112.
Commercial Census (Tokyo: Ministry of International Trade and Industry, 1981–1989).
4   Czinkota, Michael R. & Woronoff, Jon *Unlocking Japan's Markets*, Charles E. Tuttle Company, 1991, pp. 114.
5   Czinkota, Michael R. & Woronoff, Jon *Unlocking Japan's Markets*, Charles E. Tuttle Company, 1991, pp. 103.
Retailing in the Japanese Consumer Market (Tokyo: JETRO Marketing Series 5, [undated]) pp. 42–3.
6   Czinkota, Michael R. & Woronoff, Jon *Unlocking Japan's Markets*, Charles E. Tuttle Company, 1991, pp. 125.
7   Czinkota, Michael R. & Woronoff, Jon *Unlocking Japan's Markets*, Charles E. Tuttle Company, 1991, pp. 125.
"Japan's Distribution System: The Next Major Trade Confrontation?" *Japan Economic Institute*, March 17, 1989, pp. 8.
8   Czinkota, Michael R. & Woronoff, Jon *Unlocking Japan's Markets*, Charles E. Tuttle Company, 1991, pp. 125.
Retail Distribution in Japan, Tokyo: Dodwell Marketing Consultants, 1988, pp. 45.
9   Czinkota, Michael R. & Woronoff, Jon *Unlocking Japan's Markets*, Charles E. Tuttle Company, 1991, pp. 125.
U.S. International Trade Commission Report, pp. 43.

CHAPTER 10
CUSTOMS LAW AND THE IMPORT AND EXPORT OF GOODS

by George L. Miller

INTRODUCTION

Key to the effective and efficient cross-border transportation of goods are the controls placed on international trade through the imposition of customs regimes. These include not just the administration and regulation by customs bureaus, but also the myriad of trade law and regulations promulgated and administered by a plethora of governmental bodies, all in the name of fostering some goal or policy deemed to be in the interest of the regulating country.

In the case of Japan, not unexpectedly, the customs regime is complicated, difficult to master, potentially time-consuming and unavoidably expensive. This chapter explains the major elements of border entry and exit controls Japan has imposed on international trade. Daunting as the Japanese regime may appear to first-time importers, the reader should be encouraged to learn that, in most cases, imports and exports can be efficiently processed in Japan.

The Customs Bureau of the Ministry of Finance is the entity charged with enforcing border regulation of international trade in Japan. The Bureau is authorised to permit the import and export of goods under the Customs Law and to collect duties and taxes on imported goods under the Customs Tariff Law. Those laws form merely the underpinnings of the Bureau's control of trade and are, in and of themselves, relatively simple. Complexity upon complexity are layered on through Cabinet Ordinances, regulations and administrative practice that impose considerable paperwork requirements and, hence, processing delays and expense. Imported goods in particular are subject to stringent controls and regulation every step of the process from the moment of arrival until the final release from the unique-to-Japan *hozei* warehouse.

It is unfair to lay the blame solely on the Bureau for the cost and time required to effect customs clearance in Japan. For many commodities, the permit and licensing requirements (which, not surprisingly, are directed largely at imports and not exports) — imposed by no less than 30 statutes, ranging from the Explosives Control Law to the Forest Seeding Law — are the real culprits.[1] The

Bureau is easiest to blame as, under law, it may not release imported goods until all paperwork requirements are satisfied, including import permits and licenses. The permit and licensing requirements can be, in many cases, impossible to overcome and in all cases are time consuming and expensive. Fortunately, the permit and licensing requirements apply to comparatively few product classifications.

IMPORT PROCEDURES

REGULATORY AGENCIES

In addition to the Bureau which administers the Customs Law, and collects duties and taxes under the Customs Tariff Law, there are other agencies that, depending on the commodity, can influence the clearance process. The basis for regulation of trade by Japanese agencies derives from the Foreign Exchange and Foreign Trade Control Law (FEL). The FEL establishes the foundation for control over imported goods and imposes on various government bodies the obligation to establish specific trade regulations. These bodies include:

Ministry of International Trade and Industry — MITI's influence on trade, especially imports, remains significant despite a reduction of its impact on economic policy generally in Japan. MITI remains the primary source of standards, sets import quotas and administers trade regulation. For example, Import Notices promulgated by MITI are the single most important source of import quota regulation.

Ministry of Health and Welfare — Like most countries, Japan places special emphasis on laudable public policy objectives like the safety and security of foodstuffs, pharmaceuticals, cosmetics and electrical appliances. MHW administers the myriad regulations in Japan controlling ingredients and formulations of foods, drugs, cosmetics and appliances. Import licenses for regulated items must be obtained from MHW. MHW labeling and package marking requirements must also be satisfied.

Ministry of Agriculture, Forestry and Fisheries — MAFF regulates the trade of plants and animals. For example, the Staple Food Control Law grants MAFF regulatory control over such foodstuffs as rice and wheat. Certain regulated items require licenses issued only by MAFF.

While the above-mentioned ministries provide the lion's share of regulation, other agencies, including the Ministry of Posts and Telecommunications, the Japan Salt and Tobacco Public Corporation and Prefectural Labour Standards Bureaus, have similar powers for a smaller universe of goods. Determining which agency to contact and at what level for licenses and permits is a difficult task best left to professional customs clearance brokers.

IMPORT PROCEDURES AND REQUIREMENTS

The Japanese approach to procedural regulation of imports is tripartite. There are three fundamental players directly regulated in the import process: the carrier, the warehouse operator and the customs broker (representing the importer). Regulations strictly controlling the actions of each player ensure total control by the Bureau over the import process through a stringent system of checks and balances.

Goods on arrival in most cases are transported to a *hozei*, similar in many ways to a bonded warehouse.[2] There they remain until release instructions are given, separately, to the carrier, warehouse operator and broker. On arrival at the warehouse, the goods are "bonded in" and the necessary paperwork for clearance is prepared by a customs broker.

Paperwork requirements can be summarised as follows:

(i)   A commercial invoice and certificate of origin are required in all cases. Note that invoices must be signed in duplicate on the shipper's letterhead. Certificates of origin are required if the importer wishes to take advantage of preferential tariffs; in some cases U.S. origin goods can obtain the benefit of preferential tariffs without this certificate.[3]

(ii) Depending on the commodity, import licenses/permits, import quota allocation certificates and/or phytosanitary certificates may be required.

(iii) The Importer Identification Number is required for clearance under Japanese automated clearance systems.

(iv) Brokers will often require a power of attorney to act on behalf of a consignee.

Brokers are instrumental in gathering the required paperwork although some items, such as import licenses, may require significant participation on the part of the consignee and, in many cases, the shipper as well.

Brokers will also prepare a "Declaration" which states the particulars of a shipment and formally "declares" to the Bureau the existence of the goods and the desire to import same into Japan.[4] Included with the Declaration is a classification of the goods by the broker and a rating of the goods to determine the appropriate duties and taxes to be paid. The Declaration, with supporting paperwork, is filed with Customs officers who review the declaration and may actually inspect the goods themselves. Goods that are actually inspected by a Customs officer are relatively small in proportion to the total amount of goods imported. The Bureau imposes selection standards that vary from time to time. Goods that fall within these standards will automatically require inspection.

Release of goods in the form of a "permit to import" is not given by the Bureau until duties and taxes have been paid and a receipt evidencing payment is produced. Duties are calculated in accordance with the Customs Tariff Law.[5] Taxes vary depending on the commodity. At a minimum, the Japanese Consumption Tax of 3% is levied. Other taxes, ranging from a Liquor Tax to a Playing Cards Tax, may be applied in lieu of or in addition to the Consumption Tax.[6] Depending on the agreement negotiated with the broker, the broker may advance duties and taxes on behalf of the importer thereby speeding up the clearance process.

Clearance time is heavily dependent on the nature of the commodity, mode of transport and proficiency of the broker. In the normal case, goods arriving by surface transport may require between five and 16 business days for clearance from the date of arrival.[7] Air shipments may require between one and a half and five business days.[8] Some air express shipments can be cleared within hours. Items requiring licenses or permits are sometimes significantly delayed due to a failure by the importer to provide on time the required paperwork and information. Once again, it must be pointed out that the actual time required by the Bureau to effect clearance is relatively minimal. Delays and expense are primarily due to: (i) the cumbersome relationship among the three players in the clearance process, (ii) the passing of reams of paper among these players, the Bureau, the importer and the responsible ministry, and (iii) import licensing and permit requirements.

IMPORT LICENSES

Import licenses are obtained through foreign exchange banks and are required for the following commodities[9]:

- toxic substances
- explosives
- pharmaceuticals
- salt
- chemicals

– high pressure gas
– alcohol
– quota items

Licenses are not issued where proof of compliance with licensing requirements is absent. With some commodities, this could require significant discussion, and in some cases, negotiation with the appropriate regulator. Brokers often play an instrumental role in obtaining required licenses and permits.

QUOTA ITEMS

Certain goods are subject to import quotas.[10] These include agricultural products, arms, fishery products, farm products under government food control systems (i.e. rice), narcotics and processed foods. For goods covered by quotas, importers must obtain from MITI prior to importation an import allocation certificate. Handling of quota items can be quite complicated.

QUARANTINE ITEMS

Certain items, primarily perishables like fruits and vegetables, require phytosanitary certificates issued by the appropriate regulator.[11] Even with such certificates, items may be subject to quarantine requirements on arrival. Plants, soils, animals and meats all require certificates and are subject to quarantine on arrival pending inspection by the Bureau. In general, clearance procedures for perishable products are expedited. Once again, use of customs brokers often is necessary to ensure fast and accurate clearance.

TECHNICAL STANDARDS

Technical standards imposed by MITI and other regulators are a constant source of friction for exporters to Japan.[12] These standards, arguably imposed for the sake of safety, must be satisfied before the Bureau will issue a permit to import. Brokers can assist in completing the paperwork requirements in many cases, but for certain goods, the importer will have to rely on technical consultants to work through bureaucratic reluctance to approve goods that have attributes not well known in Japan.

POSTAL MATTERS

The import clearance system for postal matters is completely different from that imposed on general cargo. The self-assessment system (see discussion that follows) is not used for postal matters. Items arriving by mail are reviewed individually by inspectors employed by the Bureau. Duties are assessed item by item by Bureau employees and not brokers. This discrepancy in clearance procedures, especially in a marketplace that has postal authorities acting more and more like private enterprise in providing value-added transportation services normally associated only with the private sector, has resulted in a much lower level of adherence in the case of postal matters to import license requirements and the collection of duties and taxes. The Bureau simply does not have the manpower to provide the same level of clearance scrutiny that is provided for non-postal imports through the self-assessment system which requires the necessary assistance of a great many professional and highly trained customs brokers.[13]

DUTIES AND TARIFFS

ASSESSMENT PROCEDURES

With certain minor exceptions, the Japanese duty collection system is based on the principle of "self-assessment".[14] The importer, in its declaration to the Bureau, determines the correct amount of duty to be paid. The Bureau will accept this declaration, subject to its right to investigate more closely and impose an amount it deems to be correct. Exceptions to this general rule include: (i) unaccompanied goods; (ii) postal matters; (iii) countervailing and anti-dumping duties; and (iv) items for which duties have been pre-assessed. In the foregoing instances it is the Bureau that determines the correct amount of duty after examination.

VALUATION OF GOODS

The importer's declaration must state the value of the goods imported. The value must be a CIF (Cost, Insurance, Freight) value.[15] The Bureau may challenge the value stated in the importer's declaration. In determining an appropriate valuation, the Bureau will first look at the sales price between the buyer and seller and add on a reasonable charge for transportation and insurance. Where it is impossible to ascertain the sales price between the buyer and seller, the Bureau will compare the goods at issue with transaction costs of similar imported goods.[16] Failing that, the Bureau will look at the selling price for domestic goods of a similar nature. In the extreme case, the Bureau may request a special Cabinet Order as to the appropriate valuation and/or duty.

DUTY AND TARIFF RATES

Japan employs the Harmonised Commodity Description and Coding System in coding imports for the purpose of determining applicable duties. The "Harmonised Tariff" system has been designed to aid the free flow of international trade by providing exporters and importers with some certainty as to the amount of applicable duties. One need only know the Harmonised Code number of a specific good to calculate the appropriate duty in any country adopting this classification system.

Tariffs are based on the schedules promulgated under the Customs Tariff Law (CTL).[17] The CTL provides special duty rates for personal effects as well as special valuation methods for various types of imported goods including special imported goods (goods that cannot be valued using the methods stated above), and deteriorated or damaged goods.

Japan is a member nation of the World Trade Organisation. Japan is also a member nation of the General Agreement on Tariffs and Trade. Japan offers Most Favoured Nation status to the majority of its trading partners, including the United States. Japan also offers preferential tariffs to many developing nations.[18]

COUNTERVAILING AND ANTI-DUMPING DUTIES

Japan imposes special duties to protect domestic producers: countervailing duties and anti-dumping duties. The actual practice in Japan results in infrequent use of these protective devices, but countervailing and anti-dumping investigations, primarily undertaken by MITI, are not unheard of.

Countervailing duties are imposed on imported goods having the benefit of a subsidy in production/sale and which (i) threaten to cause material injury to an industry in Japan; or (ii) may retard the growth of a particular industry in Japan.[19] Countervailing duties are actually surcharges that are applied on top of the tariff rate that would otherwise apply to the goods in question. The amount of the surcharge is generally equal to (but not more than) the amount of the subsidy granted in respect of the goods. Any person having an interest in the import of goods meeting the scrutiny criteria stated above may bring to the government's attention a claim of injury, either actual or threatened. The government will make appropriate investigations, which must be concluded within one year of commencement. The government, prior to completing an investigation but after a finding of fact or reasonable inference that a subsidised import has caused or threatened material injury, may demand from the importer a security in the amount of estimated countervailing duties. Upon the completion of the investigation, the security will be released, less any countervailing duties actually assessed.

Dumping is the sale of goods for export at a price that is less than the price of similar goods in ordinary commercial transactions in the exporting country *and* where the importation and sale of such goods in Japan may cause or threaten injury to industry in Japan. The Bureau may impose anti-dumping duties on offending goods equal to the difference of the "normal" value of the goods and declared value of the goods on import. Anti-dumping duties are imposed in addition to tariffs otherwise imposed on the imported goods and are payable by the importer. Procedurally, anti-dumping investigations are nearly identical to countervailing duty investigations.[20]

HOZEI SYSTEM

The Japanese *hozei* system has been a source of much confusion and the target of some United States regulators who want to open the Japanese market to imported goods. The *hozei* system itself is logical and not unlike bonded warehouse systems found throughout the world. Much of the confusion over this system and its characterisation (perhaps unfairly) as a trade barrier lies not so much with the system itself, but with the manner in which Japanese regulation forces the three major players in the import process (the carrier, the warehouse and the broker) to interact through the *hozei* system.

In the *hozei* system,[21] all products imported into Japan must be held in a government licensed bonded area, a *hozei*, from the point of disembarkation until formal customs clearance release. The imported goods must be retained in the *hozei* until appropriate duties are paid and clearance is effected after all paperwork is in order. While in the *hozei*, the goods are deemed to be under the control of Customs (but risk of loss is generally shared by the carrier and the warehouse operator as a matter of contract).

There are instances when imported goods may not have to be held in a *hozei*. Unforeseeable circumstances like accidents or damage to the goods, or excess imports leaving no room in established *hozei* may require alternative, temporary storage. Temporary landings due to ship/aircraft breakdown may require temporary warehousing. In these instances, the captain of the vessel is charged with the safekeeping of the goods and must report the nature of the incident and disposition of the goods without delay. Special fees and charges may be imposed in the event temporary warehousing outside a *hozei* is required. The goods must be removed from the temporary warehouse within the period designated by the Bureau. If the goods fail to reach the designated location, the importer will be assessed duties.

The *hozei* system consists of five categories: *Hozei* Bonded Area; *Hozei* Shed; *Hozei* Warehouse; *Hozei* Manufacturing Warehouse and *Hozei* Display Area. Activities permitted in each different type of *hozei* are mandated by law, but more than one activity may be undertaken in any given *hozei* type after receiving special approval from the Bureau. For example, *hozei* are not typically meant to be a location for the checking, sorting or packing of goods, but these activities are often conducted in *hozei* with the permission of the Bureau so long as the activities do not interfere with the statutory mandated functions of that particular *hozei*.

In most instances, *Hozei* bonded areas are generally located in premises owned or administered by the government or alternatively, premises designated by the Ministry of Finance (of which the Bureau is a part). The persons authorised to conduct, control and administer activities in a *hozei* that has been designated by the Ministry of Finance must follow strict operational guidelines as designations can be revoked at the Ministry's discretion.

Hozei sheds are used for the temporary storage, loading, unloading and transportation of imported goods. The purpose of sheds is to provide a location at which imported goods can obtain customs clearance in a prompt manner. Imported goods may not remain in the *Hozei* shed for more than one month.

Hozei warehouses are long term storage facilities where imported goods may be held for up to two years after entry approval (not to be confused with customs clearance) is granted.

Hozei manufacturing warehouses are bonded areas at which imported goods may be processed or manufactured upon permission of the Bureau. Imported goods can generally be kept for no more than two years in these facilities. If domestic goods are used in combination with imported goods in the manufacturing process in these facilities, the domestic goods may be recharacterised as imported goods and the value thereof may be taken into account in determining the final import price of the manufactured good for the purpose of determining the appropriate duty.

Hozei display areas are places at which imported items may be exhibited or demonstrated. The Bureau will determine the period of time any given imported item can remain in a display area. If the imported item is not removed within the approved time period, the Bureau may assess duties on the item from the approved date of removal.

EXPORT REGULATION

Export regulation in Japan is noticeably less arduous than import. Nonetheless, the Bureau imposes a stringent export clearance system to ensure compliance with applicable law and regulation. Like import procedures, there are many players in the export process, with more than one law and ministry having a hand in the process. Generally, however, export processing, when left to the hands of professionals, is relatively fast.

REQUIRED DOCUMENTATION

Export processing requires a contract for carriage, commercial invoices and, where required, export licenses. In certain instances, Inspection and Design Certificates are required for export clearance. For certain goods, the permit to import from the destination country may also be required.

REGULATED ITEMS

The following items may not be exported from Japan without a license:

- Military weapons
- Military ordnance
- Missiles
- Nuclear reactors

Export licenses are also required for electronic goods and certain other items to the following countries:

- Iraq
- Serbia
- Croatia
- Montenegro
- Bosnia-Herzegovina

Please note that the items subject to license and countries to which restrictions may apply can change with very little notice. As a rule of thumb, Japanese export controls have, to date, followed relatively closely those controls imposed by the United States. There are exceptions, however, so the use of trained professional brokers is strongly encouraged.

INSPECTION CERTIFICATES

The following items require that the exporter obtain from MITI an inspection certificate:

— textiles and textile products
— kitchenware
— toys
— cameras

DESIGN CERTIFICATES

Exporters of the following goods must obtain design certificates from MITI:

— furniture
— watch bands
— marking pens
— kitchenware

Inspection and Design Certificates are holdovers from the 1950s and 1960s when MITI was very conscious of the reputation of Japanese products for quality. Query whether there remains a need for regulation of this sort.

EXPORT REPORT

Export Reports must be filed with the Bureau whenever items having a value in excess of ¥3,000,000 are exported.

CUSTOMS BROKERAGE

The customs process in Japan would not work without the existence of the customs brokerage industry. The self-assessment system places the burden of legal compliance on the importer who in nearly all cases is not sufficiently trained in the intricacies of the law and attendant regulation to effect customs clearance in a timely and efficient manner. The broker, therefore, is absolutely essential to both the clearance of imported goods into Japan and the export of goods from Japan.

Brokerage firms are licensed by the Bureau to represent importers and exporters before the Bureau. As of this writing, there are over 980 licensed brokerages in Japan. There are brokers in all Japanese ports. The largest brokers tend to be divisions of freight forwarders who provide an "integrated" service to their customers.

License requirements for brokerages are quite strict. Among the many requirements is that a brokerage must have at least one licensed customs broker. Individuals who desire to become customs brokers must pass a licensing examination which traditionally has a very low pass rate.

The self-assessment system used in Japan imposes on the broker the very large burden of ensuring compliance with appropriate law and regulations. The broker is, necessarily, very cautious and careful to ensure that all documentation, especially the "declaration" made to the Bureau to secure customs clearance, is wholly accurate and complete. Deficiencies in the documentation can and do result in intensified scrutiny by Bureau officials of the subject shipment and the broker alike. In extreme cases, the Bureau can suspend, temporarily or permanently, the broker's (or brokerage's) license. The threat of informal and formal censure works well to ensure a thorough vetting by the broker of all shipments tendered to the Bureau for clearance. On the other hand, importers and exporters pay for this very painstaking review in the form of higher costs and increased clearance time.

Importers are well advised to select brokers that have special expertise in the type of goods at issue. As stated above, the myriad of ministries and agencies that enforce the over 30 statutes governing the import of goods make the clearance process complex. It will serve the importer well to use brokers who are experienced in the nature of the goods to be imported and have close relationships with the regulators of those types of goods.

DEVELOPMENTS IN CUSTOMS LAW AND PRACTICE

The Ministry of Finance and the Bureau are very conscious of the fact that the clearance process in Japan may be outdated. The MOF is closely reviewing the process and, especially in clearance of air cargo, is considering several steps that will improve clearance times and reduce costs. There are several reasons behind this modernisation approach. The MOF and the Bureau realise that they cannot cope with the ever increasing number of imports (primarily) given budget restraints. There is also an understanding that Japanese exporters, which already are at a competitive disadvantage due to the dramatic increase in the value of the yen over the past few years, require faster and less costly access to foreign markets. Reducing clearance times by eliminating paper and increasing reliance on automated systems may be the answer.

Several of the steps that may be taken over the next few years to improve clearance times and reduce costs are:

Increase of de minimis values Presently, shipments having a declared value for customs clearance of less than ¥10,000 are cleared quickly and duties and tax are not imposed. The Bureau is considering raising this amount to remain competitive with other countries. The United States, for example, has a de minimis amount of USD$200.

Low value clearance Items having a declared value for customs clearance of ¥201,000 and less are eligible for expedited clearance procedures (so long as they are not on a restricted list). These expedited procedures still require significant processing time. The Bureau is contemplating changes to the expedited procedures that would reduce significantly, and perhaps eliminate, documentation requirements for low value goods.

Increase in duty free imports In conjunction with the general world-wide easing of trade restraints as evidenced by increased interest in the WTO and APEC, it is possible that Japan, along with its major trading partners, will increase the number of goods that may be imported without duty and for other goods, reduce the amount of duty imposed.

Pre-clearance Japan is still a long way from effecting the "pre-clearance" of imported goods, but the Bureau is reviewing the possibility of such a system. Pre-clearance permits the clearance of goods before arrival. Through the use of state-of-the-art automated systems, the Bureau can today receive electronic reproductions of all shipments to be imported tomorrow. The Bureau can apply its standard screening processes to these shipments and select the shipments it wants to inspect or which require additional documentation. All other shipments can be released immediately on arrival. Pre-clearance has the very positive effect of eliminating the need to handle the goods in a *Hozei* warehouse, thereby cutting out a significant amount of time and costs. No longer required with pre-clearance are the machinations necessarily resulting from the tripartite interaction among the carrier, warehouse and broker with the Bureau.

STEPS TO ASSURE EFFICIENT CUSTOMS CLEARANCE

Customs clearance in Japan needn't be more than a minor imposition for most categories of goods, so long as the shipper and importer have prepared themselves beforehand. The following steps will go a long way to accomplishing the clearance process in Japan as quickly and as inexpensively as possible:

— Select a good broker experienced in the items to be imported.

— Make certain all shipping documentation is accurately prepared and accompanies each shipment.

— Alert the importer that the goods are en route and communicate constantly to ensure the importer has obtained import licenses/permits, where required.

---

1 "Procedures for Customs Clearance of Imported Goods" Attachment 1; JETRO Import Promotion Meeting, February 25, 1981; "JETRO SUMMARY"
2 Customs Law, Article 31
3 Customs Law, Article 68
4 Customs Law, Article 67–2
5 Customs Law, Article 67
6 JETRO Summary, Attachment 6
7 Id., Attachment 5
8 Ibid.
9 JETRO Summary, Attachment 1
10 Ibid.
11 Ibid.
12 Matsushita, Mitsuo, *Japanese International Trade and Investment Law*, University of Tokyo Press, 1989, p. 64
13 Customs Law, Article 76
14 Customs Tariff Law, Article 3
15 Id., Article 4
16 Id., Article 4–2
17 Id., Article 3
18 JETRO Summary, p. 3
19 Customs Tariff Law, Article 8
20 Id., Article 9
21 Customs Law, Chapter 4 and Cabinet Order for the Enforcement of the Customs Law, Chapter 4

CHAPTER 11

INTELLECTUAL PROPERTY LAW
by Masashige Ohba

INTRODUCTION

The Japanese government and Japanese industries are well aware of the importance of intellectual property. The progress of the world economy in this century, especially the rapid growth and expansion of the Japanese economy, has relied heavily on the improvement of scientific technology. The laws of intellectual property play an important role in encouraging innovation and promoting research and development of technologies useful to industry.

The Japanese government also realises the need to harmonise intellectual property laws to achieve smooth and fair trading in global economic activities. This attitude is reflected in frequent revisions and new enactment of laws relating to intellectual property in recent years.

Therefore, those who are interested in intellectual property law should pay careful attention to revisions of laws or enactment of new laws, and the exceptions to which old laws still apply.

PART I – TYPES OF INTELLECTUAL PROPERTY RIGHTS

Japan has been a member of the Paris Union for Protection of Industrial Property since 1899. Japan also is a member of the Berne Convention, Universal Copyright Convention, and many other intellectual property-related conventions.

As a member country of these conventions, the protection of intellectual property rights in Japan is similar to that of other advanced countries and is extended to foreign nationals.

RIGHTS PROTECTED BY REGISTRATION WITH THE JPO

Monopoly rights on certain types of industrial property can be established through complying with the Japan Patent Office (JPO) procedures, including registration for rights to inventions, designs and trademarks under the following laws:

(i)   Patents on Inventions — The Patent Law

(ii) Utility Model Rights — The Utility Model Right Law

(iii) Designs — The Design Law

(iv) Trademarks — The Trademark Law

ADDITIONAL PROTECTION OF OTHER INTELLECTUAL PROPERTY RIGHTS

Other types of intellectual property which are protected by Japanese law without involving the JPO are as follows:

(i)   Registered trade names and corporate names — The Commercial Code

(ii) Trade names, corporate names, service marks, unregistered trademarks, source of origin, business reputation, etc. — The Unfair Competition Prevention Law

(iii) Copyrights — The Copyright Law

(iv) Trade secrets, technical know-how — The Unfair Competition Law, the Civil Code, the Commercial Code and the Criminal Code

(v)   Computer programs and circuit layout — The Copyright Law, the Patent Law (this requires involvement of the JPO), the Unfair Competition Prevention Law, the Civil Code or Criminal Code, and the Law concerning Lay Out of Circuits in Semiconductor Chips may be applied, depending upon the nature of required protection.

The following are brief explanations of the nature, requirements and protective scope of these intellectual property rights.

PATENTS

Concept and Requirements

Subject matter of patents:

There is practically no limitation on the subject matter of patents, except:

(i)   those substances to be produced transforming the atomic nucleus; or

(ii) those inventions that are against public order or good morals, or which may harm public health.

Biotechnology with genetic recombination and computer software may also be the subject matter of a patent, so far as the following requirements are met.

Patent requirements

(i) To be patentable an invention must be a "highly advanced creation of a technical idea by which a natural law is utilised" (Art. 2), and it shall be "industrially applicable" (Art. 1 & Art. 29, Para. 1).

(ii) To be patentable an invention must have novelty. An invention is not novel if, prior to the filing of the patent application (or the priority date) (a) it had been publicly known or (b) worked in Japan or (c) if it was described in a publication distributed in Japan or in a foreign country (Art. 29, Para. 1).

(iii) As an exception to Art. 29, Para. 1, a grace period of six months is given to an inventor or his/her assignee who conducted experiments, or disclosed an invention in published literature, or disclosed it in an academic convention specifically designated by law, or if such disclosure was made by the actions of another party against the will of the person having the right to obtain patent priority (Art. 30).

(iv) Patentable inventions require an inventive step. There is no inventive step if the invention could have been easily inferred before the filing of the application on the basis of prior art by a person who had ordinary skill in the art to which the invention pertains (Art. 29, Para. 2).

Application Process

The patent application process is described in Part II, "Procedures at the Patent Office."

Protection and Remedies

Term of Patent Right

A patent right comes into existence by registration with the Patent Office and expires 20 years after the date of filing the application (Art. 67).

An extension of the patent term for up to five years may be permitted, if exploitation of the patented invention was delayed due to the need to obtain government approval for reasons of safety, such as approval for pharmaceutical products.

Remedies for Infringement

A patentee or registered exclusive licensee can:

(i) enjoin the unauthorised working of the patented invention (Art. 100); and

(ii) recover damages suffered due to infringement (Art. 102).

Limitations on Enforcement

A patent right cannot be extended to prohibit experiments or research. Also a patentee or registered exclusive licensee cannot invoke his/her rights to seize (Art. 69):

(i) machines or equipment installed in ships or aircraft passing through the territory of Japan;

(ii) products that existed before the filing date of the application for the patents.

Scope of Compensation

Damages may be computed based on (i) lost profit, (ii) the profit gained by the infringer from the infringing activity, or (iii) reasonable compensation (royalty).

With respect to compensation for the patentee, it is possible for such compensation to be retroactive to the time when the patent applicant gave notice to the possible infringer after the patent application had been laid open (Art. 65-3, Para. 1). But the payment of such compensation becomes due only after the registration of patent (Art. 65-3, Para. 2).

A claim for past damages is retroactive for three years, but 10 years is allowed for a claim on the basis of unjust enrichment (royalty equivalent).

UTILITY MODEL RIGHTS

Concept and Requirements

Subject Matter of Utility Model Right

Registered utility model rights protect the mechanical shape and structure, or a combination of both, of articles (Art. 1 of the Utility Model Law). The permitted subject matter is narrower in scope than the subject matter of patent: a process or chemical substance cannot be covered by a utility model right.

Utility Model Requirements

(i)   Until recently, utility model rights in Japan were treated like patents. Historically, the procedures for obtaining and enforcing these rights were similar to those for patents except that the subject matter of utility model rights is limited to structural articles and its life is shorter than that of a patent.

(ii) The revisions of the Utility Model Law made in 1993, which came into force on January 1, 1994, changed the nature of utility model rights, and they have become quite different from patent rights.

Under these new revisions, a utility model right is registered without substantive examination, except for formal requirements.

(iii) The requirements for a valid utility model right, such as novelty and advancement, are still similar to those for a patent, though the level of the requirement of advancement is lower than for a patent, and many provisions of the Patent Law are still applied *mutatis mutandis*.

(iv) An application for a utility model right is convertible to a patent application or an application for design right, and vice versa.

Application Process

The utility model right application process is described in Part II, "Procedures at the Patent Office."

Protection and Remedies

Term of Utility Model Right

The life of a utility model right is six years from the date of application (Art. 15). Formerly it was 10 years from publication for opposition or 15 years from the filing date, whichever comes first. This rule is still applicable to those utility model rights granted before the revision of the Utility Model Law in 1993.

To exercise a registered utility model right, the title holder shall obtain a "Report of Technical Evaluation" by an examiner of the JPO (Art. 12). A court action or other enforcement of this right against a possible infringer can be taken only after sending a warning letter with submission of the report of technical evaluation (Art. 29-2).

In the same manner as a patent holder, the holder of a utility model right or an exclusive licensee can enjoin infringing acts and recover damages.

DESIGN RIGHTS

Concept and Requirements

Subject Matter of Design Rights

The "design" in the Design Law means shape, pattern or colour, or a combination of these in any article, which produces an aesthetic impression through the sense of sight (Art. 2 of the Design Law).

The design to be registered for a design right registration shall be creative and novel and also be capable of being industrially utilized (Art. 3).

Design Right Requirements

The novelty requirement is similar to that for patents, but there are some differences. Namely, with respect to prior arts known outside Japan, not only those designs described in the published literature but also designs known (not described in a published literature) in foreign countries or similar to ones known or described in published literature cannot be registered as a design registration (Art. 3, Para. 1).

As an exception to the novelty requirements, a six month grace period is given in cases similar to those in which a grace period is given for a patent (Art. 4).

Application Process

The design right application process is described in Part II, "Procedures at the Patent Office."

Protection and Remedies

Term of Design Right

A design right comes into existence when it is registered and expires 15 years after the date of registration (Art. 21).

Scope of Protection

(i) The owner of a design right or the registered exclusive licensee can enjoin unauthorised use of the design for business purposes (Art. 23). In addition, the damages caused by infringement can be recovered.

(ii) The scope of protection of design rights extends to designs confusingly similar to the registered design. The registered owner and the registered exclusive licensee can also enjoin unauthorised use of designs similar to the registered design.

TRADEMARKS

Concept and Requirements

Subject Matter

Japanese law now accepts the registration of trademarks not only for goods but also for services (service mark) (Art. 2).

Trademark Requirements

(i) The trademark registration system also gives priority to the first applicant (Art. 8). The prior use principle is not in effect in Japan.

Therefore, it is important to file an application for trademark registration before marketing an article bearing such a trademark in Japan. (Those trademarks which are not registered but are well-known in Japan may be protected under the Unfair Competition Prevention Law.)

(ii) Registered trademarks which have not been used for more than three years can be invalidated. In addition an application to renew the registration of a trademark that has not been used will be rejected (Art. 19, Para. 2).

(iii) If a trademark has been widely known in Japan, a third party's application for registration of the same or a similar trademark will be rejected (Art. 4, Para. 1, Item 10).

Prior Use

Mere prior use of a trademark is not sufficient to upset another person's trademark registration, although prior use may be used as a defense against an infringement action (Art. 32).

Limitations on Trademark Registration

Trademark registration cannot be obtained for the following marks (Art. 3):

(i) a common name of the goods or services;

(ii) a mark which is customarily used with respect to the goods or services;

(iii) a mark comprised only of a mark indicating in a customary manner the place of origin, the place of sale, quality, raw material, effect, use, quantity, shape, or price of goods, or the method or time of manufacture, processing or use of such goods or services;

(iv) a mark which indicates only a commonplace family name or title

(v)   a mark which is simple and commonplace; or

(vi)   a mark by which customers cannot identify goods or services relating to someone's business.

Registration may be granted as an exception in the cases described in (iii), (iv), or (v) above, if the mark is recognised by consumers as the trademark relating to a specific business entity after repeated use thereof.

Names and Public Symbols

National flags, symbol marks of local governments or other international or domestic public organs, and other similar marks, including those prescribed in Art. 6-3 of the Paris Convention, and publicly known names of other persons and marks, cannot be registered as trademarks (Art. 4).

Associated Trademarks

Trademarks similar to a registered trademark can be registered as associated trademarks by the same person.

Registration Process

The trademark application process is described in Part II, "Procedures at the Patent Office."

Protection and Remedies

Term of Registration

A trademark comes into existence when it is registered and expires 10 years after the date of registration (Arts. 18 & 19).

This term can be renewed for another 10 years (Art. 19, Para. 2), and can be renewed repeatedly at each expiration by filing an application for renewal of registration within six months before the expiry of the current term (Art. 20).

Remedies for Infringement

(i) The trademark owner and exclusive licensee can enjoin unauthorised use of the trademark on articles or services in the same class (Arts. 25 & 36). The scope of a trademark extends to those trademarks which are confusingly similar to the registered trademark (Art. 37).

(ii) The trademark owner and the registered exclusive licensee can also request compensation for damages from infringers (Art. 38).

Assignment

Under Japanese law, a trademark can be assigned, provided that (Art. 24):

(i)   associated trademarks should be collectively assigned;

(ii)   separate assignments of the same trademark may be made for each designated type of goods or service; and

(iii) the assignment shall be published in a daily newspaper 30 days before registration of the transfer.

It is also possible to grant a license, exclusive or non-exclusive, by agreement (Arts. 30 & 31).

REGISTERED TRADE NAMES AND CORPORATE NAMES (COMMERCIAL CODE)

A trade name or corporate name can be registered only when there is no registration of the same name in the same business in the same city, town or village. The trade names or corporate names registered in the Company Register will be protected against those who use confusingly similar names (Arts. 20, 21 & 22).

UNFAIR COMPETITION PREVENTION LAW

Concept and Requirements

Under this law the following business activities are considered unfair competition:

(i)   Free riding on another's reputation by creating confusion with other business, by using a trade name, corporate name, trademark, service mark or other indication of source of good or service or business entity that is the same or confusingly similar to others which are well-known in Japan, regardless of whether such other marks have been registered;

(ii)   False or misleading indication or representation as to the origin, quality, quantity of contents, manufacturing method, usage, etc. of merchandise;

(iii) False statement which denigrates a competitor's reputation;

(iv) Slavish imitation of the configuration of another's good, except where such other's good has used the same configuration more than three years after marketing thereof or where such shape is common or necessarily required for the same kind of good; and

(v)   Violation of trade secrets (This will be explained in the discussion of "Trade Secrets and Know-how" below).

Protection and Remedies

Those who suffer damages to their business interests by such an activity may request the court to enjoin such activity and to award compensation of damages, and in some cases ((a) and (b) of (1) above) criminal action may be requested.

COPYRIGHTS

Concept and Requirements

Subject Matter

Works of art that creatively express a thought or emotion in the fields of literature, science, fine arts or music, are protected by the Copyright Law.

The works protected by this Law are enumerated in Arts. 10, 12 and 12-2 as follows:

(i)   verbal works, such as novels, scenarios, essays or lectures;

(ii)   music;

(iii)   dance or pantomime;

(iv)   fine arts such as pictures, woodcut prints or sculpture;

(v)   architecture;

(vi)   diagrams such as maps, drawings, charts, models having a scientific nature;

(vii)   cinema;

(viii) photographs;

(ix)   computer programs (see Computer Software below);

(x)   collective works such as creative selection or arrangement of materials by editors; and

(xi)   data bases involving creative efforts in selecting and composing information.

Secondary Works

To produce secondary works by translating, arranging, transforming, dramatising, cinematising an original work, a license from the owner of copyright of the original work is required. However, the owner of the original work has rights over such secondary work, similar to the rights of a secondary author (Art. 28).

Author's Rights

The author of the original copyrighted work or his/her assignee or licensee, is entitled to (Arts. 21–27):

(i)   reproduce the work;

(ii)   stage and perform the work;

(iii) broadcast;

(iv)   publicly recite his/her literary work;

(v)   publicly exhibit fine arts;

(vi)   screen and distribute;

(vii) lease reproduced works of art; and

(viii) translate and adapt.

Neighbouring Copyrights include (Art. 89):

(i)   the right of performance;

(ii)   the right of making records; and

(iii) the right of broadcasting.

Protection and Remedies

Creation of Right

The copyright comes into existence when a work of art is completed; there is no need for registration in order to effect it. There is a registration system for copyrights, but these registrations are especially required for setting up the right to publish a reproduced work of art or other rights and licenses derived from the copyright against third parties. Such registration is also necessary to prove an assignment and assert it against third parties (Art. 77).

Rights of Foreign Authors

The Japanese Copyright Law protects the works of authors who are nationals of a country that is a member of the Universal Copyright Convention, or whose works are first published in a country which is a member of that convention, or the Berne Convention (Art. 6).

Any performance, recording and broadcasting in member countries of WTO shall also be protected in Japan (Arts. 7, 8, 9).

Duration of Copyright

The duration of a copyright is generally 50 years from the publication of the work, but where an individual person is the author, the duration is the author's life plus 50 years after his/her death (in cases of joint authorship the death of the last) for the benefit of heirs. However, for foreign nationals of a member country of the Berne Convention, the length of time for protection is reciprocal with each member country up to 50 years (Art. 51 or Art. 58).

Collective Exercise

In Japan collective exercise of copyrights is conducted by the Copyright Association. Authors, musicians and other artists join this association, and the association, on behalf of the members, collects the royalties from persons who are in the business of continuously using works of art or performing music.

TRADE SECRETS AND KNOW-HOW

Concept

Trade secrets are important assets to any company. Their economic value is symbolically assessed in the form of the royalty charged for know-how licenses or as a capital investment.

Definition of Trade Secret

A trade secret is defined as "manufacturing methods or sales methods or other technical or business information" that are:
(i)   useful in a commercial activity;
(ii)   maintained as a secret; and
(iii)   not known to the general public.

Violation of Trade Secrets

There are three types of trade secret violations:
(i)   accessing or taking away the materials embodying the secret information, when done in an illegal manner;
(ii)   unauthorised disclosure or use of trade secrets held in custody by virtue of a contract such as a know-how license; and
(iii)   unauthorised disclosure or use of trade secrets by employees of the company.

New Protection for Trade Secrets

A recent amendment of the Unfair Competition Prevention Law offers more effective protection of trade secrets in addition to more conventional methods of contractual protection.

Under the amended Unfair Competition Prevention Law, there are two noticeable improvements:
(i)   The proprietor or holder of the trade secrets can request the court to enjoin the infringer from disclosing or using the secret information. Formerly it was only possible, as a remedy for breach of contract, to recover damages.

(ii) The above protection may be extended against third parties who acquired the secret information knowingly or with a lack of knowledge due to gross negligence about unauthorised activity of the assignor of the information.

(iii) Third parties who know or should have known of the above violations are also liable, but those bona fide third parties who obtained the trade secrets in the ordinary course of business may continue to use them.

COMPUTER PROGRAMS AND CIRCUITS

The protection of technologies, both soft and hard, relating to computers is now becoming an increasingly important area of intellectual property.

There are many ways to approach the various aspects of protecting rights concerning computers.

Conventionally, computer programs are protected as secret know-how by contracts, and this protection has recently been reinforced by the Unfair Competition Prevention Law. Now, the legislation providing the most effective ways of protecting rights concerning computers, and which can also be used to enforce such rights against third parties, are:

(i) the Copyright Law;

(ii) the Patent Law; and

(iii) the Semiconductor Integrated Circuit Law.

Protection by the Copyright Law

Computer programs are protected by the Copyright Law as a "work of art" (Art. 10, Para. 1, item 9; Art. 2, Para 1, item 10-2).

The protection of computer programs does not extend to (Art. 10, Para. 3):

(i) program languages;

(ii) rules for using program languages; or

(iii) algorithms.

An idea or concept behind a program cannot be protected, as the Copyright Law protects only the expression embodied in works of art.

The registration of computer programs is handled by an organisation designated by the Minister of Culture, which is separate from ordinary copyright registration (Law concerning Special Treatment of Registration of Programs). The registration is not a requirement for effecting the copyright, but an assignment or license of the copyright can be asserted against third parties if it is registered. The registration of programs may also be used for proving the date of completion, author and contents, should a problem arise.

Protection by the Patent Law

Computer-related inventions are protected by the Patent Law and the number of such patents is increasing explosively.

The technical idea behind a program may be patented either as a process patent or as a device in combination with hardware, so far as it meets the requirements for a patentable invention, namely, the "creation of a high level technical idea utilising natural law" which is useful in industry.

Most of the programs for process patents take the form of a flow chart.

Computer circuits can be patented in the same manner as other electrical equipment.

Protection by the Law Concerning Semiconductor Integrated Circuits

The layout of the integrated circuits in a semiconductor chip is protected by this Law.

The right to utilise the layout of circuits comes into existence by its registration and continues to exist for 10 years. The proprietary right shall vest in the company that employed the employee who originally designed the layout, unless otherwise agreed.

Assignment of this right except by succession, or granting an exclusive license or non-exclusive license or assignment of such licenses cannot be asserted against third parties without registration.

The registered proprietor or the exclusive licensee can enjoin infringing acts and recover damages.

Contractual Protection by the Civil Code and Commercial Code

Contracts are the conventional means for protecting the secrecy of computer software. However, a non-disclosure agreement cannot afford protection against third parties, and reverse engineering may reveal the software. Therefore, the protection afforded by the above is increasingly necessary.

PART II — PROCEDURES AT THE PATENT OFFICE

APPLICATION PROCEDURES

Patents, utility model rights, design rights and trademarks have the common feature that all must be applied for and examined by the JPO (except utility model rights, for which substantial examination need not be made) and all of these rights come into existence by registration with the JPO.

The first filed application for these industrial properties will prevail. For patents and utility model rights the first application in a foreign country may be used for priority claims in accordance with the Paris Convention and Patent Cooperate Treaty (PCT).

The unique procedures for each type of rights are as follows:

(i)   Early publication of application by being laid open (*Kokai*) only applies to patents. *Kokai* will be made automatically after 18 months from the filing date, or in the case of applications filed under the Paris Convention, from the priority date.

(ii) In the registration procedure for trademarks, the mark is examined and published for opposition, and only after the elapse of the opposition period or overcoming oppositions will the trademark right be registered. In the case of patents, utility model rights and design rights, the publication is made only after the right has been granted and registered.

(iii) Utility model rights are registered without substantive examination.

There are many other minor differences depending upon the nature of the right. However, the basic structure of JPO procedures can be understood by following the procedure for patent applications. The application procedure for patents is the basis for all other applications and in fact the other laws apply the Patent Law *mutatis mutandis* in some cases.

A chart of the application procedures for patents is provided as *Schedule 1*, for utility model rights as *Schedule 2*, for design rights as *Schedule 3*, and for trademarks as *Schedule 4*.

INVALIDATION ACTIONS

The JPO has primary jurisdiction over invalidation actions for industrial property rights registered with the JPO. In Japan the validity of registered trademarks, patents, utility model rights or designs cannot be argued in infringement actions before the court, though in a preliminary injunction case the court will consider the probable validity in deciding whether to issue the injunction.

Any interested party can file an invalidation action with the JPO against the registered owner of a patent, utility model right, design right, or trademark.

With exception for certain types of invalidation, actions must be brought within five years of registration (Art. 47, Trademark Law). There is no time limit for filing an invalidation action with respect to patents, utility models, trademarks or designs. No one can institute an invalidation action on the same basis as a former case in which the decision was final and conclusive.

The defeated party may appeal to the Tokyo High Court and further to the Supreme Court.

PART III — LICENSE AGREEMENTS

GENERAL POLICY ON TECHNOLOGY TRANSFER

In principle, under Japanese law the parties are free to enter into any license agreement, either domestic or international, concerning any intellectual property, including both registered and non-registered rights, and may agree to any terms and conditions unless it is against public order.

Still there are certain restrictions from the aspect of Antimonopoly Law, and certain steps should be taken under the Foreign Exchange and Foreign Trade Control Law for international license agreements.

The economic growth of Japan and the success of Japanese industries have relied heavily on the introduction of advanced technologies from western countries, especially from the U.S., by means of patent and know-how licenses. Japan's balance of trade in technology is still negative, i.e., payments exceed receivables, though the recent tendency of newly-entered license agreements shows that exports of technologies are exceeding imports.

In the 1950s and 1960s, the conclusion of international patent and know-how license agreements was heavily controlled by the Japanese government. Such agreements required government approval under the old Foreign Investment Law in accordance with the policy of saving foreign currency funds and promoting native industries. These controls have been gradually removed and now only a few procedures for filing documents remain.

REQUIREMENTS OF NOTIFICATION OR APPROVAL

IMPORT OF TECHNOLOGIES

Notification to the Government through the Bank of Japan under the Foreign Exchange Control Law

(i) Technologies requiring advance notification (three months — 14 days in advance)

Advance notification is required only in cases involving special technologies, such as aircraft, weapons, explosive, nuclear power, or space research, except if the following exemptions apply:

Those licenses to a subsidiary of which 50% or more of the equity is owned by the licensor; or those for which remuneration is less than ¥100 million or offset with a cross license.

(ii) Technologies requiring an ex post facto report (within 15 days after conclusion)

With respect to all technology introduction other than (a) above, any license of a registered design right, registered trademark, technical know-how, or computer software requires filing a report.

(iii) Those requiring no report

Unregistered designs and trademarks can also be licensed but are not required to be reported.

Notification to the Japan Fair Trade Commission

Under the Antimonopoly Law an ex post facto report within 30 days after conclusion of an agreement is required for the following license agreements (imports):

Exclusive license on patents, utility model rights, design rights, copyrights on computer programs.

Exemptions: licenses of one year or less; licenses between associated companies, one of which owns 50% or more equity of the other; licenses for which the subject matter's business scale is less than a 10% share of the Japanese market, or is ranked 5th in Japan or below and has no retail price term; licenses concerning trademarks.

EXPORT OF TECHNOLOGIES

Foreign Exchange and Foreign Trade Control Law Related Notification.

(i) There is a list of certain technologies for which the advance approval of the Government (MITI) under the Foreign Exchange and Foreign Trade Control Law is required (concerning COCOM).

It is not always clear which technologies are included. Borderline cases require advance consultation with the authorities.

(ii) All licenses for technologies other than the listed ones, or licenses for merely using patents and other registered industrial property rights can be freely made and are not required to have any approval.

Notification to the Japan Fair Trade Commission under the Antimonopoly Law:

Same as for import of technologies (above).

JFTC GUIDELINES UNDER THE ANTIMONOPOLY LAW

The latest guidelines, issued in 1989, classified the terms into three categories, namely: (i) in principle not an unfair trade practice; (ii) may be considered as an unfair trade practice; and (iii) highly likely to be considered an unfair trade practice.

In the case of (i), unless otherwise proved unfair, it is considered legal as an admissible restriction.

In the case of (ii), an examination of actual effect of the restrictive terms and situation requiring such terms will be needed for determination of legality.

In the case of (iii), unless a justifiable reason for the restriction is provided, it is considered illegal. The following explanation indicates the type of restrictions falling into these three categories for different types of licenses.

i) Patent License

Restrictions admissible in principle
(a) Generally admissible
   (i)   separately licensing to manufacture, use, sell, etc.;
   (ii) limiting the period to less than the life of patents;
   (iii) limiting the practicing geographic area;
   (iv) limiting the technical field;
   (v)   minimum quantity of production, sales or use.
(b) Restrictions admissible depending upon circumstance or subcondition.
   (vi) the obligation of report of improved invention and cross-license on a non-exclusive basis if such obligation is balanced between the parties;

(vii) the obligation to purchase materials, components, etc. from supplier designated by the licensor, if necessary to guarantee the quality of licensed products;

(viii) the restriction of export of licensed products to certain countries, if the licensor has a patent right, or is granting an exclusive license or distributorship or developed market in such countries;

(ix) the restriction of export price or quantity, or limiting export only through designated person if the situation is the same as mentioned in viii) above;

(x) the calculation of royalty based on the price of final products or whole process in cases where the licensed patent is related only to a component or one step, or based on the price of materials or components required for the patented product or process, if such method of calculation is convenient or necessary;

(xi) the package license of plural patents, if necessary for guaranteeing the effectiveness of licensed patent;

(xii) payment after the expiration of patent, if it is considered installment payments of royalty;

(xiii) the licensor's right to terminate the license when the licensee challenges the validity of patent; and

(xiv) the obligation to use best efforts to exploit the licensed patent.

ii) Restrictions which may be considered an unfair practice

(i) the restriction of handling competitive products or using competitive technology during the terms of licensing agreement;

(ii) the restriction of sales channels;

(iii) the obligation to inform the licensor of the licensee's knowledge or experience regarding licensed patent or to grant licensor a non-exclusive license, except in the case of (i) (b) (vi);

(iv) the obligation to use trademark, etc. designated by the licensor;

(v) the restriction of quality of patented products, raw materials or components, etc., except where necessary for guarantee of the quality;

(vi) the obligation to purchase raw materials, components from (i) (b) (vii);

(vii) the restriction of export of the licensed products, except the case of (i) (b) (viii);

(viii) the restriction of export price or quantity of the licensed products, except the case of (i) (b) (ix);

(ix) the calculation of royalty based on the price of products or service other than the patented product or process, except the case of 1(a)(x);

(x) the package license of plural patents, except in the case of (1)(b)(xi);

(xi) an unjust unilateral termination clause, except in the case of (1)(b)(xiii); and

(xii) the restriction on contesting the validity of a licensed patent.

iii) Restrictions which are in principle an unfair trade practice

(i) the restriction of resale price of the licensed products by the licensee;

(ii) the restriction of sales price of the licensed products by the licensee;

(iii) the restriction on handling competitive products or using competitive technologies after termination of the licensing agreement;

(iv) the obligation to use the licensed technology or obligation to pay royalty after termination of the licensing agreement, except the case of (1)(b)(xii);

(v) the restriction of research and development of technology concerning licensed or competing technologies; and

(vi) the obligation of the licensee to assign to or grant exclusive license for the licensor with patents concerning improved or applied invention.

ii) Know-how License

In most cases the standards applied to patent license agreements will be applied to know-how license agreements.

Restrictions admissible in principle

(i) non-disclosure obligation;

(ii) restrictions on handling competitive products or using competitive technology after termination of the agreement, but only for short period if it is required for securing unauthorised disclosure or use of know-how; and

(iii) termination of the license by the licensor if the licensee challenges the agreement, regardless of whether the licensed know-how become publicly known.

Restrictions which may be considered an unfair trade practice:

Restriction from contesting whether the licensed know-how has become publicly known.

Restrictions which are in principle considered an unfair trade practice:

An obligation to pay a royalty, or non-use after the licensed know-how becomes public knowledge through no fault of the licensee.

iii) Other Intellectual Properties

There are no special guidelines concerning licenses for other intellectual properties, but similar restrictions may be considered unfair in similar situations.

PART IV — ENFORCEMENT

COURT ACTIONS

Types of Legal Actions and Remedies

A legal action against an infringer of intellectual property rights can be brought in the courts. The types of actions and remedies which may be sought are:

(1) *Kari-Shobun* (preliminary injunction) — enjoining the infringing activities temporarily;

(2) *Honso* (main lawsuit)
   (a) permanent injunction enjoining the infringing activities permanently;
   (b) destroy the infringing products, materials or devices useable only for infringement;
   (c) compensation for damages.

The Courts

An action shall be started at the district court having jurisdiction, then may be appealed to the high court, and finally may be appealed to the Supreme Court.

The Japanese judicial system consists of the Supreme Court, and below it eight High Courts and 50 District Courts.

The Tokyo District Court, in which almost 50% of the intellectual property right cases in Japan are brought, is the most important among the 50 district courts. It has a special industrial property division, the 29th Civil Division. The Osaka District Court, which handles about 20% of the intellectual property rights cases in Japan, also has an intellectual property division, the 21st Civil Division.

The Tokyo High Court, which is the appellate court for the Tokyo District Court and the 10 district courts neighbouring Tokyo, has three intellectual property divisions that handle appeals connected with infringement actions. The Tokyo High Court also has exclusive jurisdiction over appeals from JPO decisions. The judges, even in the special divisions, are not required to have any technical background. In the intellectual property divisions of the Tokyo High Court, the Tokyo District Court and the Osaka District Court, several assistant investigators from the JPO are assigned to assist the judges with technical matters.

Warning Letter and Statutory Limitations

Usually the first step taken by the owner of an intellectual property right or exclusive licensee is to send a warning letter to the infringing party. In case of utility model rights, a warning letter with submission of a report of technical evaluation by a JPO examiner is the prerequisite for such action. It is customary in Japan to send such a warning letter by content-and-delivery certified mail.

Except for utility model rights, the warning letter is not a prerequisite for taking legal action. However, it can have the following effects:

(1) It may cause voluntarily cessation of infringing acts;

(2) It may induce license negotiations;

(3) A demand for compensation for damages by such letter effects an extension of the time limit for initiating an action for claiming such compensation (suspends the ending of the period of statutory limitation).

But this last effect will expire if no court action is taken within six months after the warning letter is received by the infringer. The statutory limitation period is three years for torts, and 10 years for unjust enrichment. This means compensation for damages can be claimed retroactively for three years or 10 years from the time compensation is demanded by a court action.

Japan has no equitable defense of laches as in Anglo-American law. Therefore lawsuits can be instituted at any time during the life of the patent, trademark, design right, etc. The statutory limitation is concerned only with compensation for damages.

If a notice of claim under a patent is given after it is laid open but before the registration, the period for compensation is retroactive to the date of such notice, when action is taken after the registration of patent.

Kari-Shobun (Preliminary Injunction)

(i) A preliminary injunction order may be sought either before bringing the main lawsuit or while a main suit is pending. If the infringement is very clearly evidenced by prima facie evidence, it is possible that the court will issue an injunctive order. Because of an injunction's critical effect on the defendant, the courts are very careful and usually proceed with a series of hearings before they will issue such an order.

In a case of very clear infringement of a design, trademark or copyright or unfair compensation, a preliminary injunction order may be issued relatively easily. However, in the case of patent or utility model rights or in computer software cases, the courts will be more strict and careful. If the court finds some delicate and difficult technical problem is involved, it will tend to postpone the decision or urge the claimant to bring a *Honso* (main lawsuit), or the hearings may take as long as a main lawsuit does. The plaintiff will usually then proceed with the main lawsuit, leaving the application for the preliminary injunction pending. This practice is especially true in the Tokyo and Osaka Courts.

(ii) If a preliminary injunction order is to be issued, the court will request the claimant to make a deposit of guarantee money, either by cash, bank guarantee or national bond. The amount of this deposit will be determined solely by the judge in charge, but the concept is that it should cover the amount of damages faced by the enjoined party, who may afterward obtain a favourable judgment in the main lawsuit. The amount can vary widely depending upon the case and may range from ¥1 million to ¥100 million.

Honso (Main Lawsuit)

(i) Commencement

The main lawsuit starts with the filing of a complaint. The complaint must be accompanied by a power of attorney and a corporate certificate, which prove the existence of the plaintiff corporation and the authority of the representative director who signed the power of attorney, and also a revenue stamp amounting to a sum of about 0.5% of the disputed value or property which is the subject of the suit. This revenue stamp is an official filing fee. Service of process is conducted by the court clerk or court bailiff. The court clerk will mail or have the court bailiff deliver the complaint together with a writ of summons to the defendants.

(ii) Examination Procedures

(a) The first hearing will be held within one or two months after the filing of complaint and thereafter a series of hearings will be held at intervals of approximately two months. The entire trial will generally last about three years in patent infringement cases of ordinary complexity, but in very complicated cases it will last longer. Trademark cases are normally concluded much more quickly. At the hearings the attorneys exchange briefs and engage in a verbal discussion of the issues before the judge as well as submit supporting documentary evidence.

(b) After the issues have been clarified through a series of hearings, the court will examine witnesses based on requests by the parties and if it feels such examination is necessary. An on-site inspection, inspection of the objects concerned, or the appointment of a neutral expert may be done at the request of the parties and the discretion of the court. Examination of witnesses and evidence is also conducted at court hearings.

(c) In Japan there is no concentrated continuous trial, nor is there a jury system or discovery as in the U.S.

(d) In cases involving complicated technology, the court will sometimes hold an informal meeting for explanations. Attorneys may use any means, such as drawings, video, slides or demonstration of actual devices, to explain the technology.

(e) The court in intellectual property cases consists of three judges. However, the court occasionally appoints a commissioned judge from among the three judges hearing a case and that sole judge proceeds with preliminary proceedings in order to clarify the points at issue and put the parties' allegations or assertions in order.

In such cases the commissioned judge will conduct the preliminary proceedings in a conference room in an informal manner. In that way both parties can speak frankly so that the judge can grasp the points at issue. When the commissioned judge satisfactorily arranges both parties' assertions, the preliminary proceedings will be closed. Such preliminary proceedings may be continued for one or two years, with sessions at intervals of about two months. After they are finished the case will return to ordinary hearings at the court room.

After all proceedings have been completed, judgment may be rendered within a few weeks. In fact, however, it usually takes several months or more.

Appeal to Higher Courts

The defeated party can appeal to the high court having jurisdiction over the district court that gave the original judgment.

The appeal procedure in Japan is not a mere legal review of the judgment of the first instance. It is possible to make new assertions and submit or produce new evidence, expand the demand of compensation, or change the gist of the claim during the appeal procedure. Consequently, the appeal procedures take just as long as the trial at first instance. However, if there are no or fewer issues in dispute concerning facts, and the appealed issue is a point mainly concerning a legal question, the judgment may be given within a relatively short time.

A further appeal to the Supreme Court must be based on grounds prescribed in the law. The grounds for appeal to the Supreme Court include constitutional problems or legal error by the lower court. The Supreme Court has only rarely reversed a high court's judgment in cases involving patents or other intellectual property rights.

Compromise

Because infringement actions, especially in patent cases, take a very long time before a final judgment, in most cases it is wise to settle by compromise.

Statistics show that in the intellectual property division of the Tokyo District Court and the Osaka District Court the number of judgments given in any one year is equal to only about 25% of the new cases filed. This means that nearly 75% of the cases are either withdrawn or settled by compromise before judgment is given.

After appeal is made to the High Court, many cases are settled by compromise. This also decreases the number of cases in which the High Court gives a final decision in infringement actions, especially in cases involving patent and utility model rights.

In contrast, trademark infringement cases are generally settled very early. In many cases trademark disputes will be settled by a warning letter and without any legal action. This is because trademark infringement or design infringement is very clear even for laymen in many cases and the parties will settle or cease the infringing use upon receipt of a warning letter. Even if the problem is brought to court, the judgment will be given relatively quickly compared with patent and utility model cases. Unfair competition law cases are also generally completed much faster than patent cases.

With respect to copyright, computer program cases are usually similar to patents, and other works of art are more similar to design rights or unfair competition cases in terms of their complexity.

CUSTOMS OFFICE ACTION

Border relief is an effective means for protecting intellectual properties if infringement of importing goods is proved and recognised by the Customs Bureau. The Customs Tariff Law provides in Art. 21, Para. 1, Item 5 and Art. 21, Para. 2 that the Customs Bureau can forfeit, or destroy, or return to the country of export any imported articles that infringe any patent, utility model right, design right, trademark, copyright, neighbouring right or circuit layout right.

With respect to trademark and copyright, there have been many cases in which the imports of articles was stopped. However, there have been few in which patent infringement was discovered by the Customs Bureau, as these cases usually involve complicated technical questions.

Formerly, this action could be taken at the discretion of the Customs Bureau, though this was usually done upon the request of the interested parties.

Newly introduced measures via amendments to the Customs Tariff Law (effective from 1995) are as follows:

i) Identification procedures (Art. 21 Para 4-6)

    The Customs Bureau can forfeit, destroy, or return imported articles by reason of infringement of an intellectual property right only after and as a result of the identification procedures.

    Commencement of these procedures should be notified to the interested parties, such as proprietor and importer, requesting an explanation of facts and supporting evidence.

ii) Prohibition of Importation of Infringing Articles

    (a) Proprietors of a trademark, copyright or neighbouring right can file an Import Prohibition Application with supporting evidence (Art. 21-2 Para 1).

        The Customs Bureau should then decide and give notice to the petitioner whether it will commence the procedures for identification of infringement, or reject the application with a statement of the reason for not commencing such procedures (Art. 21-2 Para 2-3).

    (b) Proprietors of intellectual properties other than mentioned in (a) above, such as patent, utility model rights, design rights, or circuit layout rights, can submit an Import Prohibition Information. In such cases, the Customs Bureau is not required to decide whether to proceed with the identification procedures, which are optional.

iii) Deposit of Guarantee Money
 When a petition for the identification procedures is filed, the Customs Bureau may order the petitioner to deposit a guarantee for covering damages caused by delaying customs clearance due to the recognition procedures (Art. 21-3).

CONCLUSION

This chapter was accurate at the time of writing. The reader should be aware, however, that revolutionary changes in technology and the trend toward global harmonisation of intellectual property laws require rapid and repeated changes in said laws. In case of specific questions about an area of intellectual property law, it is always advisable to consult an expert practitioner in that area as to the current state of the law.

Schedule 1: Chart of Examination and Appeal Procedure for Patents

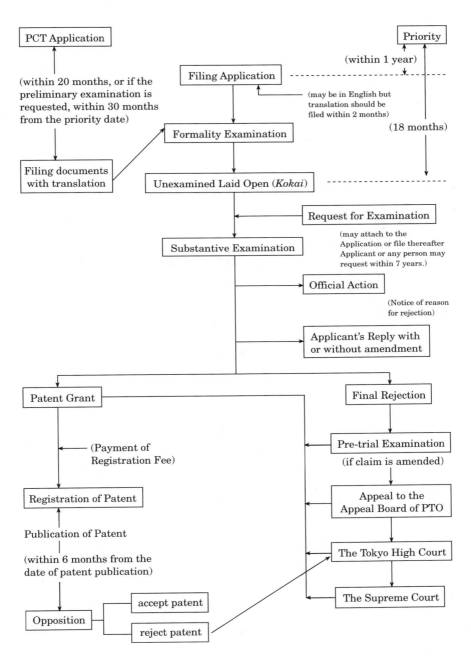

Schedule 2: Chart of Registration Procedure for Utility Model Right

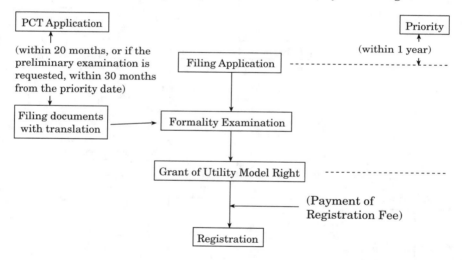

Schedule 3: Chart of Examination and Appeal Procedure for Design in Japan

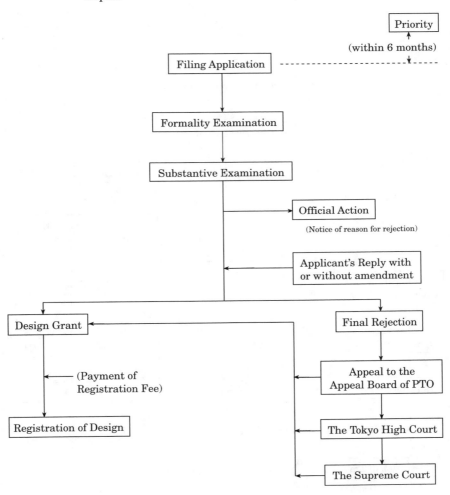

Schedule 4: Chart of Examination and Appeal Procedure for Trademark in Japan

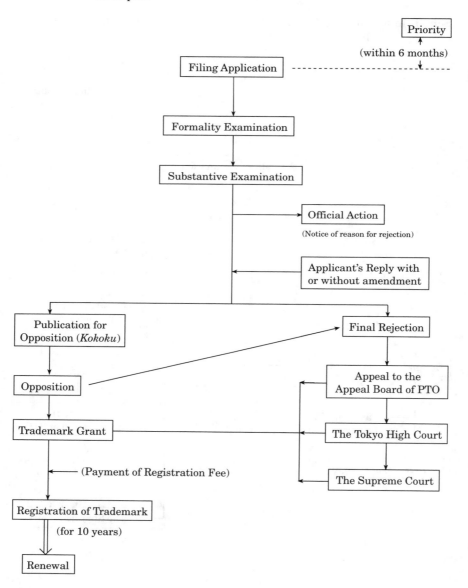

CHAPTER 12

THE JAPANESE TAX SYSTEM
*by W. Temple Jorden**

INTRODUCTION

SOURCES OF LAW

Article 84 of the Japanese Constitution requires that there be a statutory basis for all taxes. General rules concerning the implementation and interpretation of all tax statutes are to be found in such laws as the National Taxation General Rules Law, the National Tax Collection Law, and the National Tax Criminal Violation Law. The basic substantive tax statutes are the Income Tax Law (ITL), primarily for individuals, and the Corporation Tax Law (CTL), for corporations and other juridical entities. These statutes are supplemented by the Income Tax Law Enforcement Order and Corporate Tax Law Enforcement Order, both of which have been issued by the Cabinet and are subject to frequent amendment, and Ministerial Orders, issued and amended by the Ministry of Finance (MOF). Special rules and tax incentives relating to the ITL, CTL, and other basic statutes are set forth in the Special Tax Measures Law (STML), the Special Tax Measures Law Enforcement Order, and subordinate Ministerial Orders.

The National Tax Administration (NTA) also issues "basic circulars" for the purpose of ensuring uniformity of application of the tax laws. Although such circulars do not have the force of law, they represent an extremely important source of guidance concerning the NTA's current interpretation of statutes and orders. The NTA also occasionally issues so-called "individual circulars" which are technically limited in scope to specific fact patterns, but which can also be a helpful guide to current NTA thinking.

Finally, it is a principle of Japanese constitutional law that treaty provisions will take precedence over domestic statutory law. Thus, tax treaties can have an important impact on Japanese taxation of residents of countries that have concluded such treaties with Japan.

ADMINISTRATION

General supervisory authority for the administration of all Japanese tax statutes is vested in the MOF. As a practical matter, the MOF also plays a dominant role in the drafting of new tax legislation as well as in the formulation of tax policy. Actual tax administration is conducted by the NTA, which is technically independent of the MOF. Most day-to-day tax administration is handled at one of the roughly 500 local tax offices in Japan, which are supervised by one of the 11 regional tax bureaus (located in such major cities as Tokyo, Osaka, and Nagoya). Each of those bureaus is subject to the general supervision of the NTA itself.

INDIVIDUAL INCOME TAX

RESIDENCE

The manner of taxation of individuals under the ITL depends initially on the residence status of the individual involved. Briefly, an individual who qualifies as a non-resident is subject to tax only on his/her Japan-source income, and even in that case, at low fixed rates. However, if an individual qualifies as a resident for tax purposes, she will be subject to full tax rates on her income from sources in Japan, and, depending on certain circumstances, from sources outside Japan as well. In principle, the tax status of individuals is unrelated to nationality: an expatriate residing in Japan is subject to most of the same rules as a Japanese national.

In brief, a resident is any person who has a domicile in Japan or who has resided in Japan continuously for more than a year. An expatriate who enters Japan and who is likely to stay for more than a year due to employment is considered a Japanese resident from the date of his/her arrival in the country. Obversely, if the expatriate can demonstrate that the anticipated duration of her stay in Japan is less than one year, she will be deemed to be a non-resident.

A further distinction within the category of residents generally permits expatriates to benefit from a preferential arrangement: any resident who qualifies as a "non-permanent" resident (as defined below) is not subject to Japanese tax on her income from sources outside Japan unless such income is either remitted into or paid within Japan. Such an individual could therefore escape Japanese taxation on income paid and derived from services performed abroad. In addition, passive income sourced outside Japan (*e.g.,* interest, dividends, capital gains, rents, etc.) would escape taxation provided it was neither remitted into or paid in Japan. All other residents are subject to tax on worldwide income.

Non-permanent residents are residents who do not intend to

remain permanently in Japan and have not lived there for a continuous period of more than five years. Since the Japanese tax authorities presume that foreign nationals do not intend to reside permanently in Japan, the length of the period of continuous residence in Japan is generally dispositive of the issue of non-permanent residence, unless the expatriate has been granted a permanent residence visa or, in some circumstances, elects to be treated as a permanent resident. Resident Japanese nationals are presumed to intend to remain in Japan permanently and are therefore treated as permanent residents.

GROSS INCOME

Tax under the ITL is calculated separately for the following income categories, although in some circumstances losses in one category can be applied against the net income in another category:

(i) Ordinary income (comprised of (i) employment income, including all forms of remuneration from an employer and pensions, but excluding lump-sum retirement payments, (ii) interest income, (iii) dividend income, (iv) rental income, (v) business income, including all income arising from the operation of a sole proprietorship and most forms of partnership, (vi) capital gains from the sale of assets other than real property, (vii) "occasional" income (*e.g.,* prizes and gambling winnings), and (viii) miscellaneous income (*e.g.,* royalties and interest on personal loans) is generally aggregated and taxed at normal rates.

(ii) Short-term capital gains, and all business and miscellaneous income, arising from the sale of real property are taxed at a rate equal to the higher of 40%, or 110% of the marginal rate that would be applicable if the gain were added to ordinary income.

(iii) Long-term capital gains from real property are taxed at significantly more favourable rates than those applicable to short-term gains, especially with respect to a personal residence.

(iv) Slightly more than 50% of lump-sum retirement income is excluded from taxation, while the remainder is taxed at ordinary rates.

(v) Forestry income qualifies for special tax benefits, which serve the purpose of permitting income averaging over a five-year period.

EXCLUSIONS

A variety of economic benefits are excluded, completely or partially, from ordinary income under the ITL or subordinate regulations. Of those exclusions, the following are usually of particular interest to expatriates in Japan:

Housing Benefits

Rent in Tokyo and other large urban centres for housing normally considered appropriate for foreign personnel may range from $2,000 to $20,000 per month. Although a direct subsidy from an employer for such rent will be taxed in full as ordinary income, it is possible to avoid this tax burden if the employer rents the housing and sublets it to his/her director or employee. In the case of an employee, as little as 5% of the market rent paid by the employer will be taxed as a benefit-in-kind to the employee. The taxable benefit-in-kind for a director, on the other hand, is 35% of market rent (if the housing is partially used for business purposes (*e.g.*, business receptions)), representing an income exclusion of 65% of the actual rent.

In April 1995, the NTA issued a circular stating that director accommodations with floor space in excess of 240 square metres would henceforth be considered sufficiently "extravagant" to warrant full taxation of market rent as a benefit-in-kind. That is not to say that accommodations of 239 square metres will automatically escape scrutiny. The NTA has reserved considerable discretion to deem other types of housing (*e.g.*, housing with swimming pools attached) to be "extravagant", and thus fully taxable. Note, however, that the recently-issued circular only addresses housing for directors. The treatment of housing for employees does not appear to have been affected, although a tendency in that direction as well is likely.

Commuting Expenses and Provision of Company Car

A reasonable amount of actual commuting expenses (up to ¥50,000 per month) is excluded from employment income, as is the gratuitous provision of a company car to a director or employee of a company, with or without a driver, to the extent the car is used primarily for business purposes. This business-purpose test has, to date, been interpreted liberally by the tax authorities.

Business Travel and Moving Expenses

Allowances intended to cover business trip expenses, in Japan or abroad, are not taxable to the extent that they are reasonable, depending on the nature of the trip and the status of the employee or director involved. The moving expenses of a director or employee, both to and from Japan, may be assumed directly or reimbursed by an employer without constituting taxable income.

Home Leave Allowance
An expatriate may also receive an allowance covering the travel expenses arising from "home leave" alone or with family, including the costs of round-trip airfare and lodging expenses, provided the allowance is established under the employer's work rules and is granted no more than once a year.

Educational Expenses
Although educational expenses paid by an employer for the benefit of an employee's child will, in principle, be taxed as income to the employee, the NTA has informally ruled that "donations" paid by corporate employers to certain international schools in Japan in lieu of tuition will not constitute taxable income for the employee. Such donations may also be deductible for the employer, so long as total donations (including but not limited to educational donations) for the business year do not exceed a total amount equal to 1.25% of net profits plus 0.125% of the employer's stated capital.

DEDUCTIONS

Japanese tax law allows various deductions from gross individual income in Japan. By means of such deductions, the effective rate of tax on income from employment can be considerably reduced. The deductions mentioned below relate to national tax under the ITL and are far from exhaustive: only deductions likely to be of interest to an expatriate have been included.

Basic Deduction
Each taxpayer's standard deduction is ¥380,000.

Deductions for Dependents
Although there are no joint returns in Japan and each family member must, in principle, file a separate return for his/her income, a taxpayer can deduct ¥380,000 for each dependent family member who is living with the taxpayer on the last day of the calendar year, provided that family member did not receive more than ¥380,000 in income (¥1.03 million, if limited to employment income). The same person may not be claimed as a dependent on more than one tax

return. If an individual's annual net income does not exceed ¥10 million, and her spouse earned less than ¥50,000, a special additional spousal deduction of ¥380,000 is permitted.

Employment Income Deduction

Under the ITL, the following standard deduction is available to taxpayers with employment income. The calculation of the deduction, as a function of earned income, is as follows:

Salary income (¥)	Standard deduction (¥)
0 to 1,625,000	650,000
1,625,001 to 1,800,000	0 + 40% of salary income
1,800,001 to 3,600,000	180,000 + 30% of salary income
3,600,001 to 6,600,000	540,000 + 20% of salary income
6,600,001 to 10,000,000	1,200,000 + 10% of salary income
10,000,001 and above	1,700,000 + 5% of salary income

Although employee/taxpayers do have an option to claim actual employment-related expenses in place of the above standard deduction, in view of the generosity of the standard deduction, exercise of the option is a rare phenomenon.

Medical Expenses

Medical and dental expenses (net of insurance benefits) of the taxpayer and her dependents in excess of ¥100,000 (or 5% of her income, whichever is greater), but no more than ¥2 million, are deductible.

Insurance Premiums

Premiums payable under a variety of insurance policies are deductible, subject to the following limitations:

(i)   Social Insurance

Social insurance premiums (including health, unemployment and accidents) are deductible to the extent actually paid to appropriate government organisations.

(ii)   Life Insurance

Premiums paid under life insurance policies or qualified pension plans for the benefit of a taxpayer or family members are deductible up to a ceiling of ¥50,000, provided the policies or plans (1) are with companies recognised in Japan or are arranged through brokers recognised in Japan and (2) satisfy a

300

number of other stringent requirements.

(iii) Health and Home Insurance

Deductions for premiums paid under casualty and private health insurance policies covering the taxpayer or live-in relatives are deductible up to ¥3,000 for short-term, and ¥15,000 for long-term, policies. Such insurance must be taken out with an insurance company or broker licensed in Japan.

INHABITANTS TAX

The national income return (or reports from the employer in the event no return is required) serves as the basis for calculation of the local inhabitants tax (which is comprised of both prefectural and municipal taxes). The inhabitants tax is paid in either of two ways, direct payment in four installments or withholding by the employer on a monthly basis, commencing in June of the year following that in which the taxed income arose. This tax is not payable with respect to a particular year unless the taxpayer was a resident of Japan on January 1st on the following year. Since the inhabitants tax rate can be as much as 15% of taxable income (see below), leaving Japan prior to the end of a calendar year can be extremely beneficial. If an expatriate leaves Japan after January 1st of a given year, however, he/she will not only have to pay the entire amount of inhabitants tax for the previous year but also any portion of the tax for the year prior to that which has not yet been withheld. In sum, departing Japan in early January rather than late December can mean the difference of as much as 17 months' inhabitants tax.

TAX RATES

The following table sets out the current tax rates for various income brackets:

Income bracket (¥)	National tax rate (%)	Local tax rate (%)	Aggregate rate (%)
0 to 2,000000	10	5	15
2,000,001 to 3,300,000	10	10	20
3,000,001 to 7,000,000	20	10	30
7,000,001 to 9,000,000	20	15	35
9,000,001 to 18,000,000	30	15	45
18,000,001 to 30,000,000	40	15	55
30,000,001 and above	50	15	65

Thus, national and local taxes are collected at a top marginal rate of 65% with respect to income over ¥30 million. The rate for local taxes is the sum of prefectural and municipal taxes.

GIFT AND INHERITANCE TAXES

INHERITANCE TAX

Although the Japanese Civil Code provides for a variety of wills, they are not generally used in Japan. Thus, the property of a decedent is normally inherited by the statutory heirs. Wills accepted in other countries will usually be admitted to probate under the Hague Convention on the Conflicts of Laws Relating to the Form of Testamentary Dispositions.

In Japan, it is the statutory heirs or legatees (jointly referred to as "heirs") who are taxed, under the Inheritance Tax Law, on that portion of the decedent's property which they receive; there is no analogue to an "estate" under Anglo-American law. Statutory trusts do exist in Japan, but are inappropriate as tax planning vehicles. Foreign trusts, on the other hand, are occasionally used for tax planning purposes by expatriate beneficiaries resident in Japan.

Heirs who are residents of Japan (including non-permanent residents) are taxed on all inherited property, regardless of the location of that property or the residence of the decedent. Non-resident heirs will be taxed only on property located in Japan, and, again, the residence of the decedent is irrelevant.

In brief, domestic situs rules provide that physical location is dispositive with respect to both real and personal property (including currency), although debts and shares are generally considered to be located where the debtor or issuer resides. A corporate issuer is considered to be located in the jurisdiction in which it has its head office or principal place of business. Other forms of property are deemed located at the decedent's domicile. If applicable, treaties (*e.g.,* the U.S.-Japan Estates, Inheritances and Gifts Convention) may conflict with, and take precedence over, the above domestic rules.

Resident heirs within the estate tax jurisdiction of Japan are taxable on all inherited property and gifts received within three years of the decedent's death. The aggregate value of all such property and gifts received by all heirs is reduced by a basic exemption equal to ¥50 million plus ¥10 million for each statutory heir, regardless of whether such heirs in fact receive anything. Thus, the basic exemption amount would remain the same regardless of the content of a decedent's will, and the actual heirs would be taxed on their pro rata portion of the net amount of the decedent's property and gifts.

Heirs can qualify for a variety of credits, of which the most notable is the spousal credit. This credit permits a spouse to receive a credit equal to the entire amount of tax payable on his/her statutory share, which can range from one-half of the decedent's "estate" to the entire "estate", depending on the existence of other statutory heirs.

Tax rates under the Inheritance Tax Law range from 10% (for property valued at no more than ¥8 million) to 70% (for property valued at more than ¥2 billion).

GIFT TAX

Gift taxation comes within the scope of the Inheritance Tax Law. As in the case of inheritance, it is the recipient of a gift, and not the donor, who is taxed. Residents of Japan are taxed on all gifts received, while non-residents will only be taxed on gifts of property located in Japan, applying the situs rules under the Inheritance Tax Law or an applicable treaty.

Each recipient qualifies for a single annual exemption of ¥600,000 which applies to the total amount of gifts from all donors. The gift tax is severely graduated and ranges from 10% (for gifts up to ¥1.5 million) to 70% (¥100 million and over).

CORPORATE TAX

INTRODUCTION

Japanese corporations (i.e. corporations with a head or principal office in Japan and other juridical entities (jointly referred to below as "corporations")) are subject to tax at the following levels:

(i) Corporate tax, which is levied by the national government, and

(ii) Local taxes, which are comprised of inhabitants taxes, levied by both prefectural and municipal governments, and enterprise tax, which is levied by the prefectural government.

Corporate tax under the CTL is generally computed at a rate of 37.5% on net earnings. Small corporations capitalised at ¥100 million or less, however, are taxed at a rate of 28% on the first ¥8 million of income. A branch of a foreign corporation is taxed at the same rates, based on the capitalisation of the corporation as a whole.

GROSS INCOME

Unless expressly excluded by statute, all income of non-public corporations is assumed to be business-related and taxable under the CTL, and is generally reported on a so-called "realisation", or modified accrual, basis. Among the varieties of taxable income are (1) sales income, (2) non-operating income (including interest and royalties), (3) income deemed realised in the course of mergers or liquidations, (4) income from trust assets, and (5) foreign exchange gains and losses.

Full or partial exclusions are permitted for (1) intercorporate dividends, (2) asset appreciation arising in the course of certain types of transactions (e.g., exchanges of certain like property), and (3) refunds of non-deductible taxes (e.g., national corporate tax and inhabitants taxes, but not enterprise taxes).

Since consolidated reporting is not permitted in Japan, both transnational and domestic transactions between affiliates are scrutinised carefully. In the domestic realm, the tax authorities have the power, under CTL provisions relating to donative transfers and family corporations, to impute income to corporations failing to report arm's-length income in their transactions with domestic affiliates. Transnational transactions between affiliates are covered by the transfer pricing provisions of the STML, which were first issued in 1986 and will be discussed below.

Finally, Japanese corporations are allowed a variety of tax credits, the most notable of which are (1) a credit for taxes withheld by payors pursuant to the ITL (e.g., on intercorporate dividends) and (2) direct and indirect foreign tax credits.

DEDUCTIONS

One of the distinctive features of the Japanese corporate tax system is its liberal provision for tax-free reserves. Simply by way of example, such reserves may be created for bad debts, employment retirement allowances, extreme price fluctuations, and even losses on computer repurchases.

In addition, more traditional deductions are permitted for a wide range of business expenses, although subject to severe limitations in the case of contributions, entertainment expenses, and "excessive" compensations deemed to be similar to dividends, for example.

Net operating losses may be carried forward five years and back one year, provided a so-called "blue return" was filed for the year in which the losses arose (and, in the case of a carryback, the year to which the losses are to be carried back). A "blue return" is a return using a standardised accounting method the filing of which is a privilege granted by the tax office with jurisdiction over a corporation. Applications for that privilege must be filed prior to the year regarding which the blue return is to be filed or, in the case of a newly-established corporation or branch, within three months of establishment. Since the right to take advantage of loss carryforwards and carrybacks, a number of tax-deductible reserves and other tax incentives, and accelerated depreciation for certain assets is conditioned on filing a blue return, timely application for the right to file such returns is of considerable importance to foreign branches and subsidiaries in Japan.

REORGANISATIONS

General

Although, in principle, corporate reorganisations will result in the realisation of income on the transfer of appreciated property, there are some important exceptions to this rule in the context of mergers and spin-offs.

Mergers
(i)   Shareholders

Shareholders of corporations subject to a merger may be taxable on any actual or constructive dividends or capital gains arising from the merger. Shares of a surviving corporation distributed in the course of the merger are normally valued at par rather than fair market value.

(ii)   Merged Corporation

In the event that the shareholders of a merged corporation receive shares or other property in exchange for their shares in the merged corporation, not only may they be taxed on any capital gains arising from the exchange, the merged corporation itself will be taxed on its "liquidation income" at a flat 33% rate. Liquidation income refers to any residual assets distributed by a liquidating corporation which have not been previously taxed under the CTL. In the context of a merger, such income would be equal to the excess of the value of property received by the merged corporation's shareholders (par value in the case of shares of a surviving corporation) over the total paid-in capital and capital surplus of the merged corporation.

Since liquidation income would not arise in the event that a wholly-owned subsidiary were merged into its parent, it is common in Japan for merger partners to arrange for the shares of the target corporation to be acquired initially by the other and then merged into the parent by means of an up-stream merger. Such a procedure is permitted, provided the former shareholders of the acquired corporation pay tax in Japan on their capital gains or are shielded from such tax under an applicable tax treaty.

(iii) Surviving Corporation

The valuation of assets transferred to a surviving corporation is largely left to the discretion of that corporation (provided it is not less than book value). The excess of the value assigned to such assets over any shares or other property transferred to shareholders of the merged corporation (or any shares of the merged corporation written off as part of an upstream merger) will constitute merger income taxable to the surviving corporation. As a result, it is common for surviving corporations to revalue assets received in a merger up to, but not over, the book value of such shares or other property, thus taking advantage of a tax-free step-up in basis.

Spin-Offs

Although a contribution-in-kind to the capital of a corporation would normally result in the realisation of income for the shareholder, Article 51 of the CTL permits a carryover of basis in the event (1) the assets in question are contributed at the time of incorporation and (2) the transferor is a 95% shareholder. The benefits of this provision are available to foreign corporations intending to reorganise a branch into a Japanese subsidiary. They are also available to Japanese corporations establishing foreign subsidiaries.

All subsequent transfers of shares issued in connection with an Article 51 spin-off must be at fair market value.

TRANSFER PRICING

Japan's transfer pricing regime for international transactions between affiliates was first introduced in 1986 in the form of a new provision of the STML (now Art. 66-4). The general policy of the Japanese government has been, and continues to be, to adhere to the arm's length standard. It has joined other countries in such international organisations as the OECD in urging that a transactional standard be retained, and has opposed the adoption of comparative profit or formulary methodologies. Tax officials in Japan perceive themselves as occupying an intermediate position between a number of European countries (most notably, the United Kingdom) that believe transfer pricing adjustments to be appropriate only in cases of clear abuse, and the United States, which is seen as attempting to use transfer pricing adjustments as a way of increasing revenues. Since 1993, however, the NTA has become sufficiently aggressive to make transfer pricing an important dimension of business planning for foreign entities that intend to conduct business in Japan through affiliated entities.

Under current Japanese rules, the permitted methodologies for both inventory sales and other transactions are (1) the comparable uncontrolled price (CUP) method, (2) the resale price method, (3) the cost-plus method, and (4) other methods. There is no preference among the first three of the above methods, but the use of an "other" method is premised on the unavailability of suitable comparables under those three methods.

Japan's income tax treaties contain provisions similar to those in the OECD Model Convention under which the competent authorities of Japan and the treaty partner may resolve double taxation issues arising from transfer pricing disputes, and there are procedures under domestic law for interested parties to invoke the government-to-government "mutual agreement" process. This process can be extremely time-consuming, ranging from approximately six months to more than two years in difficult cases.

The NTA has also introduced a so-called "pre-confirmation" system similar to the advance pricing agreement procedure in the United States. To date, the disclosure requirements have proven so time-consuming and otherwise burdensome that only a few pre-confirmations have been successfully concluded in Japan. Since the NTA is expending considerable effort to make the system more effective, however, there is room for optimism that it may become a viable option for Japanese taxpayers in the near future.

TAX HAVENS

In 1992, Japan's tax treatment of controlled foreign subsidiaries located in tax havens was modified in important ways. Pursuant to amendments to the STML, a system based on prior designation of low-tax countries (LTCs) by the MOF was abandoned in favour of a case-by-case system whereby any foreign subsidiary can be deemed to be located in an LTC if the effective corporate tax rate in that country is less than or equal to 25%.

Under the tax-haven regime currently in effect, if a "related foreign company" (i.e., a foreign company more than 50% owned or controlled by Japanese residents [or affiliates of such residents]) has its head office or principal place of business in an LTC, it will be considered a "designated foreign subsidiary" (DFS), and its major Japanese shareholders (*i.e.,* Japanese residents or corporations which, separately or together with affiliated individuals or corporations, own 5% or more of the DFS) will be required to report their undistributed profits as income. However, if a controlled foreign subsidiary is located in an LTC for commercial, non-tax purposes (*e.g.,* a significant portion of its income does not arise from the ownership of securities or intellectual property and its business is primarily conducted in the LTC or with unrelated parties), it may escape being characterised as a DFS.

LOCAL CORPORATE TAXES

Inhabitants Taxes
Inhabitants taxes are imposed at both the prefectural and municipal levels, and, at each level, consist of (1) a per capita levy and (2) a corporate levy.

The per capita levy is calculated on the basis of capitalisation and number of employees, and can range from ¥20,000 to ¥800,000 at the prefectural level, and from ¥50,000 to ¥3 million at the municipal level.

Corporate levies are determined by applying the prefectural and municipal tax rates against the amount of corporate tax payable by a corporation. Such rates vary slightly depending on the location of the corporation's operations, but must fall within the following ranges: 5-6% for prefectures and 12.3-14.7% for municipalities. Tokyo, for example, applies the maximum combined rate of 20.7% for a corporation capitalised at over ¥100 million or having a corporate tax liability of over ¥10 million. Since this combined rate is applied to the national corporate tax amount, it represents a tax rate of over 7% on net reported income.

Enterprise Tax
Enterprise tax is levied on the profits of corporations located in Japan. This tax is collected by the prefectural governments and is calculated on essentially the same income base as the national corporate tax, with some minor differences. The tax rates are graduated and range from 6%, for income up to ¥3.5 million, to 12%, for income over ¥7 million. The prefectural governments have the discretion to increase these rates by an additional 10%. Since the enterprise tax for a given year is deductible for the purposes of calculating both national and local corporate taxes for the following year, the top effective marginal

tax rate for corporate, inhabitants (including per capita), and enterprise taxes is approximately 50%.

TAXATION OF NON-RESIDENTS

GENERAL

Normally, the threshold issue in determining whether a non-resident individual or foreign corporation (jointly referred to as "non-resident") is subject to taxation in Japan is that of whether that non-resident maintains a "permanent establishment" in Japan. If it does, it be will be subject to tax at full graduated rates under the ITL, for individuals, or the CTL, for corporations, on at least a significant portion of its Japan-source income attributable to the activities of the permanent establishment. If the non-resident does not maintain such a permanent establishment, it will normally be subject only to withholding tax, and only on certain varieties of income sourced in Japan. Finally, there are a few exceptional types of income that will be taxable at full rates regardless of whether or not the non-resident has a permanent establishment.

The following discussion will centre on the concept of "permanent establishment", and the implications of having one, under domestic law. It cannot be stressed too strongly, however, that tax treaties are a crucial source of law regarding the permissible limits of Japanese taxation of non-residents. Whenever a tax issue arises concerning a resident of a country with which Japan has a tax treaty, it is highly likely that the treaty will have an impact on the resident's ultimate tax liability in Japan.

TAXATION OF RESIDENTS WITH A PERMANENT ESTABLISHMENT IN JAPAN

The term "permanent establishment" is not used in Japanese tax legislation. However, since Japan's tax regime for non-residents is largely based on the conceptual framework in the OECD Draft Income Tax Convention of 1963 (OECD Convention) and since the concept, "permanent establishment," is a central one in the OECD Convention, it is common for commentators on Japanese taxation to use the term as shorthand for three types of presence in Japan which will result in full graduated taxation on income sourced in Japan (or at least that Japan-source income "attributable" to the activities of that "presence" in Japan).

The three types of presence referred to above are: (1) fixed places of business (*e.g.*, offices or branches), (2) construction, installation, assembly, or similar activities carried out over more than one year, and (3) contracting, fills-order, and negotiating agents. Without an applicable treaty, the maintenance of a fixed place in Japan (Category 1) will result in a non-resident's being taxable at regular graduated rates on all of its Japan-source income, regardless of whether or not it is "attributable" to its permanent establishment. The existence of a permanent establishment in categories (2) or (3) will result in regular taxation of attributable Japan-source income only. All other Japan-source income of a non-resident maintaining a permanent establishment in the latter categories would be taxed as if the non-resident did not have a permanent establishment. We will now turn to a fuller discussion of Categories (1) and (3).

Fixed Place of Business

Normally, whether or not a fixed place of business exists for Japanese tax purposes is not a difficult issue. If a non-resident maintains a place of business, office, or warehouse, or even a mine or quarry, it will constitute a fixed place of business. It should be borne in mind, however, that this concept is interpreted broadly by the tax authorities. For example, there is a Basic Circular to the effect that even a hotel room regularly used for business purposes should be considered a fixed place of business.

There are a number of exceptional cases under both domestic law and/or tax treaties where a fixed place of business will not be considered a permanent establishment. The more important exceptions are described below.

(i)   Auxiliary Activities

Both domestic and treaty law exempt from permanent establishment status fixed places of business which are used for such auxiliary activities as advertising, promotion, the supply of information, basic research, and market surveys. It is important to stress, however, that this exception only applies to fixed places of business performing auxiliary activities for the company of which it is a constituent part, and only for that company. It does not apply when such activities are performed for the benefit of a separate company, even if that company is an affiliate. In the latter case, the fixed place of business (normally a branch) performing auxiliary services for another company would have to report arm's length income in Japan.

(ii) Purchase of Goods

Under domestic law, a fixed place of business (normally a branch) used solely for purchasing goods for the corporation of which it is a part is not considered a permanent establishment. Care should be taken, however, to ensure that the branch send goods directly to its head office (or another office of the same corporation) and that third parties not take control of the goods immediately on delivery abroad. If the branch continues to control the goods prior to delivery to customers abroad, there is significant danger that the branch will be deemed to be engaged in selling activities as well, and therefore constitute a permanent establishment.

(iii) Storage, Display, Delivery, etc.

In general, the exception for fixed places of business that merely store, display, or deliver goods, or maintain a stock of goods for processing by other parties is a function of treaty law. A non-resident engaging in such activities through a fixed place of business in Japan will very likely be deemed to have a permanent establishment under domestic law.

Agents

(i) Contracting Agent

A contracting agent is one who has, and habitually exercises, the authority to conclude contracts in Japan on behalf of a foreign principal. The mere purchase of goods for a foreign principal, however, would not be sufficient to constitute a contracting agent for these purposes.

(ii) Fills-Order Agent

Under Japanese domestic law, an agent who merely maintains goods for the purpose of meeting the requirements of customers and delivers such goods to customers will be deemed to constitute a permanent establishment. This is in contrast with most OECD-type treaties, which exempt such "fills-order" agents from permanent establishment status.

(iii) Negotiating Agent

A negotiating agent is one who, though he/she may not satisfy the criteria for being a contracting agent, exclusively or principally on behalf of a non-resident "secures orders, negotiates, or performs other important acts leading toward the conclusion of contracts." The "negotiating agent" concept represents an attempt to expand the scope of "contracting agent" to include agents who play a substantially identical role. Thus, nominal limitations on an agent's authority or crude attempts to ensure that all contracts are formally executed abroad may not be sufficient to allow an agent to escape characterisation as a permanent establishment.

Although domestic law is not as explicit as OECD treaties in exempting agents of an independent status from being characterised as a permanent establishment, the language in the Enforcement Orders relating to acting "exclusively or principally" for a foreign principal is normally interpreted to exclude most types of agents (*e.g.*, brokers and general commission agents) who would be characterised as independent agents for tax treaty purposes.

(iv) Exceptions

The exceptions in both domestic law and treaties relating to fixed places of business (described above) do not, on their face, apply to agents, although some treaties expressly provide that agents engaged only in the purchase of goods for a non-resident principal will not constitute a permanent establishment. It would seem to follow that a dependent agent habitually engaged in the conclusion of contracts relating to auxiliary activities (*e.g.*, advertising or market research) or storage, display, delivery, or processing of goods *would* be deemed to be permanent establishment. In fact, although the tax authorities in Japan are likely to subject such agents to strict scrutiny, if it were concluded in an audit that the activities of an agent were actually limited to the above exempted realm, it is unlikely that the agent would be deemed to be a permanent establishment.

TAXATION OF NON-RESIDENTS WITHOUT A PERMANENT ESTABLISHMENT IN JAPAN

Source Rules

A non-resident is, in principle, taxable only on domestic source income. Whether or not that non-resident has a permanent establishment in Japan will only have an impact on the manner in which, the base on which, and the rates at which, that income is taxed. The ITL defines domestic source income as income falling in one of the following 12 categories:

Category I (Business or Assets Income)
Income arising from a business carried out in Japan, or the use, possession or transfer of assets in Japan, or other income to be provided by Cabinet Order

Category I-2 (Gains from Transfers of Rights in Land)
Since 1990, income realised from transfers of rights in land have been treated as a category of income separate from the rest of Category I.

Category II (Income from Providing Personal Services)
Income earned as compensation for personal services by an individual or corporation engaged in Japan in the business of providing personal services (*compare* Category VIII)

Category III (Rental Income)
Income arising from leasing land, buildings, other real property, or rights thereto in Japan

Category IV (Interest)
Interest on (1) bonds issued by Japanese government entities or domestic corporations or (2) deposits with a corporation with a place of business in Japan, and income distributions from a trust to which Japanese business has been entrusted.

Category V (Dividends)
Dividends from domestic corporations

Category VI (Interest on Business Loans)
Interest on business-related loans or similar transactions with a person engaging in business in Japan

Category VII (Royalty and Rental Income)
Royalties for the use of intellectual property, consideration for transfers of such property, and income from the rental of machinery or equipment

Category VIII (Remuneration for Personal Services)
Income (including deferred income) earned by an individual as consideration for the performance of personal services in Japan. (Because this item of income is only received by individuals, it is not included among the *11* items of Japan-source income listed in the CTL.)

Category IX (Prizes)
Prizes awarded in connection with advertising by a business in Japan

Category X (Annuities)
All payments arising from life insurance policies and annuity and pension agreements, and similar contracts

Category XI (Income from Savings Transactions)
Income arising from a variety of savings or investment transactions not covered under other income categories, including futures and other derivatives

Category XII (Distributions by Silent Partnerships)
A silent partnership is a contractual arrangement permitted under the Commercial Code, pursuant to which a proprietor (similar to a general partner) will operate a business in Japan without revealing the interests of "silent" partners, who may be non-residents. This category

applies to distributions to 10 or more silent partners. If there are less than 10 silent partners, distributions are generally interpreted as coming within the scope of Category I above.

Gross Tax and Withholding Tax

Entirely distinct from the regular, graduated rate taxes on net income under the ITL and CTL discussed above (the "net tax"; also referred to as the "composite tax" in Japan), is a tax on gross income (the "gross tax"; also referred to as the "separate tax" in Japan) applicable in principle to non-residents' Japan-source income not subject to net tax.

Inasmuch as withholding at source by a payor resident or domiciled in Japan is normally the only way in which the gross tax is collected, and since a non-resident payee is almost never under an obligation to file a gross tax return even if the payor fails to withhold properly, there is a justifiable tendency among tax practitioners in Japan to refer only to the withholding tax when discussing the gross tax liability of a non-resident. It should not be forgotten, however, that it is possible to have a gross tax liability without a corresponding withholding obligation (*e.g.,* payments of Japan-source income by a person not resident or domiciled in Japan), and there are withholding obligations that apply to income that is also subject to net tax, which will be discussed in the next section.

Under Article 164(2)(ii) of the ITL, only income in Categories IV through XII is subject to the gross tax. Yet, under Article 212, all income in Categories I-2 through XII is, in principle, subject to withholding. It follows that income in Categories I-2, 2, and 3 are subject to withholding but not to the gross tax. In fact, income in those categories is always subject to net tax, and any taxes withheld with respect to such income is merely credited towards the non-resident's ultimate net tax liability.

Japan currently has a three-tier system of withholding rates. Income in Category I-2 qualifies for a preferential rate of 10%, Categories IV and XI (interest and analogues thereto) are subject to a 15% rate, and all other income within the scope of Article 212 of the ITL is subject to a rate of 20%.

Net Tax

As indicated above, a non-resident with income in Categories I-III will be subject to net tax and will be required to file a net tax return. In addition, there is a separate withholding tax with respect to income in Categories I-2 through III which can, if paid, be credited against a non-resident's net tax liability. The net tax liability with respect to Categories I-III is basic, however: a non-resident with income in those categories will always be liable for net tax, regardless of whether or not it maintains a permanent establishment or whether or not withholding has been effected.

CONSUMPTION TAX

The Japanese consumption tax, introduced in 1989 under the Consumption Tax Law, is a form of value-added tax intended to tax the net value added at each stage of the production and distribution chain. It applies to all sales or rentals of goods and the provision of services in, and the importation of goods into, Japan. The current consumption tax rate is 3%. On April 1, 1997, this rate is scheduled to be increased to 4%, in conjunction with the introduction of a separate local consumption tax of 1%.

The consumption tax is imposed on all individuals and corporations (regardless of residence) which receive income from domestic taxable transactions or clear goods from customs, provided that taxpayers with taxable sales of less than ¥30 million are completely exempted, and those with less than ¥50 million in taxable sales are partially exempted. A number of significant types of transactions are not considered taxable transactions, including payments of dividends, insurance premiums, and contributions, transfers of land and securities, and exports.

Ordinarily, the consumption tax is paid at each stage in the distribution chain, starting with the producer or importer, and each taxpayer is allowed to credit any consumption tax deemed paid on taxable inputs. Only the consumer, who technically does not pay the tax, does not receive such a credit. It is because the consumer is likely to bear the economic burden of the tax that it is called a consumption tax.

OTHER TAXES

It would be an understatement to say that the foregoing is not an exhaustive treatment of the Japanese taxation system. Not only is there much more that could be said about the topics addressed, there are many other types of taxes that have not been mentioned at all, including acquisition taxes on automobiles, excise taxes on petroleum products, tobacco, liquor, sugar, utilities, airfares, meals at restaurants, and mineral baths, and a host of registration and licensing fees. The following list could be of particular interest to any non-resident planning to do business in Japan:

FIXED ASSET TAX

This tax is imposed by municipalities on the owner of land, buildings, and business-related machinery at a rate between 1.4 and 2.1% of appraised value (normally significantly lower than market value).

REAL PROPERTY ACQUISITION TAX

This is a prefectural tax imposed on the acquirer of land or buildings at a rate of 4%, subject to some variations, of appraised value.

SECURITIES TRANSACTION TAX

This tax is imposed on the transferor of stocks, bonds, and other securities located in Japan immediately before transfer at a rate of 0.3% of the transfer price of shares, or at significantly lower rates for other securities.

STAMP TAX

This is a tax payable at the time of execution of a wide variety of contracts or other instruments (e.g., promissory notes and articles of incorporation) in amounts varying from ¥200 to ¥600,000.

SUMMING UP

INDIVIDUAL TAXATION

The nominal tax rates applicable to individuals under the ITL and local inhabitants taxes are high by international standards, ranging from 15 to 65% in the aggregate. A variety of available exclusions and deductions can result in significant reductions in the effective individual tax rates, however.

Non-resident individuals are taxable only on their Japan-source income, and, even then, usually only at low fixed rates. Non-permanent residents (*i.e.,* residents who have lived in Japan for a continuous period of five years or less) are taxable on income sourced outside Japan unless such income is remitted into or paid within Japan. Permanent residents (*i.e.,* most resident Japanese nationals and other residents who have lived in Japan for more than five years) are taxable on worldwide income.

GIFT AND INHERITANCE TAXES

In Japan, it is the recipients of gifts and inherited property who are taxed, at severely graduated rates ranging from 10% to 70%. Recipients who are residents of Japan will be taxed on all received property, while non-resident recipients will be taxed only on property with a situs in Japan.

CORPORATE TAXATION

Domestic corporations and corporations with some other statutorily-defined nexus with Japan are subject to (1) corporate tax under the CTL, (2) withholding (or gross) tax under the ITL, or (3) local taxes (notably inhabitants and enterprise taxes), depending on the circumstances. Applicable withholding/gross tax rates range from 10% to 20%, while combined corporate and local taxes may exceed 50%.

TRANSFER PRICING AND TAX HAVENS

The Japanese tax authorities have the statutory weapons to attack tax abuse based on transfer pricing or the use of tax havens, and have been using those weapons with increasing frequency recently.

CONSUMPTION TAX

Japan introduced a 3% consumption tax (a form of value-added tax) in 1989, and is scheduled to increase the rate to 5% (including local consumption tax) in 1997. This tax applies to all sales or leases of goods, the provision of services, and imports.

OTHER TAXES

There are many other types of potentially significant taxes in Japan, including the fixed asset tax, real property, and other acquisition taxes, the securities transaction tax, a wide variety of excise taxes, and the stamp tax.

* The author wishes to thank Shinichi Kobayashi for reviewing an earlier draft of this chapter, and for his many helpful comments.

CHAPTER 13

LITIGATION, ARBITRATION AND THE LEGAL PROFESSION IN JAPAN
by Charles R. Stevens

LITIGATION AND ARBITRATION

One hundred and fifty years ago civil litigants were sometimes tortured for having the effrontery to disturb magistrates with their annoying disputes. While the modern civil litigant in Japan is no longer physically tortured, litigation remains a torturously expensive and protracted process. Arbitration in Japan is not much better.

NEGOTIATING SETTLEMENTS

In Japan, as in much of Asia, it is considered better to settle a dispute than to litigate or arbitrate it.

- Settlement promotes social harmony, a general ideal in Japanese society.

- Settlement means that neither side "wins" or "loses" the dispute.

- Settlement is expected in Japanese business society, where litigiousness is viewed as a dangerous characteristic of the business pariah or the gangster (or of the foreigner who doesn't know any better).

- Perhaps more importantly, settlement avoids the expenses, delays and injustices inherent in litigation or arbitration in Japan (described later).

THE IMPORTANCE OF THE PERIOD BEFORE INITIATION OF FORMAL PROCEEDINGS

In Japan it is expected that settlement will occur *before* a lawsuit or arbitration is formally initiated since the actual filing of a suit or arbitration is considered so hostile an act that settlement thereafter becomes much more difficult. In the United States initiation of suit or arbitration is often used as a negotiating tactic to bring the other party to the table for settlement discussions. In Japan such a negotiating tactic usually destroys any will on the Japanese side to settle any time soon.

BLUSTER, SHOUTING AND OTHER BAD (WESTERN) MANNERS

Bad manners are so far removed from acceptable behaviour among businessmen that a Japanese party will often "tune out" whatever message the hapless foreigner thinks that he/she is sending by the bad manners. More sophisticated Japanese will also know that extreme bad manners show loss of control that can be exploited.

ADVANTAGES OF BEING THE UNPREDICTABLE FOREIGNER

There are, however, real advantages in being a foreigner in any settlement negotiation with a Japanese party.

First, almost by definition the foreigner is unpredictable, unlikely to behave with sensitivity to the nuances of Japanese business society and, therefore, often to be a bit more indulged than a Japanese opposite party, who can be safely expected not to do anything mutually self-destructive. This extra margin to placate the foreigner can be a real negotiation advantage if it is not overplayed.

Second, a foreigner may think of doing hostile acts that are unthinkable in Japan (litigation or arbitration) or may do things abroad that are not possible in Japan (foreign litigation, especially litigation involving intrusive discovery, or initiation of trade or antitrust complaints).

Finally, the settlement documentation and the language of settlement negotiation will almost always be English, a powerful advantage giving more control to the foreigner.

LITIGATION IN JAPAN

For the potential litigant the most important fact about litigation in Japan is that litigation calendars are very clogged. In 1995 only 2,852 judges handled approximately 130,000 new civil cases per year (excluding family matters) and tens of thousands of new criminal matters.

Among industrialised countries Japan has very few judges when compared with the number of persons in its general population.

Population of Industrialised Countries and Numbers of Judges

30 May 1994

	Population	**No. of Judges**	**Population for Every Judge**
United Kingdom	57,800,000	31,205	1,852
Germany	80,200,000	17,932	4,472
France	56,600,000	4,633	12,217
United States	255,600,000	29,846	8,564
Japan	124,760,000	2,852	43,745
Korea	44,300,000	1,238	35,784

Source: 1994 No. 12 Vol. 45 Jiyu to Seigi (Liberty and Justice).

The result is that very overburdened judges don't have time to have meaningful hearings in the great preponderance of civil cases. Hearings are usually held before a single judge (although in especially complicated cases the court may, at its discretion, convene a panel of three judges). Oral arguments typically take place in short monthly sessions where over-worked counsel frequently assert facts and legal arguments to a harassed judge barely able to review the file. Systematic testimony by witnesses with opportunity for cross-examination is rare. Documentary proof is limited by inadequate means of compelling production of documents. Most ordinary civil cases requiring a full trial proceed at the pace of one brief hearing a month for three to five years. If the civil case is complicated, it is not unusual for such a trial to take five years or longer. Much of the time of the judge is consumed in constantly urging the parties to settle the case to get it off of the court calendar. Even after a decision at the District Court level, appeals can take many years.

Filing fees for civil litigation are geared to the amount claimed. Consequently, it can be very costly to file a complaint in a commercial litigation. In 1994 the filing fee for a claim of about $5,000,000 was slightly more than $16,000. In practice this means that a party initially claims smaller amounts until it seems that the litigation is coming out favourably, whereupon it amends its claims to something closer to the actual damages suffered.

Finally judgements, when they are awarded, will seem very low to most foreign litigants. It is inconceivable that any judgement in Japan will award damages in the Yen equivalent of tens or hundreds of millions of dollars, no matter what the damages actually suffered. Part of the reason for this may be the filing fees mentioned above. Another reason is that punitive levels of damages are considered to be criminal sanctions, not appropriate in civil cases in Japan.[1] Other reasons undoubtedly include the cautious bureaucratic mentality of career jurists to whom large awards are likely to be personally shocking.

FOREIGN LITIGATION INVOLVING JAPAN

The best method for a foreign party to use to litigate against a Japanese party is to avoid the problems outlined above by

(i) bringing suit in a foreign court and then, if successful,

(ii) enforcing the foreign court's judgement in the Japanese courts.

Article 200 of the Japanese Code of Civil Procedure provides that final and binding judgements of foreign courts are valid in Japan if they fulfil four basic conditions:

(i)   the jurisdiction of the court that rendered the foreign judgement must not be disallowed by laws and orders or by treaty;

(ii)   where the defeated defendant is a Japanese person, such defendant received service of summons or any other orders necessary to commence the action through means other than publication or such defendant has responded to the action, whether or not summons was served;

(iii)   the judgement of the foreign court is not contrary to Japanese public order and good morals;[2] and

(iv)   there are guaranties of comity.

Foreign judgements have been enforced regularly by the Japanese courts. A suit for enforcement of a foreign judgement can be completed in one or two years, as contrasted with a civil suit in Japanese court that might take more than five years before judgement.

   A foreign court also permits use of methods of discovery which in most cases are greatly superior to those available in Japan. In United States courts, in particular, documentary discovery and discovery by way of depositions are two methods which are superior to anything available in Japan. A major danger with foreign discovery (especially U.S. discovery) is, however, that it must be conducted in such a way so that any resultant judgment is not deemed unenforceable by a Japanese court because the judgment does not comply with Article 200, especially that it is not contrary to "Japanese public order and good morals."

In the case of U.S. depositions the depositions leading up to the judgement must not have violated Japanese sovereignty by being conducted in Japan in a manner contrary to the U.S. Japan Consular Convention. The Japanese government and Japanese judges may take the position that Japanese sovereignty and "Japanese public order and good morals" have been violated if:

(i) U.S. attorneys travelling to Japan for the deposition have not applied for and obtained special deposition visas from the applicable Japanese consulate or

(ii) the deposition is not conducted under the auspices of U.S. Embassy or Consulate, i.e. literally in a deposition room in the Embassy or a Consulate under the supervision of a U.S. consular officer whose duties include supervising depositions.

Deposition rooms exist in five U.S. facilities in Japan (in the Embassy in Tokyo and in the U.S. Consulates in Osaka, Fukuoka, Sapporo and Naha), and they are usually fully booked many months in advance. Blocking them out for days or weeks of extensive depositions is extremely difficult. Depositions conducted in other more convenient locations such as hotels or *bengoshi* (licensed Japanese lawyers) offices are subject to later attack as violative of the Consular Convention, and, thus, of Japanese sovereignty, public order and good morals.

ARBITRATIONS INVOLVING JAPAN

Another way of avoiding the delays of litigation in Japan is by deciding a dispute by arbitration. Japan is a signatory of the New York Convention on the Recognition and Enforcement of Foreign Arbitral Awards, and international arbitration awards are enforceable in the Japanese courts.[3]

Many *bengoshi* argue that representation of a party before an arbitration tribunal in Japan by a foreign lawyer is a violation of the unauthorised practice of law provision in Article 72 of Japan's Lawyer Law, a criminal provision the violation of which might make the arbitral award unenforceable in a Japanese court and might also subject the foreigner lawyer to Japanese criminal penalties. These arguments are made with particular insistence if the dispute being arbitrated involves important issues of Japanese law. In 1996, the Japan Federation of Bar Associations passed a resolution and consented to a legislative amendment which, when passed by Japan's Diet, will allow foreign lawyers to represent parties in international arbitrations in Japan in most cases.

Because of the history of *bengoshi* protectionism on arbitrations, in the last few decades most draftsmen of international commercial contracts involving Japanese parties and arbitration clauses have been careful to provide that arbitration will occur outside of Japan. This has meant that in recent years there have been fewer than 10 arbitrations per year before the Japan Commercial Arbitration Association, Japan's leading international arbitration organisation. In contrast, in recent years there have been hundreds of arbitrations per year before the China International Economic and Trade Arbitration Commission (CIETAC), China's leading arbitration organisation.

Most Japanese and foreign parties will also wish to avoid adoption of arbitration clauses that put the place of arbitration in the home jurisdiction of the responding party. Such clauses for many years and for unknown reasons were very popular in arbitration clauses involving Japanese parties. They undesirably leave the choice of place to the happenstance of who is first to file the arbitration request.

THE JAPANESE LEGAL SYSTEM, AND THE LEGAL PROFESSION

Japanese legal history is too huge a subject to go into in depth here[4], but there are several important historical facts that do have great importance for the modern role of the legal profession in Japanese society.

ABSENCE OF LAWYERS BEFORE 1868

The first historical fact of great importance is that there were no lawyers in Japan before the beginning of the Meiji Restoration in 1868. Criminal and civil law was administered by a professionally trained group of *samurai* magistrates in charge of a system that relied on written laws and edicts published[5] by various levels of feudal government, on social custom in matters involving social relationships, on commercial custom in cases involving commerce, and on case precedent based on case records available to the magistrates. A Japanese *samurai* magistrate of the 18th century reasoned to his conclusions using analogies drawn from prior cases or custom much in the same way that his English counterpart did in the English courts of the 18th century. The difference was that in Japan there were no lawyers to state both sides of the case. The parties sometimes attempted to argue their own cases and sometimes were assisted by those related to them in the feudal hierarchy or kinship, but as the only possessor of sophisticated legal training and as the only person with ready access to laws, decrees and case precedents, the magistrate decided unaided (and unhampered) by counsel.

The whole Western concept of the lawyer was seriously misunderstood in pre-Meiji, Tokugawa Japan:

"Prior to 1867 there was not a single statement in Japanese literature accurately depicting the role of the lawyer as it existed in the Western World. The first reference, in 1811, adverted to the lawyer as a "natural philosopher." An 1854 work perhaps came somewhat closer to reality when it described the lawyer as one who accompanied stupid people to court and wrote documents for them." Rabinowitz "The Historical Development of the Japanese Bar" 70 *Harv. L. Rev.*, 61 (1956).[6]

The total absence of lawyers before 1868[7] had two important effects on the modern profession: (i) a feeling of inferiority and lack of legitimacy based on the lack of any sort of professional history or ancient tradition and (ii) a subservience to the post-1868 procuracy which, along with the judiciary, had inherited the superior, law-defining role of the Tokugawa magistrates. Indeed after 1868 and until post-war reforms under the American Occupation, the *bengoshi* part of the legal profession[8] was regulated by the Ministry of Justice and was not fully independent of government control.

THE IMPORTANCE OF A NAME: *BENGOSHI*

After lawyers began to appear in the new Japanese courts they were eventually termed *bengoshi*, three ideographs which mean literally "a gentleman who speaks in defence (or in protection)." This new Japanese word was created with the intent of translating the English word "barrister" or the French word "avocat". The word quite literally connotes the litigation role of a lawyer.

Most Japanese *bengoshi* still spend all or most of their time on litigation matters. Almost no Japanese *bengoshi*, except for the very few internationally practising *bengoshi* discussed below, merely counsel clients with no involvement in litigation.

LAW AS A COURSE OF ACADEMIC STUDIES

After 1868 the new ruling elite in Japan quickly concluded that for Japan to become modern quickly the old custom and precedent-based Tokugawa system had to be discarded almost in its entirety,[9] and a code system had to be quickly put in its place. The intent was to make Japan almost instantly modern in law with a Continental-style code system. This also led to a Continental-style emphasis on law studies as an undergraduate academic discipline, and from the late 19th century until the present day the most prestigious undergraduate "major" in Japan is law. In Japan every year LL B graduates are extraordinarily numerous and go on to dominate the highest levels of the Japanese career bureaucracy and industry. In 1994 there were 43,577[7] graduates from the law faculties in Japanese universities, a number larger than the annual number of 1994 graduates from law schools in the United States - a country with twice as large a population.

THE JUDICIARY

The courts of original jurisdiction in Japan are the 50 District Courts. The most important and largest District Court is the Tokyo District Court. Appeals from the District Courts and appeals from quasi-judicial government agencies are taken to the High Courts of which there are eight, located in various geographic centres. Finally, appeals from the High Courts and special "leaping appeals" from the District Courts (involving the constitutionality of legislation, for example) can go to the Supreme Court of Japan.

In addition to the normal court system described above, there are speciality courts: 50 Family Courts, which handle family matters and juvenile delinquency cases, and 575 Summary Courts, which handle petty civil and criminal matters.

Except for the justices of the Supreme Court, most Japanese judges have spent their entire careers on the bench. The Supreme Court justices are appointed from the ranks of distinguished judges, attorneys, procurators, and civil servants. The judiciary is an independent third branch of the government, and its affairs are administered by the Secretariat of the Supreme Court of Japan. After graduation from the Legal Research and Training Institute, described below, the young judge normally spends 10 years as an assistant judge before becoming a full judge. After becoming a full judge he/she is gradually promoted upward in the judicial hierarchy as he/she becomes older, hopefully reaching the level of High Court Judge, Chief Judge of a District Court, or Chief Judge of a major Division of a major District Court before his/her retirement. As an assistant judge and as a full judge he/she is rotated regularly to various courts, and almost every experienced judge has spent some time in the remote provincial District Courts in Hokkaido, Northern Honshu or Shikoku, as well as in the busier and more famous District Courts in Tokyo and Osaka. The Japanese judge is, in short, a kind of judicial bureaucrat.

BENGOSHI

Prior to reforms which occurred after World War II aspiring *bengoshi* were not permitted to attend the elite government institute for training young judges and procurators which eventually became the Legal Research and Training Institute in the post-war period. In the reforms of the judicial system which occurred during the American Occupation, the *bengoshi* successfully lobbied for a system which required judges, procurators and *bengoshi* to attend the Institute prior to being admitted to their respective parts of the legal profession. In practice this has meant that the total of new entrants to the ranks of judges, procurators and *bengoshi* has been limited by the less than 750 available spaces at the Institute.[11] The small trickle of graduates has been the only source of legal professionals necessary to run the court system in a country with a population of over 120 million.

Annually almost 23,000 persons take the Institute's entrance examinations although the passing rate is less than 3.5% because of the small number of places in the Institute. With such a low passing rate even the most talented students from the best Japanese universities must plan to take the Institute's entrance examinations in several successive years before the examinations are passed. In 1994, for example, the average age of those admitted was 27.95, meaning that the entrant took the examination six or seven years in a row and many others took the examinations for ten or more years before achieving success.

The gruelling entrance examination system has the effect of making professional monopoly all the sweeter to those who eventually succeed. Many older Japanese *bengoshi* assert that it also leads to odd, narrow and repressed characters for those younger *bengoshi* who have spent so much of their youth in dry cramming.

The curriculum of the Legal Research and Training Institute focusses heavily on litigation and procedure, both civil and criminal. The legal apprentices are given opportunities to work in the court system, the procuracy, and *bengoshi* offices, to sample career opportunities and to gain further training. They are not significantly trained in analytic thinking, which one hopes is the heart of American law school training. In contrast to the entrance examination, once a legal apprentice gains admission to the Institute, he/she is virtually assured of graduation. The passing rate for the examination necessary for graduation from the Institute (the functional equivalent of an American bar examination) has been 100% in recent years.

Each year about 10%–15% of the Institute's graduates elect to become judges, 10%–15% elect to become procurators, and the rest become *bengoshi*. The individual *bengoshi* goes on to practice, usually in a small law office, often starting out in an apprentice-like relationship under a senior attorney and then branching out into his/ her own satellite practice, sharing space with his/her former mentor, or leaving and setting up a new office on his/her own. The concept of large, corporation-like law firms is foreign to Japan and even large numbers of Japanese *bengoshi* who ostensibly practice as a "firm" are often a collection of sole practitioners or proprietorships sharing the same space.

Japanese *bengoshi* are concentrated in the Kanto area which embraces Tokyo and Yokohama and in the Kinki area which embraces Osaka, Kobe and Kyoto.

Geographic Distribution of Japanese Bengoshi — 1994

	Number	**Percentage**
Kanto region	8,366	57.4
Kinki region	2,769	19.0
Chubu region	960	6.6
Chugoku region	478	3.3
Kyushu region	826	5.7
Okinawa region	189	1.3
Tohoku region	417	2.8
Hokkaido region	326	2.2
Shikoku region	253	1.7

Source: 1994 No. 12 Vol. 45 Jiyu to Seigi (Liberty and Justice).

Major islands in the Japanese archipelago, such as Kyushu, Shikoku and Hokkaido, have *bengoshi* populations of only 826, 253, and 326 respectively. Prefectures such as Nagano, Fukushima, Gifu, Kagoshima, Tochigi, Mie, Nagasaki, Yamaguchi, Aomori, Ehime, Iwate, Akita, Yamagata, Oita, Nara, and Miyazaki have a *bengoshi* population of less than (and sometimes *much* less than) 100 *bengoshi* per prefecture.

Day-to-day what do Japanese *bengoshi* do? Certainly the 3,057 or so who are in the provinces concern themselves mostly with litigation, civil and criminal, with some counselling and some negotiations related to property law and commercial problems, and occasionally with some aspect of public service, such as serving on locally elected or appointed governmental bodies. However, few *bengoshi* have gone into national politics. Only 38 out of 763 Diet members in 1985 were *bengoshi*, less than 5% of the Diet.[8] In the provinces most of the 3,057 practised in small offices as single practitioners, in shared office space as single practitioners or in small offices of two or three *bengoshi*.

Of the remaining 11,135 or 76% of all Japanese *bengoshi* who practised in the Kanto or Kinki regions in 1994, relatively few engaged in any form of international practice. For instance, 925 *bengoshi* aspired enough to international practice to have themselves listed in the *1995 Martindale-Hubbell Law Directory*.[13] Of those listed in the *1995 Martindale*, 375 had foreign law degrees (LLM's, MCL's, etc.), and 117 had foreign bar qualifications, including 111 who qualified in New York.

The remaining 10,000 or so Kanto and Kinki *bengoshi* had practices not too dissimilar from their rural counterparts, with strong litigation orientation and little or no contact with foreign legal problems.

FOREIGN LAWYERS

During the immediate post-War period international practice in Japan was dominated by American lawyers who had been admitted to the Japanese Bar during the Occupation. In 1955 admission of foreign lawyers was halted, with those already admitted given grandfather status.[14]

With the growth of Japan's economic importance beginning in the early 1970s major international law firms based in the United States and the United Kingdom began to lobby the Japanese government to re-open the Japanese Bar to foreign lawyers. After 10 years of constant trade pressure, primarily from the United States, in 1987 Japan inaugurated a new system for admission of foreign lawyers to the Japanese Bar. Under the new system foreign lawyers can be admitted in Japan to practice the law of their home jurisdiction.[15] Under amendments effective on January 1, 1995 they can also form joint enterprises with Japanese *bengoshi* to render local law advice (through such *bengoshi*).

At the end of the 1980s, when the "bubble" economy was at its height, many of the leading international firms from London, New York and other cities in the United States rushed to establish offices in Tokyo. Japanese acquisitions in North America and Europe supplied a strong initial stream of practice to these firms, but such acquisitions largely ceased after the bursting of the "bubble".

Foreign firms in Tokyo have also been active in documenting international financial transactions structured by Japanese and foreign financial institutions in Tokyo. Since most international financial documentation is governed by English law or New York law, the limitation of their activities to advice on foreign law has not been a serious handicap to foreign attorneys in documenting financial work in Japan. On the other hand the shift of financial activity from Tokyo to the rest of Asia (particularly Hong Kong and Singapore) in the 1990s has hurt the practice of the Tokyo offices of foreign law firms and of *bengoshi* firms that specialise in international financial matters.

As a result of these negative economic factors, the number of admitted foreign lawyers in Japan has fallen from approximately 90 at its height in 1990–91 to 75 in 1995.[16] Many foreign firms have scaled back in Tokyo, and some prominent firms have even closed their Tokyo offices.[17]

OTHER LEGAL PROFESSIONALS

It would be incorrect to conclude that because *bengoshi* are extremely few in number in Japanese society and because *bengoshi* are litigation oriented, there are very few members of the legal profession in Japanese society. Any population statistics on the Japanese legal profession must also include the following:

Legal Profession in Japan

	Type of Professional	Population
1.	*bengoshi*	15,223
2.	*zeirishi* (licensed tax practitioners)	60,752
3.	*benrishi* (licensed patent practitioners)	3,646
4.	*shiho shoshi* (judicial scriveners)	16,956
5.	*gyosei shoshi* (administrative scriveners)	35,345
6.	corporate in-house legal specialists	6,000
7.	judges	2,852
8.	procurators	1,173
9.	law professors	2,500 (approx)
	TOTAL	**144,447**

Source: 1994 No. 12 Vol. 45 Jiyu to Seigi (Liberty and Justice).

Excluding judges, procurators, and law professors and assuming a Japanese population of about 125 million, for every "legal professional" there were 864 persons in the general Japanese population. Figures for other industrialised countries are as follows:

Population of Industrialised Countries and Numbers of the Lawyers
30 May 1994

	Population	No. of Lawyers	Population for Every Lawyer
United Kingdom	57,800,000	83,300	694
Germany	80,200,000	67,112	1,195
France	56,600,000	23,000	2,461
United States	255,600,000	799,960	320
Japan	124,760,000	15,223	8,195
Korea	44,300,000	2,813	15,748

Source: 1994 No. 12 Vol. 45 Jiyu to Seigi (Liberty and Justice).

There are many different types of "lawyers", and types of lawyers in one society do not necessarily correspond to types of lawyers in another. The figures cited most frequently are a comparison of numbers of persons in the population of the United States for each "lawyer" (about 320 for every "lawyer") to 8,195 persons in the Japanese population for every *bengoshi*. The more accurate comparison is probably 320 in the American population for every lawyer to 863 persons in the Japanese population for every legal professional. Judging from the figures for the European countries, the United States and France are the two extremes, not the United States and Japan.

If we compare litigators by comparing barristers in Great Britain with *bengoshi* in Japan, there are about 10,000 persons in the population of England, Wales, and Scotland for every barrister and 8,195 persons in the population of Japan for every *bengoshi*. These figures are remarkably similar, and the comparison is not inappropriate since some barristers (such as those who primarily act as consultants) do not litigate frequently, just as some *bengoshi* (e.g. the international practitioners) do not litigate frequently. But what do other Japanese legal professionals do? Are their roles really comparable to that of lawyers in the United States or Europe?

ZEIRISHI

Licensed tax practitioners (*zeirishi*) advise on tax problems of individuals and corporations and negotiate on tax questions on behalf of private clients with the various taxing entities of the Japanese government. They are qualified either by passing a difficult national examination or by prior service with the tax bureaucracy. Probably because of the latter form of qualification, they are much more numerous than *bengoshi*. In their counselling role their activities are quite similar to tax specialist lawyers in the United States.

BENRISHI

Licensed patent practitioners (*benrishi*) concern themselves with filing patent applications, challenges before the Japan Patent Office, and trademark registrations. Their activities are analogous to those of attorneys and patent agents in the United States. They essentially "push" all the paper that passes through the Japanese patent system.

SCRIVENERS

Scriveners provide a very important means by which Japanese society overcomes a shortage of *bengoshi*. *Shiho shoshi* (judicial scriveners) are licensed professionals who prepare documents necessary for the day-to-day life of the courts, the Legal Affairs Bureau of the Ministry of Justice (where, for instance, articles of incorporation and qualifications to do business are registered), and other judicial or legal institutions. *Shiho shoshi* also regularly complete the documentation necessary for registration of real estate transactions. *Gyosei shoshi* (administrative scriveners) are licensed professionals who draw up documents for presentation to government offices at the national, prefectural, and municipal level. Examples include driver's licence and car registration applications and applications for many types of technical government permissions (e.g. construction permits). *Tsukanshi* (customs scriveners) are specially licensed to draw up documents necessary for customs procedures. In addition to drawing up the necessary documents, all of the above scriveners (*shiho shoshi, gyosei shoshi,* and *tsukanshi*) regularly represent their clients in necessary negotiations connected with the documents and all give legal advice on their areas of specialty. In the words of one knowledgeable observer, ". . . in some localities, especially where there are shortages of [*bengoshi*], judicial scriveners come very close to playing the role of 'practising attorneys of an inferior rank' . . ."[9]

CORPORATE IN-HOUSE LEGAL SPECIALISTS

Corporate legal advice is still not widely recognised as a separate professional function by the Japanese business community, and most businessmen and even some licensed professionals admit that in contract drafting and corporate law matters the legal specialist, a company employee who has specialised in legal matters without the formal training necessary for practice as a licensed professional (except for undergraduate legal training), is superior in corporate law skills to many Japanese licensed professionals. Most Japanese companies now have legal departments or sections, and many companies suspend the normal company rotation policies for legal department personnel so that they will reach the levels of expertise necessary to handle complex legal questions. The Japanese Institute of International Business Law and other such organisations have been formed by businessmen and legal academics to provide a source of continuing training for the company staff whose jobs include legal affairs.

In the early 1970s many legal department personnel were organised into legal departments (*bu*), and it has become possible for such specialists to rise to the department chief (*bucho*) level in their companies with possible future advancement to a directorship.

GRADUATES FROM LEGAL FACULTIES — THE BUREAUCRATS AS LEGAL PROFESSIONALS

Every year over 30,000 Japanese undergraduates graduate with an LL.B. degree. Some of them go on to "practise" law within corporate in-house legal departments; some join corporations and spend the rest of their careers without significant legal contacts. Others, especially the elite in the law faculties of the national universities, particularly the Law Faculty of the University of Tokyo and the Law Faculty of the University of Kyoto, take the examination for Class I Public Servants, and each year about 1,500 join the elite career bureaucracies of the Ministry of Finance, the Ministry of International Trade and Industry, The Bank of Japan, the National Police Agency, the Economic Planning Agency, the Ministry of Foreign Affairs, and other government ministries. If, as someone has said, America is a society run by lawyers, Japan is a society run by bureaucrats, and it is not too farfetched to make an analogy between the role of lawyers in Washington, D.C. and the role of bureaucrats in Tokyo. Most *bengoshi*, for instance, pick up a telephone and call the relevant Ministry when they face a difficult legal interpretation; some do not even bother to research the problem in detail before benefiting from the "free" advice. In giving free legal advice, solving problems and adjusting the society's tensions and conflicting interests, the role of the bureaucrat as an administrator and creator of Japanese law and as a counsellor on Japanese law should not be ignored when attempting to assess the role of the legal profession in Japan.

THE UNDERSIDE OF THE PROFESSION

SOKAIYA

No description of the legal profession in Japan would be complete without mentioning the underside of the profession, including *sokaiya*, *jidanya* and *jiko gakari*. *Sokaiya* (literally, "persons who attend general meetings") are professional shareholders whose traditional role in post-war Japan was to attend shareholder meetings and to ensure, for a retainer fee, by fair means or foul, that such meetings concluded within a few minutes with no embarrassment to the managements of their client companies. The *sokaiya* profession reached its height in the late 70s or early 80s. The Tokyo Metropolitan Police Department reported that in 1979 the 2,845 companies listed on the Tokyo, Osaka and Nagoya Stock Exchanges paid an estimated ¥42 billion in fees to *sokaiya*.[19] The police estimated in 1981 the 10 largest *sokaiya* groups were paid ¥63 billion.[20]

In 1982 the Commercial Code of Japan was amended to prevent attendance at a shareholders' meeting by persons holding less than 1,000 shares each and to impose prison sentences of up to six months or fines for paying or receiving special consideration in respect of attendance at shareholders' meetings, i.e. for acting as or retaining a *sokaiya*.[10]Even with the passage of the new law, however, the several hundred remaining *sokaiya* have not given up. In the 1990s violence against corporate executives (including the murder of one senior executive in 1994 and the attempted murder of several other executives) has been attributed to increased demands by *sokaiya* on their corporate "clients".

JIDANYA AND JIKO GAKARI

Finally, among the unlicensed "professionals" one should also mention the *jidanya* (settlement brokers) who are often hired as bill collectors or as persons who "induce" settlement of petty claims. Specialists in "settling" traffic accident claims are sometimes known by the separate term *jiko gakari*. *Jidanya* and *jiko gakari* draw manpower from the *yakuza* (gangsters) but are sometimes retained by very respectable "client" companies, such as insurance companies.

CONCLUSION

Where does all this leave us? Surely it is not true that Japan is a society without a significant legal profession. It is true that the numbers of *bengoshi*, procurators and judges are very few, but there are very many other groups which fill what would otherwise be a paralysing gap in Japanese society.

---

[1] For a discussion of this thought process in connection with a recent attempt to enforce a U.S. court judgment in Japan see Henderson "Comparative Law in the Japanese Courts: Punitive Damages" in 24 *Law in Japan* 98 (1991).

[2] Punitive damage awards by a foreign court are likely to be held violative of "Japanese public order and good morals". See Henderson *op. cit.* at Note 1.

[3] Arbitration awards are enforceable as long as they are not subject to attack for the usual reasons of lack of jurisdiction, lack of a proper hearing or fraud. Japanese *Code of Civil Procedure* Arts. 800 and 801. Japanese law also requires an arbitral award to be accompanied by reasons, and the foreign party intent on enforcing an arbitration award in Japan should be sure that reasons accompany the award.

[4] The best work on pre-modern Japanese law in English is Wigmore, *Law and Justice in Tokugawa Japan* (3d ed. 1970), which has been reprinted by Tokyo University Press. The Wigmore in question is the late Dean John Henry Wigmore who, in addition to his epic work on evidence, was, as a young man, the first distinguished American expert on Japanese law.

[5] In the Tokugawa Era (1603–1868) law was "published" by distributing edicts to magistrates, by handing down edicts through social hierarchy to local organisations, and by posting important (usually criminal) edicts at public cross-roads and other public places. There were no publicly available books which purported systematically to set forth "the law".

[6] See also Rabinowitz "Law and the Social Process in Tokugawa Japan" 10 *Transactions of the Asiatic Society of Japan* 38 (3rd Series 1968).

[7] Mombusho *Gakko Kihon Chosa Hokukusho* (1994) [Ministry of Education *Report on the Basic Survey of Schools* (1994)].

[8] The party breakdown in 1985 was as follows:

Liberal Democratic Party	15
Communist Party	11
Socialist Party	7
Komeito	3
Democratic Socialist Party	1
Shaminren	1
Total	38

[9] *Tanaka The Japanese Legal System 563 (1979).*

[10] *See Commercial Code Arts. 266, 294-2, and 497.*

INDEX